MCAT®

High-Yield Problem-Solving Guide

Edited by Alexander Stone Macnow, MD

KAPLAN

TEST PREP

Published by Kaplan Publishing, a division of Kaplan, Inc.
750 Third Avenue
New York, NY 10017

Printed in the United States of America

10 9 8 7 6 5 4 3 2 1

ISBN: 978-1-5062-0097-2 | Item Number: MM5055F

Preface

And now it starts: your long, yet fruitful journey toward wearing a white coat. Proudly wearing that white coat, though, is hopefully only part of your motivation. You are reading this book because you want to be a healer.

If you're serious about going to medical school, then you are likely already familiar with the importance of the MCAT in medical school admissions. While the holistic review process puts additional weight on your experiences, extracurricular activities, and personal attributes, the fact remains: along with your GPA, your MCAT score remains one of the two most important components of your application portfolio—at least early in the admissions process. Each additional point you score on the MCAT pushes you in front of thousands of other students and makes you an even more attractive applicant. But the MCAT is not simply an obstacle to overcome; it is an opportunity to show schools that you will be a strong student and a future leader in medicine.

We at Kaplan take our jobs very seriously and aim to help students see success not only on the MCAT, but as future physicians. Our team meets regularly with our Learning Sciences departments to ensure that we're using the most up-to-date teaching techniques in our resources. Multiple members of our team hold advanced degrees in medicine or associated biomedical sciences, and are committed to the highest level of medical education. Kaplan has been working with the MCAT for over 50 years and our commitment to premed students is unflagging; in fact, Stanley Kaplan created this company when he had difficulty being accepted to medical school due to unfair quota systems that existed at the time.

We stand now at the beginning of a new era in medical education. As citizens of this 21st-century world of healthcare, we are charged with creating a patient-oriented, culturally competent, cost-conscious, universally available, technically advanced and research-focused healthcare system, run by compassionate providers. Suffice it to say, this is no easy task. Problem-based learning, integrated curricula, and classes in interpersonal skills are some of the responses to this demand for an excellent workforce—a workforce of which you'll soon be a part.

We're thrilled that you've chosen us to help you on this journey. Please reach out to us to share your challenges, concerns, and successes. Together, we will shape the future of medicine in the United States and abroad; we look forward to helping you become the doctor you deserve to be.

Good luck!

Alexander Stone Macnow, MD
Editor-in-Chief
Department of Pathology and Laboratory Medicine
Hospital of the University of Pennsylvania

BA, Musicology—Boston University, 2008
MD—Perelman School of Medicine at the University of Pennsylvania, 2013

Contents

The *Kaplan MCAT Review* Team vii

About the MCAT viii

How This Book Was Created xix

Using This Book xx

Chapter 1: Behavioral Sciences   1

Regions of the Brain 2

Vision. 4

Associative Learning. 8

Language. 10

Theories of Emotion 12

Formation of Identity 14

Bipolar and Depressive Disorders 16

Social Processes. 20

Verbal and Nonverbal Communication 22

Attribution Theory. 24

Demographics. 26

Disparities in Health and Healthcare. 28

Solutions to Related Questions 30

Chapter 2: Biochemistry   37

Elements of Peptide Structure 38

Lineweaver–Burk Plots. 40

Isoelectric Focusing 44

Isomerism in Carbohydrates 48

Lipid Saponification 50

DNA Replication 52

Operons. 56

Membrane Traffic 58

Glycolysis 60

Electron Transport Chain and Oxidative Phosphorylation 62

β-Oxidation. 64

Hormonal Regulation of Metabolism 66

Solutions to Related Questions 68

Chapter 3: Biology 77

Prokaryotic Genetics 78

Menstrual Cycle 82

Stages of Embryogenesis 86

Action Potential 88

Endocrine Organs 90

The Respiratory System 92

Oxyhemoglobin Dissociation Curve 94

Immune Function 98

The Digestive System 100

Kidney Function 102

Muscle Contraction 104

Hardy–Weinberg Equilibrium 106

Solutions to Related Questions 108

Chapter 4: General Chemistry 115

Atomic Mass and Weight 116

Periodic Trends 118

VSEPR Theory and Geometry 122

Stoichiometry 126

Rate Laws 130

Reaction Energy Profiles 134

Hess's Law 138

The Ideal Gas Law 140

Molar Solubility 142

Titrations 146

Balancing Oxidation–Reduction Reactions 150

Electrochemical Cells 152

Solutions to Related Questions 155

Chapter 5: Organic Chemistry 165

Nomenclature 166

Stereoisomers 170

Hybridized Orbitals 172

Nucleophilicity Trends 174

Reactions of Alcohols 178

Identifying the Structure of an Unknown Oxy Compound 182

Enolate Chemistry. 186

Nucleophilic Acyl Substitution Reactions 190

Properties of Carboxylic Acid Derivatives 194

Phosphorus-Containing Compounds. 196

Spectroscopy 200

Extraction 204

Solutions to Related Questions 206

Chapter 6: Physics and Math   213

Inclined Plane 214

Projectile Motion and Air Resistance. 218

Thermodynamics 220

Fluid Dynamics 228

Electrostatics 232

Resistor Circuits 234

Doppler Effect 238

Snell's Law 242

Nuclear Reactions 246

Dimensional Analysis 250

Study Design. 254

Graphical Analysis 256

Solutions to Related Questions 260

The *Kaplan MCAT Review* Team

Alexander Stone Macnow, MD

Editor-in-Chief

Tyra Hall-Pogar, PhD

Editor

Bela Starkman, PhD

Editor

Laura L. Ambler

Kaplan MCAT Faculty

Uneeb Qureshi

Kaplan MCAT Faculty

Alisha Maureen Crowley

Kaplan MCAT Faculty

Derek Rusnak, MA

Kaplan MCAT Faculty

Kelly Kyker-Snowman, MS

Kaplan MCAT Faculty

Kristen L. Russell, ME

Kaplan MCAT Faculty

Jason R. Pfleiger

Kaplan MCAT Faculty

Pamela Willingham, MSW

Kaplan MCAT Faculty

MCAT faculty reviewers Elmar R. Aliyev; James Burns; Jonathan Cornfield; Nikolai Dorofeev, MD; Raef Ali Fadel; Samer T. Ismail; Elizabeth A. Kudlaty; John P. Mahon; Matthew A. Meier; Nainika Nanda; Caroline Nkemdilim Opene; Kaitlyn E. Prenger; Nicholas M. White; Allison Ann Wilkes, MS; and Tony Yu

Thanks to Kim Bowers; Tim Eich; Owen Farcy; Dan Frey; Robin Garmise; Rita Garthaffner; Joanna Graham; Adam Grey; Allison Harm; Beth Hoffberg; Aaron Lemon-Strauss; Keith Lubeley; Diane McGarvey; Petros Minasi; John Polstein; Deeangelee Pooran-Kublall, MD, MPH; Rochelle Rothstein, MD; Larry Rudman; Sylvia Tidwell Scheuring; Carly Schnur; Karin Tucker; Lee Weiss; and the countless others who made this project possible.

About the MCAT

ANATOMY OF THE MCAT

Here is a general overview of the structure of Test Day:

Section	Number of Questions	Time Allotted
Examinee Agreement		8 minutes
Tutorial (optional)		10 minutes
Chemical and Physical Foundations of Biological Systems	59	95 minutes
Break (optional)		10 minutes
Critical Analysis and Reasoning Skills (CARS)	53	90 minutes
Lunch Break (optional)		30 minutes
Biological and Biochemical Foundations of Living Systems	59	95 minutes
Break (optional)		10 minutes
Psychological, Social, and Biological Foundations of Behavior	59	95 minutes
Void Question		5 minutes
Satisfaction Survey (optional)		5 minutes

The structure of the four sections of the MCAT is further detailed below.

Chemical and Physical Foundations of Biological Systems	
Time	95 minutes
Format	• 59 questions • 10 passages • 44 questions are passage-based, and 15 are discrete (stand-alone) questions. • Score between 118 and 132
What It Tests	• Biochemistry: 25% • Biology: 5% • General Chemistry: 30% • Organic Chemistry: 15% • Physics: 25%

Critical Analysis and Reasoning Skills (CARS)	
Time	90 minutes
Format	• 53 questions • 9 passages • All questions are passage-based. There are no discrete (stand-alone) questions. • Score between 118 and 132

What It Tests	Disciplines:
	• Humanities: 50%
	• Social Sciences: 50%
	Skills:
	• *Foundations of Comprehension*: 30%
	• *Reasoning Within the Text*: 30%
	• *Reasoning Beyond the Text*: 40%

Biological and Biochemical Foundations of Living Systems	
Time	95 minutes
Format	• 59 questions
	• 10 passages
	• 44 questions are passage-based, and 15 are discrete (stand-alone) questions.
	• Score between 118 and 132
What It Tests	• Biochemistry: 25%
	• Biology: 65%
	• General Chemistry: 5%
	• Organic Chemistry: 5%

Psychological, Social, and Biological Foundations of Behavior	
Time	95 minutes
Format	• 59 questions
	• 10 passages
	• 44 questions are passage-based, and 15 are discrete (stand-alone) questions.
	• Score between 118 and 132
What It Tests	• Biology: 5%
	• Psychology: 65%
	• Sociology: 30%

Total	
Testing Time	375 minutes (6 hours, 15 minutes)
Total Seat Time	453 minutes (7 hours, 33 minutes)
Questions	230
Score	472 to 528

SCIENTIFIC INQUIRY AND REASONING SKILLS (SIRS)

The AAMC has defined four *Scientific Inquiry and Reasoning Skills* (SIRS) that will be tested in the three science sections of the MCAT:

1. *Knowledge of Scientific Concepts and Principles* (35% of questions)
2. *Scientific Reasoning and Problem-Solving* (45% of questions)
3. *Reasoning About the Design and Execution of Research* (10% of questions)
4. *Data-Based and Statistical Reasoning* (10% of questions)

Let's see how each one breaks down into more specific Test Day behaviors. Note that the bullet points of specific objectives for each of the SIRS are taken directly from the *Official Guide to the MCAT Exam*; the descriptions of what these behaviors mean and sample question stems, however, are written by Kaplan.

Skill 1: *Knowledge of Scientific Concepts and Principles*

This is probably the least surprising of the four SIRS; the testing of science knowledge is, after all, one of the signature qualities of the MCAT. Skill 1 questions will require you to do the following:

- Recognize correct scientific principles
- Identify the relationships among closely-related concepts
- Identify the relationships between different representations of concepts (verbal, symbolic, graphic)
- Identify examples of observations that illustrate scientific principles
- Use mathematical equations to solve problems

At Kaplan, we simply call these Science Knowledge or Skill 1 questions. Another way to think of Skill 1 questions is as "one-step" problems. The single step is either to realize which scientific concept the question stem is suggesting or to take the concept stated in the question stem and identify which answer choice is an accurate application of it. Skill 1 questions are particularly prominent among discrete questions (those not associated with a passage). These questions are an opportunity to gain quick points on Test Day—if you know the science concept attached to the question, then that's it! On Test Day, 35% of the questions in each science section will be Skill 1 questions.

Here are some sample Skill 1 question stems:

- How would a proponent of the James–Lange theory of emotion interpret the findings of the study cited the passage?
- Which of the following most accurately describes the function of FSH in the human female menstrual cycle?
- If the products of Reaction 1 and Reaction 2 were combined in solution, the resulting reaction would form:
- Ionic bonds are maintained by which of the following forces?

Skill 2: *Scientific Reasoning and Problem-Solving*

The MCAT science sections do, of course, move beyond testing straightforward science knowledge; Skill 2 questions are the most common way in which it does so. At Kaplan, we also call these Critical Thinking questions. Skill 2 questions will require you to do the following:

- Reason about scientific principles, theories, and models
- Analyze and evaluate scientific explanations and predictions
- Evaluate arguments about causes and consequences
- Bring together theory, observations, and evidence to draw conclusions
- Recognize scientific findings that challenge or invalidate a scientific theory or model
- Determine and use scientific formulas to solve problems

Just as Skill 1 questions can be thought of as "one-step" problems, many Skill 2 questions are "two-step" problems, and more difficult Skill 2 questions may require three or more steps. These questions can require a wide spectrum of reasoning skills, including integration of multiple facts from a passage, combination of multiple science content areas, and prediction of an experiment's results. Skill 2 questions also tend to ask about science content without actually mentioning it by name. For example, a question might describe the results of one experiment and ask you to predict the results of a second experiment without actually telling you what underlying scientific principles are at work—part of the question's difficulty will be figuring out which principles to apply in order to get the correct answer. On Test Day, 45% of the questions in each science section will be Skill 2 questions.

Here are some sample Skill 2 question stems:

- Which of the following experimental conditions would most likely yield results similar to those in Figure 2?
- All of the following conclusions are supported by the information in the passage EXCEPT:
- The most likely cause of the anomalous results found by the experimenter is:
- An impact to a man's chest quickly reduces the volume of one of his lungs to 70% of its initial value while not allowing any air to escape from the man's mouth. By what percentage is the force of outward air pressure increased on a 2 cm2 portion of the inner surface of the compressed lung?

Skill 3: *Reasoning About the Design and Execution of Research*

The MCAT is interested in your ability to critically appraise and analyze research, as this is an important day-to-day task of a physician. We call these questions Skill 3 or Experimental and Research Design questions for short. Skill 3 questions will require you to do the following:

- Identify the role of theory, past findings, and observations in scientific questioning
- Identify testable research questions and hypotheses
- Distinguish between samples and populations and distinguish results that support generalizations about populations
- Identify independent and dependent variables
- Reason about the features of research studies that suggest associations between variables or causal relationships between them (such as temporality and random assignment)
- Identify conclusions that are supported by research results
- Determine the implications of results for real-world situations
- Reason about ethical issues in scientific research

Over the years, the AAMC has received input from medical schools to require more practical research skills of MCAT test-takers, and Skill 3 questions are the response to these demands. This skill is unique in that the outside knowledge you need to answer Skill 3 questions is not taught in any one undergraduate course; instead, the research design principles needed to answer these questions are learned gradually throughout your science classes and especially through any laboratory work you have completed. It should be noted that Skill 3 comprises 10% of the questions in each science section on Test Day.

Here are some sample Skill 3 question stems:

- What is the dependent variable in the study described in the passage?
- The major flaw in the method used to measure disease susceptibility in Experiment 1 is:
- Which of the following procedures is most important for the experimenters to follow in order for their study to maintain a proper, randomized sample of research subjects?
- A researcher would like to test the hypothesis that individuals who move to an urban area during adulthood are more likely to own a car than are those who have lived in an urban area since birth. Which of the following studies would best test this hypothesis?

Skill 4: *Data-Based and Statistical Reasoning*

Lastly, the science sections of the MCAT test your ability to analyze the visual and numerical results of experiments and studies. We call these Data and Statistical Analysis questions. Skill 4 questions will require you to do the following:

- Use, analyze, and interpret data in figures, graphs, and tables
- Evaluate whether representations make sense for particular scientific observations and data

- Use measures of central tendency (mean, median, and mode) and measures of dispersion (range, interquartile range, and standard deviation) to describe data
- Reason about random and systematic error
- Reason about statistical significance and uncertainty (interpreting statistical significance levels and interpreting a confidence interval)
- Use data to explain relationships between variables or make predictions
- Use data to answer research questions and draw conclusions

Skill 4 is included in the MCAT because physicians and researchers spend much of their time examining the results of their own studies and the studies of others, and it's very important for them to make legitimate conclusions and sound judgments based on that data. The MCAT tests Skill 4 on all three science sections with graphical representations of data (charts and bar graphs) as well as numerical ones (tables, lists, and results summarized in sentence or paragraph form). On Test Day, 10% of the questions in each science section will be Skill 4 questions.

Here are some sample Skill 4 question stems:

- According to the information in the passage, there is an inverse correlation between:
- What conclusion is best supported by the findings displayed in Figure 2?
- A medical test for a rare type of heavy metal poisoning returns a positive result for 98% of affected individuals and 13% of unaffected individuals. Which of the following types of error is most prevalent in this test?
- If a fourth trial of Experiment 1 was run and yielded a result of 54% compliance, which of the following would be true?

SIRS Summary

Discussing the SIRS tested on the MCAT is a daunting prospect given that the very nature of the skills tends to make the conversation rather abstract. Nevertheless, with enough practice, you'll be able to identify each of the four skills quickly, and you'll also be able to apply the proper strategies to solve those problems on Test Day. If you need a quick reference to remind you of the four SIRS, these guidelines may help:

Skill 1 (Science Knowledge) questions ask:

- Do you remember this science content?

Skill 2 (Critical Thinking) questions ask:

- Do you remember this science content? And if you do, could you please apply it to this novel situation?
- Could you answer this question that cleverly combines multiple content areas at the same time?

Skill 3 (Experimental and Research Design) questions ask:

- Let's forget about the science content for a while. Could you give some insight into the experimental or research methods involved in this situation?

Skill 4 (Data and Statistical Analysis) questions ask:

- Let's forget about the science content for a while. Could you accurately read some graphs and tables for a moment? Could you make some conclusions or extrapolations based on the information presented?

CRITICAL ANALYSIS AND REASONING SKILLS (CARS)

The *Critical Analysis and Reasoning Skills* (CARS) section of the MCAT tests three discrete families of textual reasoning skills; each of these families requires a higher level of reasoning than the last. Those three skills are as follows:

1. *Foundations of Comprehension* (30% of questions)
2. *Reasoning Within the Text* (30% of questions)
3. *Reasoning Beyond the Text* (40% of questions)

These three skills are tested through nine humanities- and social sciences-themed passages, with approximately 5 to 7 questions per passage. Let's take a more in-depth look into these three skills. Again, the bullet points of specific objectives for each of the CARS are taken directly from the *Official Guide to the MCAT Exam*; the descriptions of what these behaviors mean and sample question stems, however, are written by Kaplan.

Foundations of Comprehension

Questions in this skill will ask for basic facts and simple inferences about the passage; the questions themselves will be similar to those seen on reading comprehension sections of other standardized exams like the SAT® and ACT®. *Foundations of Comprehension* questions will require you to do the following:

- Understand the basic components of the text
- Infer meaning from rhetorical devices, word choice, and text structure

This admittedly covers a wide range of potential question types including Main Idea, Detail, Function, and Definition-in-Context questions, but finding the correct answer to all *Foundations of Comprehension* questions will follow from a basic understanding of the passage and the point of view of its author (and occasionally that of other voices in the passage).

Here are some sample *Foundations of Comprehension* question stems:

- **Main Idea**—The author's primary purpose in this passage is:
- **Detail**—Based on the information in the second paragraph, which of the following is the most accurate summary of the opinion held by Schubert's critics?
- **(Scattered) Detail**—According to the passage, which of the following is FALSE about literary reviews in the 1920s?
- **Function**—The author's discussion of the effect of socioeconomic status on social mobility primarily serves which of the following functions?
- **Definition-in-Context**—The word "obscure" (paragraph 3), when used in reference to the historian's actions, most nearly means:

Reasoning Within the Text

While *Foundations of Comprehension* questions will usually depend on interpreting a single piece of information in the passage or understanding the passage as a whole, *Reasoning Within the Text* questions will typically require you to infer unstated parts of arguments or bring together two disparate pieces of the passage. *Reasoning Within the Text* questions will require you to:

- Integrate different components of the text to increase comprehension

In other words, questions in this skill often ask either *How do these two details relate to one another?* or *What else must be true that the author didn't say?* The CARS section will also ask you to judge certain parts of the passage or even judge the author. These questions, which fall under the *Reasoning Within the Text* skill, can ask you to identify authorial bias, evaluate the credibility of cited sources, determine the logical soundness of an argument, or search for relevant evidence in the passage to support a given conclusion. In all, this category includes Inference and Strengthen–Weaken (Within the Passage) questions, as well as a smattering of related—but rare—question types.

Here are some sample *Reasoning Within the Text* question stems:

- **Inference (Implication)**—Which of the following phrases, as used in the passage, is most suggestive that the author has a personal bias toward narrative records of history?
- **Inference (Assumption)**—In putting together her argument in the passage, the author most likely assumes:
- **Strengthen–Weaken (Within the Passage)**—Which of the following facts is used in the passage as the most prominent piece of evidence in favor of the author's conclusions?
- **Strengthen–Weaken (Within the Passage)**—Based on the role it plays in the author's argument, *The Possessed* can be considered:

Reasoning Beyond the Text

The distinguishing factor of *Reasoning Beyond the Text* questions is in the title of the skill: the word *Beyond*. Questions that test this skill, which make up a larger share of the CARS section than questions from either of the other two skills, will always introduce a completely new situation that was not present in the passage itself; these questions will ask you to determine how one influences the other. *Reasoning Beyond the Text* questions will require you to:

- Apply or extrapolate ideas from the passage to new contexts
- Assess the impact of introducing new factors, information, or conditions to ideas from the passage

The *Reasoning Beyond the Text* skill is further divided into Apply and Strengthen–Weaken (Beyond the Passage) questions, and a few other rarely appearing question types.

Here are some sample *Reasoning Beyond the Text* question stems:

- **Apply**—If a document were located that demonstrated Berlioz intended to include a chorus of at least 700 in his *Grande Messe des Mortes*, how would the author likely respond?
- **Apply**—Which of the following is the best example of a "virtuous rebellion," as it is defined in the passage?
- **Strengthen–Weaken (Beyond the Text)**—Suppose Jane Austen had written in a letter to her sister, "My strongest characters were those forced by circumstance to confront basic questions about the society in which they lived." What relevance would this have to the passage?
- **Strengthen–Weaken (Beyond the Text)**—Which of the following sentences, if added to the end of the passage, would most WEAKEN the author's conclusions in the last paragraph?

CARS Summary

Through the *Foundations of Comprehension* skill, the CARS section tests many of the reading skills you have been building on since grade school, albeit in the context of very challenging doctorate-level passages. But through the two other skills (*Reasoning Within the Text* and *Reasoning Beyond the Text*), the MCAT demands that you understand the deep structure of passages and the arguments within them at a very advanced level. And, of course, all of this is tested under very tight timing restrictions: only 102 seconds per question—and that doesn't even include the time spent reading the passages.

Here's a quick reference guide to the three CARS skills:

Foundations of Comprehension questions ask:

- Did you understand the passage and its main ideas?
- What does the passage have to say about this particular detail?

Reasoning Within the Text questions ask:

- What must be true that the author did not say?
- What's the logical relationship between these two ideas from the passage?
- How well argued is the author's thesis?

Reasoning Beyond the Text questions ask:

- How does this principle from the passage apply to this new situation?
- How does this new piece of information influence the arguments in the passage?

SCORING

Each of the four sections of the MCAT is scored between 118 and 132, with the median at 125. This means the total score ranges from 472 to 528, with the median at 500. Why such peculiar numbers? The AAMC stresses that this scale emphasizes the importance of the central portion of the score distribution, where most students score (around 125 per section, or 500 total), rather than putting undue focus on the high end of the scale.

Note that there is no wrong answer penalty on the MCAT, so you should select an answer for every question—even if it is only a guess.

The AAMC has released a hypothetical correlation between scaled score and percentile, as shown here. It should be noted that the percentile scale is adjusted and renormalized over time and thus should not be overinterpreted.

Total Score	Percentile	Total Score	Percentile
528	99	499	45
527	99	498	41
526	99	497	36
525	98	496	32
524	98	495	27
523	98	494	24
522	97	493	20
521	97	492	17
520	97	491	14
519	96	490	11
518	96	489	9
517	95	488	7
516	95	487	7

Total Score	Percentile	Total Score	Percentile
515	94	486	6
514	94	485	6
513	93	484	5
512	93	483	5
511	91	482	4
510	89	481	4
509	86	480	3
508	83	479	3
507	80	478	3
506	76	477	2
505	73	476	2
504	68	475	2
503	64	474	1
502	59	473	1
501	55	472	1
500	50		

Source: *The New Score Scales for the 2015 MCAT® Exam: An Overview of What Admissions Officers Need to Know.* AAMC. 2014: 9.

Further information on score reporting is included at the end of the next section (see *After Your Test*).

MCAT POLICIES AND PROCEDURES

We strongly encourage you to download the latest copy of *MCAT® Essentials*, available on the AAMC's website, to ensure that you have the latest information about registration and Test Day policies and procedures; this document is updated annually. A brief summary of some of the most important rules is provided here.

MCAT Registration

The only way to register for the MCAT is online. You can access AAMC's registration system at: www.aamc.org/mcat

You will be able to access the site approximately six months before Test Day. The AAMC designates three registration "Zones"—Gold, Silver, and Bronze. Registering during the Gold Zone (from the opening of registration until approximately one month before Test Day) provides the most flexibility and lowest test fees. The Silver Zone runs until approximately two to three weeks before Test Day and has less flexibility and higher fees; the Bronze Zone runs until approximately one to two weeks before Test Day and has the least flexibility and highest fees.

Fees and the Fee Assistance Program (FAP)

Payment for test registration must be made by MasterCard or VISA. As described earlier, the fees for registering for the MCAT—as well as rescheduling the exam or changing your testing center—increase as one approaches Test Day. In addition, it is not uncommon for test centers to fill up well in advance of the registration deadline. For these reasons, we recommend identifying your preferred Test Day as soon as possible and registering. There are ancillary benefits to having a set Test Day, as well: when you know the date you're working toward, you'll study harder and are less likely to keep pushing back the exam. The AAMC offers a Fee Assistance Program (FAP) for students with financial hardship to help reduce the cost of taking the MCAT, as well as for the American Medical College Application Service (AMCAS®) application. Further information on the FAP can be found at: www.aamc.org/students/applying/fap

Testing Security

On Test Day, you will be required to present a government-issued ID. When registering, take care to spell your name precisely the same as it appears on this ID; failure to provide this ID at the test center or differences in spelling between your registration and ID will be considered a "no-show," and you will not receive a refund for the exam.

You will also be required to provide an electronic thumbprint and electronic signature verification to take the exam. Some testing centers may use a metal detection wand to ensure that no prohibited items are brought into the testing room. Prohibited items include all electronic devices, including watches and timers, calculators, cell phones, and any and all forms of recording equipment; food, drinks (including water), and cigarettes or other smoking paraphernalia; hats and scarves (except for religious purposes); and books, notes, or other study materials. If you require a medical device, such as an insulin pump or pacemaker, you must apply for accommodated testing. During breaks, you are allowed to access food and drink, but not electronic devices, including cell phones.

Testing centers are under video surveillance and the AAMC does not take potential violations of testing security lightly. The bottom line: *know the rules and don't break them.*

Accommodations

Students with disabilities or medical conditions can apply for accommodated testing. Documentation of the disability or condition is required, and requests may take two months—or more—to be approved. For this reason, it is recommended that you begin the process of applying for accommodated testing as early as possible. More information on applying for accommodated testing can be found at: www.aamc.org/students/applying/mcat/accommodations

After Your Test

When your MCAT is all over, no matter how you feel you did, be good to yourself when you leave the test center. Celebrate! Take a nap. Watch a movie. Ride your bike. Plan a trip. Call up all of your neglected friends or stalk them on Facebook. Totally consume a cheesesteak and drink dirty martinis at night (assuming you're over 21). Whatever you do, make sure that it has absolutely nothing to do with thinking too hard—you deserve some rest and relaxation.

Perhaps most importantly, do not discuss specific details about the test with anyone. For one, it is important to let go of the stress of Test Day, and reliving your exam only inhibits you from being able to do so. But more significantly, the Examinee Agreement you sign at the beginning of your exam specifically prohibits you from discussing or disclosing exam content. The AAMC is known to seek out individuals who violate this agreement and retains the right to prosecute these individuals at their discretion. This means that you should not, under any circumstances, discuss the exam in person or over the phone with other individuals—including us at Kaplan—or post information or questions about exam content to Facebook, Student Doctor Network, or other online social media. You are permitted to comment on your "general exam experience," including how you felt about the exam overall or an individual section, but this is a fine line. In summary: *if you're not certain whether you can discuss an aspect of the test or not, just don't do it!* Do not let a silly Facebook post stop you from becoming the doctor you deserve to be.

Scores are released approximately one month after Test Day. The release is staggered during the afternoon and evening, starting at 5 p.m. Eastern. This means that not all examinees receive their scores at exactly the same time. Your score report will include a scaled score for each section between 118 and 132, as well as your total combined score between 472 and 528. These scores are given as confidence intervals. For each section, the confidence interval is approximately the given score ±1; for the total score, it is approximately the given score ±2. You will also be given the corresponding percentile rank for each of these section scores and the total score.

AAMC CONTACT INFORMATION

For further questions, contact the MCAT team at the Association of American Medical Colleges:

MCAT Resource Center
Association of American Medical Colleges
www.aamc.org/mcat
(202) 828-0690
mcat@aamc.org

How This Book Was Created

The *High-Yield Problem-Solving Guide* (HYPSG) project began in November 2012 shortly after the release of the *Preview Guide for the MCAT 2015 Exam*, 2nd edition. Through thorough analysis by our staff psychometricians, we were able to analyze the relative yield of the different topics on the MCAT and began constructing tables of contents for the books of the *Kaplan MCAT Review* series to which the HYPSG is related.

Writing of the books began in April 2013. A dedicated staff of 30 writers, 7 editors, and 32 proofreaders worked over 5000 combined hours to produce these books. The format of the books was heavily influenced by weekly meetings with Kaplan's learning science team.

This book was submitted for publication in May 2015. For any updates after this date, please visit www.kaplanmcat.com.

Each question in this book has been vetted through at least eight rounds of review. To that end, the information presented in these books is true and accurate to the best of our knowledge. Still, your feedback helps us improve our prep materials. Please notify us of any inaccuracies or errors in the books by sending an email to KaplanMCATfeedback@kaplan.com.

Using This Book

The *High-Yield Problem-Solving Guide*, along with the other seven books in your student kit, is the cornerstone of your prep for the MCAT. This book offers the content review, strategies, and practice that make Kaplan the #1 choice for MCAT prep. After all, twice as many doctors prepared with Kaplan for the MCAT than with any other course.

This book is designed to help you practice problem-solving by applying your content knowledge and critical thinking skills to a wide variety of practice questions. Each question aligns with one of the chapters of the *Kaplan MCAT Review* series and is presented in the worked example format in which the answer is determined through a number of logical steps. Your approach to a given question may vary from the ones presented in this book—and that's okay! The solutions presented in this book represent just one possible way that MCAT experts determine the correct answer to the question. Look for opportunities to improve your speed and efficiency with these questions, and apply what you learn in this book to your own MCAT practice. Please understand that strategy review—no matter how thorough—is not sufficient preparation for the MCAT! The MCAT tests not only your problem-solving skills but also your science knowledge, critical reading, and reasoning skills. Do not assume that simply memorizing the contents of this book will earn you high scores on Test Day; to maximize your scores, you must also improve your reading and test-taking skills through MCAT-style questions and practice tests.

RELATED QUESTIONS

At the end of each example, you'll find three related practice questions. These may be similar to the worked example presented, or may focus on different but related applications of the material. Most of these questions focus on the second of the *Scientific Inquiry and Reasoning Skills* (Scientific Reasoning and Problem-Solving), although there are occasional questions that fall into the first SIRS (Knowledge of Scientific Concepts and Principles).

SIDEBARS

The following is a guide to the three types of sidebars you'll find in the *High-Yield Problem-Solving Guide*:

- **Key Concepts**: These sidebars draw attention to the most important subtopics presented in the worked example and its related questions. If you understand nothing else, make sure you grasp the Key Concepts for any given subject.
- **Takeaways**: These sidebars draw attention to the most important takeaways in a given topic, and they sometimes offer synopses or overviews of complex information.
- **Things to Watch Out For**: These sidebars either highlight pitfalls and common mistakes students make with a given topic, or describe common applications of the topic on the MCAT. Think of these as words of warning—warning you what you might see on Test Day, and warning you what mistakes you should be careful to avoid.

In the end, this is your book, so write in the margins, draw diagrams, highlight the key points—do whatever is necessary to help you get that higher score. We look forward to working with you as you achieve your dreams and become the doctor you deserve to be!

Behavioral Sciences

Key Concepts

Behavioral Sciences Chapter 1
Forebrain
Hindbrain
Midbrain
Hypothalamus
Thalamus

Regions of the Brain

The story of Phineas Gage, who experienced significant personality changes after being impaled with a railroad spike, laid the foundation for associating the frontal lobe with personality. The forebrain is also associated with emotion and memory. What areas of the brain may be affected if one or multiple lesions are found in the forebrain, and what cognitive or life functions would be lost? Could an individual survive the loss of this area of the brain?

1 **Determine the parts of the forebrain.**

The first part of the question requires you to know the parts of the forebrain, which include the cerebral cortex, basal ganglia, limbic system, thalamus, and hypothalamus.

2 **Determine what the parts of the forebrain do.**

In order to identify what functions an individual would lose, you must first identify the normal functions of each brain area:

- **Cerebral cortex:** The outer covering of the cerebral hemispheres. It is divided into four lobes, each of which serves specific functions:
  - **Frontal lobe:** Executive function, impulse control, long-term planning (prefrontal cortex), motor function (primary motor cortex), speech production (Broca's area)
  - **Parietal lobe:** Sensation of touch, pressure, temperature, and pain (somatosensory cortex); spatial processing, orientation, and manipulation
  - **Occipital lobe:** Visual processing
  - **Temporal lobe:** Sound processing (auditory cortex), speech perception (Wernicke's area), memory, and emotion (limbic system)
- **Basal ganglia:** Coordinate muscle movements as they receive information from the cortex and relay this information to the brain and the spinal cord. The basal ganglia smoothen movements and help maintain postural stability.
- **Limbic system:** Comprises a group of interconnected structures looping around the central portion of the brain and is primarily associated with emotion and memory:
  - **Septal nuclei:** Involved with feelings of pleasure, pleasure-seeking behavior, and addiction
  - **Amygdala:** Controls fear and aggression

- **Hippocampus:** Consolidates memories and communicates with other parts of the limbic system through an extension called the fornix
- **Thalamus:** Serves as an important sensory relay station for incoming sensory information, including all senses except for smell. After receiving incoming sensory impulses, the thalamus sorts them and then transmits them to the appropriate projection areas in the cerebral cortex.
- **Hypothalamus:** A key player in emotional experience during high-arousal states, aggressive behavior, and sexual behavior. It also controls many endocrine functions as well as the autonomic nervous system. The hypothalamus serves many homeostatic functions, and its receptors regulate metabolism, temperature, and water balance.

③ Assess whether survival would be possible.

It is widely believed that an individual would survive with loss of forebrain functions, although there may be dramatic changes in quality of life, ability to take care of oneself, and mood. Individuals with significant forebrain damage may require medication to regulate mood and endocrine functions. The midbrain and hindbrain are generally believed to be required for survival. The midbrain controls the reception of sensory and motor information, whereas the hindbrain controls balance, motor coordination, breathing, and general arousal processes, such as sleeping and waking. While the functions of the forebrain are critical for interacting with others and with the world, they are not absolutely necessary for survival.

Related Questions

1. What are the parts of the hindbrain and the meaningful functions these areas serve?

2. What are the three parts of the hypothalamus and what functions does each part serve?

3. What parts of the brain make up the cerebrum? How is the cerebrum associated with Parkinson's disease and schizophrenia?

Takeaways

The brain is organized by the evolutionary order of its development, so the complexity of its functions generally increases as you move up the organ. Notice that the brain structures associated with basic survival are located at the base of the brain and that these are the first areas to develop.

Things to Watch Out For

It is easy to confuse the terminology of the brain. While the frontal lobe is part of the forebrain, the forebrain also includes many other structures. While the brainstem is the hindmost part of the brain, not all parts of the brainstem are in the hindbrain (the midbrain is separate from the rest of the brainstem). Further, the MCAT will not always group brain areas anatomically but may categorize according to the functions of various brain regions.

Key Concepts

Behavioral Sciences Chapter 2

The eye

Visual transduction

Visual processing

Central nervous system pathways

Vision

Multiple sclerosis (MS) is a common demyelinating disorder that affects the white matter of the central nervous system. The visual pathways are commonly affected; optic neuritis, which is inflammation of the optic nerve, is one of the most common presentations. Less commonly, MS may cause lesions of an entire section of the visual pathway, leading to visual field defects. What would be the visual field defect in an individual who lost function of the right optic nerve? Of the fibers crossing in the optic chiasm? Of the right optic tract? Of the right occipital lobe?

1 Determine what fibers are carried in the right optic nerve.

The right optic nerve collects the axons of neurons leaving the retina of the right eye. The nasal visual field (toward the nose) projects to the temporal retina (toward the side of the head). Similarly, the temporal visual field projects to the nasal retina. Together, all of these fibers form the right optic nerve.

If the entire right optic nerve were lesioned in MS, then all of information from the right eye would be lost. In medicine, this may be represented as shown:

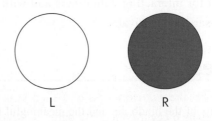

When reading visual fields, imagine that you are looking out at the world through the two circles; in this example, nothing is visible through the right eye.

2 Determine what fibers cross in the optic chiasm.

In the optic chiasm, the nasal fibers cross while the temporal fibers pass directly through to the ipsilateral (on the same side) optic tract. Remember that the nasal fibers carry information from the temporal visual field. Therefore, a lesion of the fibers crossing in the optic chiasm would knock out nasal fibers from both eyes and cause a loss of the temporal visual field from both eyes. This is called bitemporal hemianopsia, and can be represented as shown:

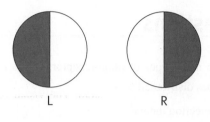

L   R

3 Determine what fibers are carried in the right optic tract.

Because of the crossing in the optic chiasm, the right optic tract carries the nasal fibers from the left eye and the temporal fibers from the right eye. These correspond to the temporal visual field from the left eye and the nasal visual field from the right eye, respectively—which is the left visual field of each eye. A complete lesion of the right optic tract would therefore cause a loss of the left visual field from both eyes. This is called homonymous hemianopsia and can be represented as shown:

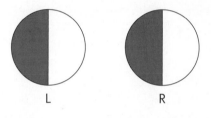

L   R

4 Determine what fibers are carried in the right occipital lobe.

The optic tracts project directly to their respective occipital lobes. Therefore, damage to the right occipital lobe will cause loss of the left visual field. Interestingly, occipital lobe lesions (which occur commonly during a stroke) are often marked by macular sparing, or survival of the central visual field in each eye, and can be represented as shown:

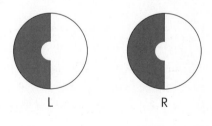

L   R

This is due to differences in circulation to the different parts of the occipital lobe, which is outside the scope of the MCAT.

Takeaways

An optic nerve carries all the information from the associated eye. The optic chiasm contains crossing nasal fibers (the temporal visual field) from each eye. An optic tract carries all the information from the opposite visual field.

Things to Watch Out For

It is very easy to misread a question about the visual system—does the answer refer to a part of the visual pathway or to a part of the visual field? Wrong answers often simply mix up *left* and *right* or *nasal* and *temporal*.

Related Questions

1. What are the two main types of photoreceptors in the retina? How are these photoreceptor types distributed?

2. What is feature detection theory?

3. What is parallel processing?

High-Yield Problem-Solving Guide questions continue on the next page. ▶ ▶ ▶

Key Concepts

Behavioral Sciences Chapter 3
Operant conditioning
Reinforcement
Punishment
Schedules of reinforcement

Associative Learning

A pigeon is placed in a cage with two buttons: blue and green. The blue button releases a food pellet after a <u>random period of time</u> if it has been pressed at least once since a food pellet was last provided, but it also inflicts an electrical shock on the pigeon each time it is pressed. The green button, when pressed, temporarily shuts off the blue button's shock mechanism until a food pellet is released. Assume that the pigeon can be taught to use these buttons. In keeping with the role of each button as an operant conditioner, what is the expected frequency at which each button will be pressed?

 Determine the types of reinforcement and punishment described.

The blue button has two consequences. One, the electrical shock, is used as a positive punishment because it adds an unpleasant stimulus that is meant to deter behavior. Remember that *positive* refers to the addition of a stimulus (the shock) and *punishment* refers to the intended outcome (to decrease behavior). The other outcome—the food pellet—is a positive reinforcer because it provides a desirable result for the bird. Remember that *reinforcement* refers to the intended outcome (to increase behavior).

The green button, on the other hand, removes an unpleasant stimulus, making it a negative reinforcer. Remember that *negative* refers to the removal of a stimulus (the shock). Because the green button prevents the shock from occurring, pressing it is also an example of avoidance learning.

 Determine the schedules of reinforcement described.

The blue button functions under two schedules as described. Because the shock occurs each time the button is pressed, it is on a fixed-ratio schedule. The food pellet is produced after an amount of time that is unpredictable, which can be described as a variable-interval schedule. The green button provides the same result each time it is pressed, even if subsequent presses within an interval are superfluous, so it too is on a constant fixed-ratio schedule.

KAPLAN

3 **Describe the frequency of the button presses in terms of their reinforcement schedules.**

Because the question asks us to assume that the pigeon can be taught how both buttons work, we can expect that the pigeon will be able to use the buttons to always avoid being shocked. Because the food reward for the blue button is on a variable-interval schedule, we expect the frequency of button presses to be relatively low but constant. A button on a fixed-ratio schedule would normally be pressed more frequently than on a variable-interval schedule, but in the scenario described, the green button only affects the consequences of the blue button. We would therefore expect the green button to be pressed only as needed: once per interval immediately after the food reward from the previous interval.

Related Questions

1. Emily wishes to stop her cat from knocking items off of a shelf, but doesn't believe in punishment. How can she use operant conditioning to decrease this behavior without punishing the cat?

2. A fetish is a nonsexual behavior or object that becomes sexualized and is often able to provide sexual satisfaction on its own. How might the principles of associative learning help to explain fetish development?

3. Ted's favorite restaurant plays the same music each day during lunch. He realizes that whenever he hears one of the songs, he feels hungry. Describe the classical conditioning stimuli and responses in this scenario. What will happen if he stops going to the restaurant?

Takeaways

There are many terms that can be used to describe an operant conditioning scenario; it's important to break down described scenarios carefully to determine what is being added or taken away (positive *vs.* negative) and what effect that will have on the target behaviors (reinforcement *vs.* punishment).

Things to Watch Out For

When presented with an operant conditioning question, be careful not to confuse negative reinforcement with punishment. Reinforcers always increase the likelihood of a behavior, and punishments always decrease the likelihood of a behavior.

Key Concepts

Behavioral Sciences Chapter 4

Aphasia
Language development
Language acquisition
Central nervous system pathways

Language

A 73-year-old male patient has recently had a stroke. While he appears to be recovering and is able to follow verbal instructions, he has lost the ability to speak. What language disorder has this patient likely developed? What part of the patient's brain has likely been damaged to cause this disorder?

 Determine the scope of possible language disorders in this patient.

Because the patient has had a stroke, he most likely has developed aphasia— a disturbance in the ability to comprehend or formulate language resulting from dysfunction in a specific brain region. Three major forms of aphasia are Broca's aphasia, Wernicke's aphasia, and conduction aphasia.

2 **Recall the characteristic symptoms of the different types of aphasia.**

When one assesses aphasia, the three most important characteristics to look for are speech comprehension, speech production, and the ability to repeat verbal information.

Speech comprehension is primarily the responsibility of the temporal lobe; more specifically, Wernicke's area on the superior temporal gyrus is involved in interpreting the content of speech. Other regions of the temporal lobe are important for interpreting other auditory stimuli, such as incident sound and music.

Speech production is primarily the responsibility of the frontal lobe; more specifically, Broca's area on the inferior frontal gyrus is involved in the coordination of the muscles of the larynx, pharynx, palate, tongue, and lips that allow for the production of speech.

The ability to repeat verbal information is the combined responsibility of Wernicke's area, Broca's area, and the arcuate fasciculus—a band of white matter that connects the two areas. While all three areas must be intact to permit repetition of speech, an isolated loss of the ability to repeat verbal information (conduction aphasia) may result from isolated damage to the arcuate fasciculus.

Identify the patient's aphasia symptoms.

This patient has intact speech comprehension, as evidenced by his ability to follow verbal commands, but has difficulty with speech production. We do not have enough information to assess his ability to repeat verbal information; however, even if a clinician tested for repetition ability, the results would be obscured by the difficulty with speech production.

4 **Match the patient's symptoms to the correct form of aphasia.**

The inability to produce speech, combined with intact speech comprehension, is characteristic of Broca's aphasia. Broca's aphasia results from damage to Broca's area; this is a very common lesion in strokes because it falls in the vascular distribution of the middle cerebral artery—the most frequently affected vessel in a stroke.

It is possible that this patient also suffered damage to the nearby arcuate fasciculus, but we do not have enough information to draw this conclusion. We have strong evidence for Broca's aphasia, which would mask the symptoms of conduction aphasia.

Related Questions

1. What is the typical timeline for language development in children?
2. What is the nativist theory of language acquisition?
3. What is the learning theory of language acquisition?

Takeaways

Broca's aphasia includes intact speech comprehension but reduced or absent speech production; Wernicke's aphasia includes intact speech production but reduced or absent speech comprehension; conduction aphasia includes intact speech production and comprehension but the loss of the ability to repeat verbal information.

Things to Watch Out For

Many cases of aphasia can incorporate attributes of the different diagnoses described in this question; major damage to both the frontal and temporal lobes could lead to loss of both speech production and speech comprehension, for example.

Key Concepts

Behavioral Sciences Chapter 5

James–Lange theory of emotion
Cannon–Bard theory of emotion
Schachter–Singer theory of emotion
Universal emotions

Takeaways

The James–Lange theory of emotion states that an emotion is the result of physiological arousal caused by a stimulus, which is then labeled by the brain as an emotion.

Things to Watch Out For

Make sure you understand the subtle differences between the James–Lange, Cannon–Bard, and Schachter–Singer theories of emotion—all three play a part in our current understanding of how emotions arise. Also remember that the spinal cord is not the only pathway for feedback from the visceral organs—the vagus nerve, which feeds directly into the medulla oblongata, performs this function as well.

Theories of Emotion

A car cuts you off as you're driving down a highway at 60 miles per hour. As a result, you feel angry. You also notice that your heart rate is elevated, your mouth feels dry, and your skin feels hot. How does the James–Lange theory of emotion account for the anger you feel as a result of the actions of the other driver?

1 Recall the James–Lange theory.

The James–Lange theory of emotion states, in brief, that a stimulus results first in physiological arousal, which leads to a secondary response in which the emotion is labeled. Thus, when a emotional stimulus is sensed, the first result is physiological arousal, which activates the sympathetic nervous system. When the peripheral organs receive this sympathetic input and respond, this response is subsequently labeled as an emotion by the brain. This theory implies that without the feedback from the visceral organs, an emotion could not be experienced.

2 Determine the relevant factors in the question that apply to the theory.

In this question, the stimulus is getting cut off by another driver while traveling at a high speed. Physiological arousal is indicated by increased heart rate, dry mouth, and increased skin temperature—the sympathetic nervous system innervates the heart and speeds up its rhythm, increases the viscosity (and decreases the flow) of saliva from the salivary glands, and increases bloodflow to the locomotor muscles and skin. The secondary response here is the conscious perception of an emotion: anger.

3 Correlate the relevant factors from the question to the theory.

The emotion of anger you experience in this situation is initiated by your perception of the driver who cuts you off. This stimulus leads to your physiological arousal in the form of changes in heart rate, salivary flow, and skin temperature. These sensations are then labeled as anger by your brain.

Related Questions

1. What is the sequence of events in the Cannon–Bard theory of emotion? *stimulus → emotion & physiological together*

2. What is the sequence of events in the Schachter–Singer theory of emotion?

3. What did Darwin have to say about emotions? How did Ekman further develop Darwin's ideas?

Key Concepts

Behavioral Sciences Chapter 6

Kohlberg's theory of moral reasoning
  development
Psychosexual development
Psychosocial development
Locus of control

Formation of Identity

Lois and Marvin debate the passing of a law that would require businesses to pay all of their employees a minimum wage that is tied to the annual rate of inflation. Lois claims that such a law is necessary because it helps to combat poverty, thereby preventing crime and civil unrest. Marvin maintains that the law is unjust because businesses have a right to operate in a way that maximizes their profits and allows them to stay in business. According to Lawrence Kohlberg, which phase and stage of moral development is each person exhibiting? Are these stages of moral reasoning expected in adults?

1 Describe the reasoning of each person.

Note that Kohlberg's theory does not focus on the ultimate decision of each individual (whether the law is good or bad, necessary or unnecessary, just or unjust), but rather the route by which one arrives at this decision. Lois's reasoning is based on the effects the law would have on society. Because her argument hinges on the prevention of crime and civil unrest, one could characterize her method of reasoning as being focused on maintaining social order.

Marvin's argument, on the other hand, is derived from the rights of an individual or entity. While his conclusion focuses on larger-scale issues (the justice of the law), his argument focuses on individual rights.

2 Match the reasoning to a phase.

Lois's reasoning focuses on societal concerns and understanding and accepting social rules. This puts her thought process squarely into conventional morality. Each of Kohlberg's phases is divided into two stages. Here, Lois's reasoning is mostly focused on societal concerns and maintaining social order, which puts her thinking into Kohlberg's stage four (often called *law and order*).

Marvin's reasoning is based on abstract principles such as justice and individual rights, meaning that it fits within the postconventional phase. More specifically, individual rights are a hallmark of stage five of Kohlberg's theory of moral reasoning (often called *social contract*).

3 Determine whether these stages are expected in adults.

Kohlberg's theory does not expect that all individuals will reach stage six of moral reasoning (*universal human ethics*). Stages one and two (*obedience* and *self-interest*) constitute preconventional thought, which is common in preadolescents. Stages three and four (*conformity* and *law and order*) constitute conventional thought, which is common in adolescents and adults. Not all adults reach stages five and six (*social contract* and *universal human ethics*), which constitute postconventional thought. Therefore, Lois and Marvin are both using moral reasoning patterns expected in adults.

Related Questions

1. A three-year-old child has begun to explore her surroundings and is learning that she is able to control the world around her. She brushes her own teeth, dresses herself, and has begun to develop personal interests. According to Erikson's stages of psychosocial development, what is the next conflict this child will face?

2. Two college roommates are constantly at odds because one is extremely messy and the other is obsessively tidy. According to Freudian analysis, how can the differences between these roommates be explained in terms of psychosexual fixation?

3. A child of busy parents is often left on his own to play and learn. According to Vygotsky, what effect would the consistent absence of a more knowledgeable other have on the child's locus of control and self-efficacy?

Takeaways

Keep in mind that the conclusion of an argument is irrelevant to determining the stage of moral reasoning. Lois and Marvin could have come to opposite conclusions and still have fallen in the same stages of moral reasoning.

Things to Watch Out For

While the differences between phases of moral reasoning are fairly clear-cut, the differences between the numbered stages can be subtle. Make sure to be able to describe the six stages clearly, and carefully examine the content of the arguments made in any moral reasoning question.

Key Concepts

Behavioral Sciences Chapter 7

Manic episodes

Depressive episodes

Bipolar I and II disorders

Major depressive disorder

Bipolar and Depressive Disorders

A 46-year-old woman is brought by her husband to the emergency room after she was found on the roof of her home, yelling incomprehensible statements at the sky. Her husband says that, over the last two weeks, she has been staying up late at night, shopping for expensive clothes that she cannot afford, and sleeping only two to three hours per night. She cannot stop talking and moves rapidly from one topic to another. When asked how she feels, she exclaims, *I'm fantastic!* Last month, she was diagnosed with depression and started on a medication for her symptoms. What diagnosis is she most likely to have?

1 Characterize the mood.

The symptoms described here are consistent with mania. Bipolar and depressive disorders were historically classified under the same umbrella of mood disorders in the previous version of the *Diagnostic and Statistical Manual of Mental Disorders* (DSM), the DSM-IV-TR. In the DSM-5, these two types of disorders have been split into separate diagnostic categories. They still share some characteristics, however, so it is useful to think of them together.

Bipolar disorders—at least their manic components—are characterized by elevated, expansive, or irritable mood. In other words, these individuals feel on top of the world or feel irritable. Depressive disorders are characterized by sadness, lack of interest, or apathy. The patient in this example clearly has an elevated mood, as evidenced by her feeling *fantastic!*

2 Determine whether the manic symptoms constitute a manic episode.

According to the DSM-5, a manic episode must include an elevated, expansive, or irritable mood as described earlier and must last for at least one week (although the duration does not matter if the episode is severe enough to warrant hospitalization). The patient must also have at least three of the following symptoms (four if the mood is only irritable):

- Easily **D**istracted
- Decreased need for sleep (**I**nsomnia)
- Increased self-esteem or **G**randiosity
- **F**light of ideas or racing thoughts

- Increased goal-directed activity or motor **A**gitation
- Increased talkativeness or pressured **S**peech
- Involvement in high-risk behavior (**T**houghtlessness)

These symptoms must cause significant impairment, require hospitalization, or be accompanied by psychosis. The mnemonic **DIGFAST** is a simple way of remembering these symptoms.

The patient in the question meets criteria for a manic episode. These symptoms have been ongoing for two weeks, she has decreased need for sleep, flight of ideas, increased goal-directed activity (purchasing clothes online), and increased talkativeness. The symptom of yelling at the sky implies psychosis, but we at least know that the symptoms are significantly impairing her home life—enough for her husband to bring her into the hospital.

3 Rule out nonpsychiatric diagnoses.

Many diagnoses in the DSM-5, including bipolar and depressive disorders, have the disclaimer that they must not be caused by substance use or an underlying illness. In this scenario, we have no indication that there is an underlying nonpsychiatric explanation for the patient's symptoms.

4 Match the symptoms to a diagnosis.

The presence of a manic episode alone is enough to make the diagnosis of bipolar I disorder; however, the patient's history of depression strengthens this diagnosis because most patients with bipolar I disorder cycle between manic and depressive episodes.

This patient was originally diagnosed with major depressive disorder. This diagnosis requires at least one major depressive episode but cannot include manic episodes. Therefore, this patient's diagnosis is more accurately reflected by bipolar I disorder than major depressive disorder.

Bipolar II disorder has similar symptoms but includes hypomanic episodes instead of manic episodes.

Takeaways

Manic episodes are at least one week of elevated, expansive, or irritable mood with at least three of these symptoms: distractibility, insomnia, increased self-esteem or grandiosity, flight of ideas or racing thoughts, increased goal-directed or agitated motor activity, increased talkativeness or pressured speech, and high-risk behavior. They cannot be accounted for by a drug or underlying disorder.

Things to Watch Out For

As with many diagnoses in the DSM-5, a patient must fit the criteria of a disorder to be diagnosed with that disorder. Other related disorders, such as bipolar II disorder and major depressive disorder, have some shared symptomatology but do not meet the criteria for bipolar I disorder.

Related Questions

1. What is a depressive episode? What diagnoses may include a depressive episode?

2. What is a hypomanic episode? What diagnoses may include a hypomanic episode?

3. This patient's bipolar I disorder was not recognized until she started medication for a major depressive episode. Why is this commonly the case?

High-Yield Problem-Solving Guide questions continue on the next page. ▶ ▶ ▶

Key Concepts

Behavioral Sciences Chapter 8

Social processes
Bystander effect
Deindividuation
Peer pressure
Social facilitation

bystander effect (handwritten)

Social Processes

At a fundraising event, a room full of people are socializing and eating hors d'oeuvres. The approximately 300 people in the room, who vary in age from 21 to 50, have all participated in fundraisers together previously. An individual in the room becomes unsteady and falls while walking toward the bathroom. Initially, no one reacts or rushes to aid the fallen person. What social phenomenon describes this scenario? Evaluate the following scenarios in terms of likelihood of response and response time: If the event had fewer attendees, what outcome would be expected? If the attendees were complete strangers, what outcome would be expected? If the attendees had prior knowledge that the fallen person suffered from a heart condition, what outcome would be expected?

1 Determine what social phenomenon is described in the text.

This scenario is an example of the bystander effect, a social phenomenon that occurs in social groups wherein individuals do not help a victim when others are present.

2 Evaluate the effect of an event with fewer attendees.

It has been shown that the number of individuals in the room (or comparable environment) is inversely related to the likelihood and timeliness of response to the victim. If fewer attendees were present, we would expect it to be more likely that an individual would come to the aid of the victim. We would also expect that the response time would be faster with fewer people present.

3 Evaluate the effect of the attendees being strangers.

The question states that the 300 individuals have interacted previously at fundraising events. Research has shown that increased cohesiveness of the group and closeness with the victim can partially mitigate the bystander effect. Groups of people who are better acquainted are more likely to uphold social responsibilities and come to the aid of the victim. If the group were made up of strangers, we could expect that the likelihood of response would be lower and response time would be slower.

4 **Evaluate the effect of prior knowledge of the victim having a heart condition.**

It has been shown that the degree of emergency or danger to the victim influences the response of the group. If individuals in the group were aware that the fallen person had a heart condition, it would increase the degree of danger perceived by those individuals, as the person might not have simply lost his or her balance, but might be experiencing a complication related to his or her heart condition—perhaps even an arrhythmia or heart attack. This would increase the likelihood of a response and decrease the observed response time.

Related Questions

1. Children were observed on Halloween while trick-or-treating. Candy was left on the porch of a home with a note saying *Please take only one piece of candy*. It was observed that children trick-or-treating alone or with one friend or sibling were very likely to take only one piece of candy, but that children in groups were dramatically more likely to take handfuls of candy. What social process is at play, and what influence does the nature of the holiday have on the observed results?

   deindividuation

2. An Olympic weightlifter is preparing for a competition and records his clean-and-jerk weights over a period of three months during his independent training sessions. He sees increases in his lifts as he progresses toward the competition, but plateaus in the final month. At the competition, he reaches a personal record, adding seven kilograms to his lift. What social process best describes the improved performance at the competition?

   social facilitation

3. Max is a high school student who has typically shown mediocre performance. He transfers to a new school and befriends a group of high-achieving students. Max's grades in his first semester are much above his previous grades. What social process describes these results?

   peer pressure? conformity?

Key Concepts

Behavioral Sciences Chapter 9

Verbal communication
Nonverbal communication
Impression management strategies
Authentic self
Tactical self

Verbal and Nonverbal Communication

> Tom is on the interview trail for medical school. He wears a tailored black suit and a pin from his premedical honor society to every interview and makes references to the influential physician–scientists with whom he's done research. At one particular school, he arrives slightly late to the interview. *Pardon me for being late*, he says. *I couldn't find where to park*. What are some of the impression management strategies Tom is using during this interview day?

1 Define impression management.

Impression management refers to a person's attempts to influence how others perceive him or her. This is accomplished through the regulation or controlling of information in social interactions. There are a number of impression management strategies that are used in specific social situations.

2 Determine what elements constitute impression management strategies.

There are two main elements of impression management in this story. First, Tom is wearing particular clothes—a tailored black suit and the pin from his premedical honor society—and creating a positive image by associating himself with influential physician–scientists. Second, he is providing a socially acceptable excuse for why he arrived late at an interview. Whether the excuse is actually true has some bearing on the label we can give to this impression management strategy.

3 Determine the strategy being used when Tom wears certain clothes and refers to specific professional associations.

The strategy of using props, appearance, emotional expression, or associations with others to create a positive image is called managing appearances. This impression management strategy usually requires a balance between presenting the authentic self—who Tom actually is—and the tactical self—who he markets himself to be when he adheres to others' expectations of him. While managing appearances can play a role in any social situation, we commonly think of its application in settings where an individual wishes to establish authority or to appear knowledgeable and trustworthy, especially in cases where a power dynamic exists.

4 **Determine the strategy being used when Tom mentions that he could not find parking.**

We are not given enough information to know whether Tom's claim that he could not find parking is true. Regardless, Tom is trying to make questionable behavior (being late for a medical school interview) acceptable through an excuse. This strategy is called aligning actions, and it is most commonly used when someone fails to live up to a particular expectation, such as being on time for an interview, scoring poorly on an exam, or missing a deadline.

Aligning actions is often associated with an external locus of control, in which someone considers personal successes or failures to be the result of factors outside of his or her control. Aligning actions also encourages others to make situational attributions about an individual's behavior, inferring that the causes of the behavior are features of the surroundings, rather than personal beliefs, attitudes, or personality characteristics.

Related Questions

1. How does nonverbal communication add to a conversation?
2. What is alter-casting?
3. What is ingratiation?

Takeaways

Aligning actions is related to excuse-making and rationalization of questionable behavior. It may be associated with an external locus of control and may be used to encourage others to make situational—rather than dispositional—attributions.

Things to **Watch Out For**

Impression management techniques can overlap, and one may use multiple impression management techniques in the same social situation. Be prepared for questions that ask about mixing these strategies.

Key Concepts

Behavioral Sciences Chapter 10

Attributions
Correspondent inference theory
Fundamental attribution error
Attributional bias

Attribution Theory

You are walking through a crowded lecture hall with a stack of books and your laptop in your arms. The next thing you know you are on the ground with your books sprawled around you and a cracked laptop after tripping over a classmate's leg. You immediately get up and yell at the person in the seat next to where you fell: *Why did you trip me? Are you trying to kill me and break my laptop?* What type of attribution have you made? What explains why you reached this conclusion? What is another type of attribution that you could have made?

1 Determine the causes for attribution and what type is made in the example.

Attribution theory explains the tendency for individuals to infer the causes of other people's behavior. There are two main categories of attributions: dispositional and situational. Dispositional, or internal, attributions are related to the features or characteristics of the person whose behavior is considered, including his or her beliefs, attitudes, and personality characteristics. Situational, or external, attributions are external and based on the features of the surrounding environment, such as threats, money, social norms, and peer pressure. In this case, when you immediately assumed the classmate was trying to trip you, you attributed the behavior to intentional malice of the person, believing that he or she tripped you on purpose out of rudeness, mean-spiritedness, or spite. This is a dispositional attribution.

2 Explain the tendency to make this type of attribution.

When examining the causes of others' behavior, there is a general bias toward making dispositional rather than situational attributions, which is known as the fundamental attribution error. In this case, the assumption was that the person deliberately meant to trip you. The fundamental attribution error is more common in negative contexts and when dealing with others whom we do not know well.

3 Consider alternative attributions and associated examples.

If you had not made the fundamental attribution error, you might have considered other external reasons for your fall by making situational attributions. You could

Takeaways

We have a tendency to blame others. When inferring causes of others' behavior, we tend to make dispositional—rather than situational—attributions. When rationalizing our own mistakes or shortcomings, we tend to assume an external—rather than internal—locus of control.

Things to Watch Out For

Think about attribution theory and fundamental attribution error any time you see one person analyzing another person's behavior. Be on the lookout for assumptions that lead to dispositional attributions.

have attributed your falling not to the person intentionally tripping you, but rather to a failure to see you when stretching his or her legs, to the person's attempt to get out of the way of another person, or to your own distraction in the crowded lecture hall, which caused you not to see the person who accidentally tripped you.

Related Questions

1. What theory describes the tendency to make dispositional attributions for behavior we see as intentional?

   external locus of control

2. When Itai wins his event at a track meet, he says it is because he trained hard and performed his best. When he loses the following week, he says it is because he had a poor lane position and the ground was soft from the rain. What describes his views of success and failure?

   success → internal
   failure → external

3. Kristin is usually at the top of the class and gets As on all of her tests. You are surprised to hear that she got a D on her latest math test. What cue are you likely to use to explain her usual behavior? What type of attribution are you likely to make for this low math test score?

   usual → internal
   low → external

Key Concepts

Behavioral Sciences Chapter 11

Demographic structure

Fertility

Migration

Mortality

Urbanization

Demographics

> A hypothetical town currently has 1000 people. Of the 1000 people, 480 are women and 520 are men; 170 individuals self-describe as white, 280 as black, 230 as Asian, and 320 as Hispanic. The crude mortality rate is 15 for every 1000 persons per year. In one year, 45 children are born, 200 Hispanic individuals leave the town, and 150 Asian individuals enter the town. How has the population changed in terms of size and racial demographics? Which factors contributed to population growth or decline?

 1 **Determine which details contribute to population size.**

Population size is affected by reproduction, death, and net migration rates. The mortality rate for the town is 15 for every 1000 persons per year and the birth rate is 45 for every 1000 persons per year. The difference in the two provides the rate of natural increase. Net migration rate is the difference between immigration into and emigration from an area. In total, 150 people immigrate into this town and 200 people emigrate from it.

2 **Evaluate the relative rates and determine whether the population size is expected to rise or decline.**

Because the birth rate is higher than the death rate, the population is expected to naturally increase. The rate of natural increase is the difference between these two, or:

$$\frac{45 \text{ births}}{1000 \frac{\text{persons}}{\text{year}}} - \frac{15 \text{ deaths}}{1000 \frac{\text{persons}}{\text{year}}} = \frac{+30 \text{ persons}}{1000 \frac{\text{persons}}{\text{year}}}$$

In addition, the net migration rate is the difference between the immigration and emigration rates, or:

$$\frac{150 \text{ immigrants}}{1000 \frac{\text{persons}}{\text{year}}} - \frac{200 \text{ emigrants}}{1000 \frac{\text{persons}}{\text{year}}} = \frac{-50 \text{ persons}}{1000 \frac{\text{persons}}{\text{year}}}$$

Adding these two rates together gives us the overall population growth rate:

$$\frac{30 \text{ persons}}{1000 \frac{\text{persons}}{\text{year}}} + \frac{-50 \text{ persons}}{1000 \frac{\text{persons}}{\text{year}}} = \frac{-20 \text{ persons}}{1000 \frac{\text{persons}}{\text{year}}}$$

Thus, this population is shrinking at a rate of 20 persons per 1000 persons per year, or 2%.

 Determine how the demographics of the population have changed.

The population was initially 17 percent white, 28 percent black, 23 percent Asian, and 32 percent Hispanic. The birth and death rates per racial demographic are not given; do not assume that these rates will be uniform across the population. While we cannot derive predictions about the changes in demographics from these rates, we can predict some qualitative changes from the migration statistics.

The percentage of Asians increased dramatically over the year, growing from 230 to 380 due to immigration. If we assume that all deaths were in this group, we know that the minimum population of Asians is 380 – 15 = 365 individuals. If we assume that all births were in this group, we know that the maximum population of Asians is 380 + 45 = 425 individuals. We can confidently say that this group will be the largest demographic in the population.

The Hispanic population, which was previously the largest, will decrease to between 105 and 165 individuals (320 – 200 = 120; 120 – 15 = 105; 120 + 45 = 165). Depending on the changes in the white population, either the Hispanic or the white population is now the smallest demographic in the population.

Takeaways

There are three main ways for a population to grow: have more babies, have fewer deaths, or have more people move into the population than out of it. There are three main ways for a population to shrink: have fewer babies, have more deaths, or have more people move out of the population than into it.

Things to Watch Out For

Be careful with the sign convention in demographics. To determine the overall rate of change in the population, subtract the mortality rate from the birth rate and then add the result to the net migration rate.

Related Questions

1. India has seen a large population growth in the past 50 years; however, the growth of Mumbai is significantly higher than in outlying areas. What migration phenomenon best explains this trend?   ↑immigration than emigration

2. The recent U.S. trend to outsource work to other countries is an example of what social shift?   outsourcing = globalization

3. Russia has a rate of natural increase of –4.93. What does this mean in terms of birth and death rates?   ↑ death rate, ↓ birth rate

Key Concepts

Behavioral Sciences Chapter 12

Race inequities in health

Gender inequities in health

Class inequities in health

Race, gender, and class inequities in healthcare

morbidity = frequency a disease appears in a population

Takeaways

It is important to be familiar with both health and healthcare trends with respect to race, gender, and class. It is more useful to be aware of the trends than to memorize specific statistics.

Things to Watch Out For

While females are more likely than men to seek out healthcare services, they often experience longer delays or more difficulty in receiving care than men.

Disparities in Health and Healthcare

Researchers studied four groups: high-income females, high-income males, low-income females, and low-income males. Which group is expected to have the best health profile? How do they differ? How do access and usage of healthcare services differ among these groups?

best = high income females

1 Determine how health profiles differ by gender.

Statistics show that females have better health profiles than males. Life expectancy for women is higher than for men. Death rates due to heart disease, cancer, chronic respiratory disease, and diabetes are higher for men. Men are also more likely to die from accidents, homicide, and suicide. While men have higher mortality rates, women tend to have higher morbidity rates.

2 Determine how health profiles differ by class.

Low-income groups have far worse health profiles than high-income groups. Low-income groups are more likely to have poor health and to die younger. They are more likely to have life-shortening diseases and to die from homicide or suicide. In addition, infant mortality rates are higher for low-income groups.

3 Determine which group is expected to have the best health profile.

According to gender and income status, the high-income female group is expected to have the best health profile.

4 Determine how usage and availability of healthcare differs among different genders and classes.

We have identified that women have better health profiles than men. Women are also more likely to utilize healthcare services. They are more likely to be insured and to have routine visits to primary care doctors, and they have a higher frequency of physician visits per year. However, women experience more difficulty with access and delays in healthcare services. Low-income groups have poorer healthcare profiles and poorer access to and utilization of healthcare services. The high-income female and high-income male groups have better access to healthcare and higher usage than both low-income groups. Females of both groups will utilize healthcare more often than their male counterparts.

Related Questions

1. How do the health profiles of white Americans, African-Americans, and Asian-Americans compare?

2. A low-income female from a small town goes to her local urgent care center. She knows all of the nurses and doctors because of the size of the town. A high-income male from out of town has more severe symptoms and has been at the urgent care center for five hours when the woman arrives, but is seen after her. What is the most likely cause for the discrepancy in care?

3. Rachel is a 35-year-old female with a body mass index of 21.3 from a low-income group. Stephanie is a 35-year-old female with a body mass index of 34.5 from a high-income group. Rachel visits her primary doctor for routine checkups more frequently and reports high satisfaction with care. Stephanie is less likely to visit the doctor and has changed primary care providers three times in the past five years. What best explains this discrepancy?

[Handwritten annotations:]
white = good
AA = worst
Asian = best

preferential treatment from in-group preferences

steph → obese
· not offered as good care
· ↓ happiness w/ physician

Solutions to Related Questions

1. Regions of the Brain

1. The hindbrain is located where the brain meets the spinal cord and includes the medulla oblongata, the pons, the cerebellum, and the reticular formation. The medulla oblongata is responsible for regulating vital functions such as breathing, heart rate, blood pressure, and digestion. The pons contains sensory and motor pathways between the cortex and the medulla. The cerebellum is at the top of the hindbrain and helps maintain posture, balance, and coordination of body movements. Damage to this area causes clumsiness, slurred speech, and loss of balance; note that these are similar to the impairments caused by alcohol, which largely affects the cerebellum. The reticular formation controls general arousal processes and alertness.

2. The hypothalamus is subdivided into three areas: lateral, ventromedial, and anterior. The lateral hypothalamus is referred to as the hunger center and contains special receptors thought to detect when the body needs more food or fluids. The ventromedial hypothalamus is identified as the satiety center and provides signals to stop eating. The anterior hypothalamus regulates sexual behavior, sleep, and body temperature.

3. The cerebrum is composed of the basal ganglia, limbic system, and cerebral cortex; it can also be divided between left and right hemispheres. The basal ganglia coordinate muscle movements as they receive information from the cortex and relay this information to the brain and spinal cord. The basal ganglia include the extrapyramidal motor system, which gathers information about body position and carries this information to the brain and spinal cord, helping to smoothen movements and steady posture. Damage to this area is associated with Parkinson's disease, which is characterized by jerky movements and uncontrolled resting tremors, among other symptoms. The basal ganglia are also believed to play a role in schizophrenia. Within the cerebrum are ventricles filled with cerebrospinal fluid that ultimately flows into the central canal in the middle of the spinal cord. Research has linked abnormally enlarged ventricles with symptoms often seen in schizophrenia, including social withdrawal, flat affect, and catatonic states. The functions of the limbic system and cerebral cortex are detailed in Step 2 of the main question.

2. Vision

1. The duplicity theory of vision states that the retina contains two types of photoreceptors: cones and rods. Cones come in three types and are used for color vision and to perceive fine details. Cones are most effective in bright light (daylight or artificial light). In reduced illumination, rods function best and allow perception only of an achromatic, lower-resolution image. Rods allow for night vision, when cones cannot function. Overall, there are many more rods than cones; however, the fovea at the center of the retina contains only cones. As one moves further away from the fovea, the proportion of rods increases and the proportion of cones decreases. Therefore, visual acuity is best in the fovea, and the fovea is most sensitive in normal daylight vision.

2. Feature detection theory states that we interpret objects by assessing specific characteristics, such as lines, shapes, or specific kinds of motion to identify something of importance *vs.* something of little value. Fishing is a good example of feature detection applied to animals: the person fishing attempts to mimic the features of something recognizable to the fish as food. Some cell types involved in feature detection are cones (for color), parvocellular cells (for shape and boundary detection), and magnocellular cells (for motion).

3. Parallel processing is the psychological counterpart to feature detection theory and refers to our analysis of different attributes of an object through separate pathways before integrating them. Parallel processing requires the interpretation of color, motion, shape, and depth as separate entities, which are then combined to create a cohesive view of the world.

3. Associative Learning

1. At first, this may seem like a paradox—decreasing behavior is the goal of punishment, after all. However, Emily can decrease the frequency of the negative behavior by reinforcing incompatible behaviors. For example, she might provide treats when the cat stays down off of the shelf or pet the cat when it is in a different room.

2. In terms of associative learning, a fetish is an example of a conditioned reinforcer. The fetish object has become paired with sexual gratification such that fixation on it and its use provide satisfaction without a specific sexual context. Once paired, the experienced gratification becomes a reward (positive reinforcer) that increases the use of the fetish object.

3. Ted has been conditioned to associate the songs played in the restaurant with the smell or taste of the food served there. The food is the unconditioned stimulus, the music is the conditioned stimulus, and the feeling of hunger is both the unconditioned and conditioned response. If Ted stops going to the restaurant, extinction of the conditioned response—a decreased feeling of hunger when hearing this music—should follow.

4. Language

1. Babies usually begin to babble in the first year of life; babbling peaks between 9 and 12 months. From 12 to 18 months, infants add about one word per month to their vocabularies. Around 18 months, there is an "explosion of language" in which the infant learns dozens of words and begins to use inflection and gestures to indicate different meanings for the same word. From 18 to 20 months, the infant also begins to use two-word sentences. From two to three years, a child beings to form three-word (or longer) sentences. By age five, children have largely mastered the rules of language.

2. According to the nativist (biological) theory of language acquisition, humans have an innate capacity for language. This capacity is sometimes referred to as the language acquisition device, a theoretical pathway in the brain that allows infants to absorb and process language rules. It is thought that this device is triggered by exposure to language. Thus, the nativist theory posits that children must be exposed to language during a critical period between the age of two and puberty in order to fully develop their linguistic abilities.

3. The learning (behaviorist) theory states that language acquisition is accomplished through operant conditioning. Caregivers repeat and reinforce the sounds that mimic their own spoken language. Thus, over time, the infant perceives that certain

sounds are highly valued and are reliably reinforced, while others have little value and are not reinforced, with the result of shaping the child's acquisition of language.

5. Theories of Emotion

1. The Cannon–Bard theory, in contrast to the James–Lange theory of emotion, states that neither the physiological arousal nor the corresponding visceral stimulation for a particular emotion is distinct enough for the brain to label that emotion. Instead, this theory states that sensory information is received and sent to both the cortex and the sympathetic nervous system simultaneously by the thalamus. In other words, the physiological and cognitive components of emotion occur simultaneously (rather than in sequence) and result in the behavioral component of emotion.

2. According to the Schachter–Singer theory of emotion, both arousal and the labeling of arousal on the basis of environmental cues must take place in order for an emotion to be experienced. The subjective experience of emotion arises from the interaction between changes in physiological arousal and the cognitive interpretation of that arousal. In the absence of any clear emotion-provoking stimuli, the interpretation of physiological arousal depends on what is happening in the environment. In other words, physiological arousal could be labeled as anger, fear, or happiness, depending on environmental cues.

3. Darwin believed that emotions are products of evolution and that as a result, emotions and their corresponding expressions are universal. Because all humans evolved the same set of facial muscles, these muscles would show the same expression when communicating an emotion, regardless of differences in society or culture. Paul Ekman identified seven universal emotions: happiness, sadness, contempt, surprise, fear, disgust, and anger. Also, his research showed that each of these universal emotions comes with a specific set of facial cues, regardless of culture or society.

6. Formation of Identity

1. As described, this child has successfully resolved the conflict of autonomy *vs.* shame and doubt. When resolved favorably, an individual feels able to exert control over the world and to exercise choice as well as self-restraint. The next conflict should be initiative *vs.* guilt, which normally occurs between ages 3 and 6. If resolved favorably, the child will feel a sense of purpose, can initiate activities, and can enjoy accomplishment.

2. Extreme tidiness and messiness, according to Freud, are two sides of the same coin: both indicate fixation in the anal stage of psychosexual development, which normally occurs between one and three years of age. The difference lies in which part of the unconscious is stronger. The tidy roommate's superego influences his behavior, whereas the messy roommate's id influences his behavior. Remember that the superego is focused on perfectionism, while the id is focused on satisfying primal, inborn urges.

3. Lacking a more knowledgeable other, this child would likely have difficulty accomplishing tasks that are within his zone of proximal development. This refers to tasks that a child cannot do on his or her own but can accomplish with the assistance of this more knowledgeable other. Consistent failure to learn new tasks could lead to a feeling of ineffectiveness and helplessness, thereby likely causing low self-efficacy. This could, in turn, lead to a persistent external locus of control, or a feeling that one's successes and failures are due to circumstance, rather than personal characteristics and actions.

7. Bipolar and Depressive Disorders

1. Depressive episodes last at least two weeks and include at least five of the following: feeling down or **sad**, changes in **S**leep patterns, loss of **I**nterest, feelings of **G**uilt, loss of **E**nergy, difficulty **C**oncentrating, changes in weight or **A**ppetite, **P**sychomotor retardation or agitation (feeling or seeming slowed down or agitated), and recurrent thoughts of death or **S**uicide. These can be remembered with the mnemonic **sadness + SIG E. CAPS**. As with manic episodes, depressive episodes must not be accounted for by an underlying disorder. Major depressive disorder, bipolar I disorder, and bipolar II disorder may all include major depressive episodes.

2. Hypomanic episodes are less severe than manic episodes. While the diagnosis of a hypomanic episode also requires three symptoms of a manic episode (four if the mood is irritable only), they do not cause significant impairment to everyday life, cannot have psychotic symptoms, and need not last as long (at least four days). Bipolar II disorder is characterized by hypomanic episodes with or without depressive episodes.

3. Manic symptoms and depressive symptoms are, to an extent, at opposite ends of the same mood spectrum. Patients who actually have bipolar I disorder or bipolar II disorder may first present with a depressive episode. Without any history of mania (at the time), the person may be diagnosed with major depressive disorder. However, treatments of depression are aimed at activating the person and increasing energy and mood. In a patient who has an underlying bipolar disorder, the activation caused by the medication can actually lead to a manic episode, unmasking the bipolar disorder.

8. Social Processes

1. The process seen with these trick-or-treating children is deindividuation. When in groups, individuals are more likely to behave in ways that they would not if they were alone. The group setting increases the anonymity of the behavior and can result in behavior that is inconsistent with a person's typical behavior. During Halloween, children are dressed up in costumes, which increases anonymity, making them even more likely to behave in atypical ways.

2. Social facilitation is at play in this example. Individuals are more likely to exhibit enhanced performance in the presence of others—especially if they already feel a high sense of self-efficacy with the task at hand. The lifter completes his training sessions independently, but during competition, judges observe him and there may be a cheering crowd. Being watched enhances his ability to perform, resulting in a new personal record.

3. Peer pressure refers to social influence placed on an individual by a group of peers or others one perceives as equals. While peer pressure is often seen as a negative influence, it can also be positive. In Max's case, the fact that his new group of friends are high-achieving students places pressure on him to perform at the level of his peers. His desire to be socially accepted by his peer group results in behavior to meet the norm—in this case, higher grades in school.

9. Verbal and Nonverbal Communication

1. Nonverbal cues serve several functions in communication, but their primary purpose is often to express emotions. Ekman's seven universal emotions are a classic example of these emotion-disclosing facial expressions that do not differ across cultures. Nonverbal communication can also be used to convey attitudes; for example, smiling at someone while maintaining eye contact conveys *I like you*. One can communicate personality traits through nonverbal communication as well; for example, someone who is outgoing may use bold, broad hand gestures, an energetic tone of voice, and voice inflection to add to verbal communication. Nonverbal cues may be culture specific: maintenance of eye contact, an acceptable amount of personal space, and the meanings of different postures or hand signals can vary between groups. In these cases, successful communication is often contingent on knowledge of cultural symbols and display rules.

2. Alter-casting is the imposition of an identity onto another person. In this impression management strategy, one assigns a role to another person. This is often done subtly by implying that a desirable quality is associated with a given behavior. Examples include a friend saying *A real friend would...* or Kaplan saying *As a good MCAT student...* in our books.

3. Ingratiation is the use of flattery or conforming to expectations to win someone over. In this impression management strategy, one may blindly agree with another person, may compliment another person before asking for a favor, or may simply try to live up to "good boy, good girl" imagery.

10. Attribution Theory

1. Correspondent inference theory describes the tendency to make dispositional attributions when behavior is seen as motivated or intentional as opposed to accidental. We tend to assume that unexpected actions are representative of an individual's personality or motives; thus, in cases when an individual unexpectedly performs a behavior that helps or hurts us, we assume that this is reflective of the person (dispositional attribution) rather than of circumstance (situational attribution).

2. Self-serving attributional bias is the tendency to attribute successes to dispositional factors and failures to situational factors. Itai sees his success as a result of hard work and personal achievement. On the other hand, he sees his failure as a result not of his own actions, but rather of lane position and track conditions. We could also say that successes are explained with an internal locus of control, whereas failures are explained with an external locus of control. It is noteworthy that in some cases of depression, self-serving attributional bias becomes reversed: the individual attributes success to situational factors (*I got lucky this time*) and failure to personal factors (*It was all my fault*).

3. When making attributions, we consider a person's behavior over time. Because Kristin has always gotten As, we expect her to continue to get As. These are consistency cues, which refer to having consistent behavior over time, as well as distinctiveness cues, which refer to having similar behavior in similar situations. On the latest test, Kristin got a D, which is not consistent with her past behavior. In this case, we are likely to attribute the behavior to situational as opposed to dispositional factors because we have familiarity with Kristin's "normal" behavior.

11. Demographics

1. While birth and death rates likely play a role in the disproportionate growth of Mumbai in comparison to outlying areas of the city, urbanization is also likely one of the main drivers of population growth. Urbanization is the migration of large groups of people to densely populated urban areas, creating cities. In fact, analysis of the outlying areas may demonstrate that these towns are actually decreasing in size as large portions of their populations move into the city for economic or social opportunities.

2. Outsourcing is an example of globalization. Globalization is defined as the increase in internationally connected systems and integration, with the tapping of foreign labor markets and increased availability of goods and services.

3. The rate of natural increase is the crude birth rate minus the crude death rate. Having a negative rate of natural increase translates to the death rate being higher than the birth rate in a population. This means that, assuming no immigration or emigration, the population will shrink at a rate of 4.93 percent per year.

12. Disparities in Health and Healthcare

1. Asian-Americans have the best health profiles of the group, followed by white Americans. African-Americans have the worst health profiles of the three. Specifically, Asian-Americans have lower mortality rates associated with cancer, heart disease, and diabetes and lower infant mortality rates than other populations. African-Americans, on the other hand, have higher mortality rates linked to cancer, heart disease, diabetes, drug and alcohol use, and HIV/AIDS and higher infant mortality rates than other populations.

2. It has been shown that preferential treatment often arises from in-group associations. The female in this story is part of the in-group because she knows everyone in the town—most importantly, the doctors and nurses who will be involved in her healthcare. The male, on the other hand, is part of an out-group, and thus, despite having more severe symptoms and spending a longer time in the waiting room or triage, still waits longer to receive healthcare services.

3. While it is expected that high-income females are more likely to visit the doctor and have better access to healthcare, obesity is potentially a factor in this case. Stephanie's body mass index puts her in the obese range (over 30). Obesity bias is an identified issue in healthcare. Obese patients are more likely to change doctors, and they report lower levels of trust in their primary care physicians. Doctors are also less likely to recommend effective weight-loss programs to obese patients, sometimes on the basis of the flawed assumption that obese patients lack the willpower to effectively lose weight. Obese patients are also less likely to be offered quality preventative care and screenings.

Biochemistry

Key Concepts

Biochemistry Chapter 1

Peptide structure
α-Helices
β-Pleated sheets
Proteases

Elements of Peptide Structure

Creutzfeldt–Jakob disease is a neurodegenerative disorder caused by a prion protein. This prion protein induces a change in secondary protein structure from α-helices to β-pleated sheets. What are possible biochemical consequences of this change in secondary protein structure?

1 Identify the characteristics of α-helices and β-pleated sheets.

α-Helices are rodlike structures in which the peptide chain coils clockwise about a central axis. The helix is stabilized by intramolecular hydrogen bonding that occurs between carboxyl oxygens and amino hydrogens located four residues away from each other. Typically, amino acid side chains point away from the helix's core, allowing for interaction with the cellular environment.

In β-pleated sheets, the peptide chains form rows that are held together by intramolecular hydrogen bonding that occurs between the carboxyl oxygen on one peptide chain and the amino hydrogen on another. Pleating maximizes hydrogen bonding in the structure.

2 Determine how structure affects function.

The structural properties of a peptide affect its function. After analyzing the structure of the protein, determine how each feature may affect the chemical properties of the protein. α-Helical structure involves extension of hydrophilic side chains away from the core of the protein toward the aqueous environment of the cell. β-Pleated sheets are less likely to assume this sort of confirmation; however, one side of the β-pleated sheet may contain hydrophobic side chains, while the other may be hydrophilic.

If we wanted to determine how structure affects protein degradation, we would need to compare the ease with which enzymes could access the amide bonds in each conformation. α-Helices are strandlike structures, while β-pleated sheets are more flat. An α-helix is more easily degraded because its peptide bonds are more accessible to *peptidases*—enzymes that cleave peptide bonds. On the other hand, β-pleated sheets are more stable and expose far fewer residues to the cellular environment.

3 **Predict how changing a protein from an α-helix to a β-pleated sheet may affect the organism.**

Prions convert proteins from a more soluble, easily degraded α-helical conformation to a less soluble, more difficult to degrade β-pleated sheet conformation. Insoluble proteins that cannot be degraded will eventually build up and form plaques, which can lead to loss of cell function and ultimately cell death. As cells die, aberrant proteins may be left behind, resulting in pockets of protein within tissues, and complete loss of function of cells, tissues, and even whole organs.

Related Questions

1. A point mutation changes a cysteine residue to an alanine residue. How might this affect protein structure? *from polar → nonpolar ; disulfide bonds?*

2. A protein is treated with a 6 M solution of hydrochloric acid. What levels of protein structure are most likely disrupted by treatment with this solution? *2nd, 3rd, maybe 4th ; prob 1st if really concentrated*

3. A point mutation causes a single leucine residue to be substituted for an isoleucine residue in the transmembrane section of a G protein-coupled receptor. How might this change affect overall protein structure and function? *both nonpolar — not big change transmembrane = nonpolar*

Takeaways

α-Helices create proteins that are more strandlike, more soluble, and easier to degrade. β-Pleated sheets create proteins that are flatter, less soluble, and more stable (harder to degrade).

Things to Watch Out For

Many questions on the MCAT integrate knowledge from multiple science areas. While the focus in this question was on the biochemistry of prion diseases, other questions could focus on the fact that they can be genetically inherited or can be spread as an infectious disease.

Key Concepts

Biochemistry Chapter 2
Enzyme activity
K_m
v_{max}
Competitive inhibitors
Lineweaver–Burk plots

Lineweaver–Burk Plots

A Lineweaver–Burk plot of *HMG-CoA reductase*, the rate-limiting enzyme of cholesterol synthesis, is shown below. Statins, such as atorvastatin (Lipitor), simvastatin (Zocor), and rosuvastatin (Crestor), are routinely used to treat patients with high cholesterol because they are competitive inhibitors of HMG-CoA reductase. How would use of a statin affect the Lineweaver–Burk plot?

$\uparrow K_m, \; V_{max} =$

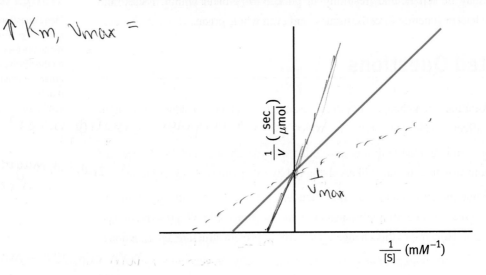

1 Analyze the axes and intercepts of the plot.

The first step for any question involving a graph on Test Day is to analyze the axes. Lineweaver–Burk plots measure reaction rate as a function of the concentration of substrate available to bind to the enzyme. In this case, the y-axis represents the reciprocal of the velocity or reaction rate, $\frac{1}{v}$, and the x-axis represents the reciprocal of substrate concentration, $\frac{1}{[S]}$. This is why Lineweaver–Burk plots are sometimes called double reciprocal plots.

The y-intercept is the reciprocal of the enzyme velocity when $\frac{1}{[S]} = 0$. If $\frac{1}{[S]} = 0$, then $[S] = \infty$. The enzyme velocity when $[S]$ is infinitely large is termed the maximal velocity, v_{max}; therefore, the y-intercept corresponds to $\frac{1}{v_{max}}$. The x-intercept in a Lineweaver–Burk plot corresponds to $-\frac{1}{K_m}$. While this information can be extrapolated from the plot data on Test Day, it is easier and faster to memorize these intercepts.

2 Determine the effect of a competitive inhibitor on v_{max}.

Competitive inhibitors compete with the substrate for binding to the active site of an enzyme. The presence of these inhibitors results in fewer active sites being available to act on the substrate, resulting in decreased enzyme activity. Competitive inhibition can be overcome by increasing the substrate concentration. Excess substrate can outcompete the competitive inhibitor, allowing the enzyme to regain v_{max}. Therefore, while it may take more substrate to reach v_{max}, the value of v_{max} itself does not change.

3 Determine the effect of a competitive inhibitor on K_m.

The Michaelis constant, K_m, is defined as the substrate concentration at which enzyme velocity equals half of v_{max} or $\frac{v_{max}}{2}$. In competitive inhibition, v_{max} is unchanged, while K_m is increased. As described in the previous step, increasing the substrate concentration allows the substrate to outcompete the inhibitor and the enzyme can regain the same maximal velocity. However, because a higher concentration of substrate is necessary to reach the same v_{max}, the K_m of the enzyme will also increase. K_m can be thought of as a measure of the affinity between an enzyme and its substrate; a higher K_m indicates decreased affinity between an enzyme and its substrate, as would be expected in the presence of a competitive inhibitor.

$$K_m = \frac{V_{max}}{2}$$

4 Predict the graphical changes in the Lineweaver–Burk plot.

In the presence of a competitive inhibitor, v_{max} is unchanged. The y-intercept of the Lineweaver–Burk plot corresponds to $\frac{1}{v_{max}}$, so there is no change expected in the y-intercept.

In the presence of a competitive inhibitor, K_m increases. The x-intercept of the Lineweaver–Burk plot corresponds to $-\frac{1}{K_m}$; therefore, an increase in K_m indicates a decrease in the magnitude of $-\frac{1}{K_m}$, resulting in the x-intercept moving closer to the origin. This can be seen in the diagram below that compares the Lineweaver–Burk plot of an enzyme in the absence of inhibitor with an enzyme in the presence of inhibitor:

Takeaways

Competitive inhibitors occupy the active site of an enzyme, but the binding of the inhibitor can be reversed if the substrate concentration is high enough. Competitive inhibition does not change v_{max}, but does increase K_m (the substrate concentration needed to achieve half-maximal velocity).

Things to Watch Out For

K_m can be easily misinterpreted. Because it is the concentration at which half-maximal velocity is reached, an increase in K_m can indicate an inefficient enzyme, the presence of an inhibitor, or a decrease in the affinity of the enzyme for its substrate.

Related Questions

↓ Km, ↓ Vmax

1. How would the Lineweaver–Burk plot change in the presence of a noncompetitive inhibitor? *(parallel lines)*

Km =, Vmax ↓

2. How would the Lineweaver–Burk plot change in the presence of an uncompetitive inhibitor?

3. If the information in the HMG-CoA reductase experiment had been represented as a Michaelis–Menten plot instead of a Lineweaver–Burk plot, what changes would be observed in the presence of a competitive inhibitor?

High-Yield Problem-Solving Guide questions continue on the next page. ▶ ▶ ▶

Key Concepts

Biochemistry Chapter 3
Isoelectric focusing
Determining isoelectric point
Electrolytic cells
Amino acids

Isoelectric Focusing

A biochemist is trying to separate glycine, glutamic acid, and lysine given the following information:

	$pK_{a,COOH\ group}$	$pK_{a,NH_3^+\ group}$	$pK_{a,R\ group}$
Glycine	2.34	9.60	—
Glutamic acid	2.19	9.67	4.25
Lysine	2.18	8.95	10.53

The three points below indicate where the three amino acids stopped migrating in the gel. Which point corresponds to <u>each amino acid?</u>

(−) cathode   anode = acidic (+)

1   2   3

K   G   E

① Identify if it is an isoelectric focusing problem.

Whenever a question gives you the <u>pK_a</u> of the substance being purified, think <u>ion-exchange chromatography</u> or <u>isoelectric focusing</u>. In the above question, we can be certain that isoelectric focusing is used because the separatory apparatus has a cathode and an anode and because we're told that each amino acid will eventually stop migrating through the gel.

② Determine the isoelectric points of the samples.

To find the pI for an amino acid, identify the deprotonation reaction that converts the amino acid with a +1 overall charge into a zwitterion with 0 overall charge; also, identify the deprotonation reaction that converts the zwitterion into a form with a −1 overall charge. The pI for the amino acid is the average of the pK_a values for these two reactions.

For glycine, the sequence of deprotonation reactions is the following:

$$NH_3^+ - \underset{\underset{H}{|}}{\overset{\overset{R}{|}}{C}} - COOH \underset{}{\overset{pK_{a1} = 2.34}{\rightleftharpoons}} NH_3^+ - \underset{\underset{H}{|}}{\overset{\overset{R}{|}}{C}} - COO^- \underset{}{\overset{pK_{a2} = 9.60}{\rightleftharpoons}} NH_2 - \underset{\underset{H}{|}}{\overset{\overset{R}{|}}{C}} - COO^-$$

The pK_a values for the reactions leading to and from the zwitterionic form of glycine are $pK_{a,COOH\ group}$ and $pK_{a,NH_3^+\ group}$ in the table given in the question. Hence, the pI for glycine is the average of these two pK_a values:

$$pI_{glycine} = \frac{2.34 + 9.60}{2} = 5.97$$

For glutamic acid, the sequence of deprotonation reactions is the following:

Glutamic acid has an acidic side chain, so there is an extra reaction corresponding to its deprotonation. The pK_a values for the reactions leading to and from the zwitterionic form of glutamic acid are $pK_{a,COOH\ group}$ and $pK_{a,R\ group}$ in the table given in the question. Hence, the pI for glutamic acid is the average of these two pK_a values:

$$pI_{glutamic\ acid} = \frac{2.19 + 4.25}{2} = 3.22$$

For lysine, the sequence of deprotonation reactions is the following:

$$NH_3^+ - \underset{\underset{H}{|}}{\overset{\overset{RH^+}{|}}{C}} - COOH \underset{}{\overset{pK_{a1} = 2.18}{\rightleftharpoons}} NH_3^+ - \underset{\underset{H}{|}}{\overset{\overset{RH^+}{|}}{C}} - COO^- \underset{}{\overset{pK_{a2} = 8.95}{\rightleftharpoons}} NH_2 - \underset{\underset{H}{|}}{\overset{\overset{RH^+}{|}}{C}} - COO^- \underset{}{\overset{pK_{a3} = 10.53}{\rightleftharpoons}} NH_2 - \underset{\underset{H}{|}}{\overset{\overset{R}{|}}{C}} - COO^-$$

Lysine has a basic side chain, so there is an extra reaction corresponding to its deprotonation. The pK_a values for the reactions leading to and from the zwitterionic form of lysine are $pK_{a,NH_3^+\ group}$ and $pK_{a,R\ group}$ in the table given in the question. Hence, the pI for lysine is the average of these two pK_a values:

$$pI_{lysinne} = \frac{8.95 + 10.53}{2} = 9.74$$

3 Determine the relative pH gradient of the gel.

Electrophoresis is always run in an electrolytic cell. Recall that electrolytic cells require an outside source of energy. The negative terminal is connected to the cathode, and the positive end is connected to the anode. This means that the anode (acidic end of the gel) will attract negative anions and the cathode (basic end of the gel) will attract positive cations.

By extension, we know that zone 1 is at a higher pH than zone 2, which is at a higher pH than zone 3.

4 Determine where the samples will migrate.

Amino acids will migrate toward their pI. At the pI, the amino acid will have zero net charge because it will be in its zwitterionic form and it will stop migrating. In this question, lysine will migrate to region 1, glycine will migrate to region 2, and glutamic acid will migrate to region 3.

Related Questions

more acidic enving →
protonated
go towards cathode

1. If a polypeptide with a pI of 6.7 is subjected to electrophoresis at pH 5, will the segment move toward the anode or cathode? *anode*

2. Why does an amino acid stop migrating when it reaches the part of the gel with a pH equal to its pI?

3. If the pH gradient of the gel were reversed relative to the electrodes, what would happen during the separation of these amino acids?

Takeaways

To solve isoelectric focusing questions, determine the pI of the samples being separated. Then, determine the orientation of the pH gradient in the gel. As a rule of thumb, anions are attracted to the anode, which is in the acidic part of the gel.

Things to Watch Out For

Be careful with problems that ask you to separate proteins. Remember that the pI of a protein cannot be determined simply by averaging the pI values of the individual amino acids. If the isoelectric point of a protein is not given, then another method must be used to separate the proteins.

High-Yield Problem-Solving Guide questions continue on the next page. ▶ ▶ ▶

Key Concepts

Biochemistry Chapter 4

Fischer projections
Carbohydrate structure
Carbohydrate terminology
Stereoisomers
Chiral centers

Isomerism in Carbohydrates

What is the relationship between the two structures presented below?

① Describe structural similarities.

Start by carefully analyzing each carbohydrate molecule, taking note of similarities between the structures. Both structures are aldoses that contain five carbon atoms and are therefore termed aldopentoses. The highest-numbered chiral carbon (located farthest from the carbonyl group) contains a hydroxyl group (–OH) pointing to the right in the Fischer projection, making the configuration D for both sugars. Remember that while D- and L-isomers of the same sugar are enantiomers, this nomenclature is relative to the stereochemistry of the highest-numbered chiral carbon in glyceraldehyde, and has no automatic correlation to the direction of rotation of plane-polarized light.

② Determine structural differences.

The only difference between the structures is the configuration of C-2. In the first structure, the –OH group points to the right, giving this carbon an (*R*) configuration, while the –OH group points to the left in the second structure, giving this carbon an (*S*) configuration.

③ Choose the appropriate terminology to describe this difference between the sugar molecules.

When describing the isomerism of sugars, there are a few words we could use to describe differences between stereoisomers. We already discussed enantiomerism in Step 1; enantiomers differ in configuration at all chiral carbons and are nonsuperimposable mirror images of each other. These two sugars are not enantiomers because they differ at only one of their three chiral carbons.

Isomers that differ at some—but not all—chiral centers are considered dia-stereomers. While this term would be an appropriate choice to describe the differences between these sugars, the MCAT tends to choose the most specific term possible to describe isomers. Epimers are diastereomers that differ at exactly one chiral carbon and can be named based on this carbon; these two molecules could be called C-2 epimers of each other.

Finally, anomers are a subtype of epimers in which the chiral center that differs between the two sugars is the anomeric carbon (the chiral center that is created by ring closure of the sugar, in which one of the hydroxyl groups attacks the carbonyl carbon in a nucleophilic addition reaction). These molecules cannot be considered anomers of each other because they are in their straight-chain forms.

Thus, these molecules are epimers, a subtype of diastereomers. These structures are D-ribose (on the left) and D-arabinose (on the right).

pyranose = sugars in 6 membered ring

furanose = sugar in 5 mem ring

Takeaways

Carbohydrate isomerism utilizes unique terminology. On Test Day, you must be familiar with the specific vocabulary associated with carbohydrates (aldose, ketose, furanose, pyranose, epimer, anomer, and so on).

Things to Watch Out For

Take the time to identify the distin-guishing characteristics of each sugar structure. Checking the relative (*not* absolute) configurations of each chiral carbon can prevent you from missing important details.

Related Questions

1. Mutarotation is the interconversion between the α- and β-cyclic forms of a sugar. In solution, the α and β forms are in equilibrium. What is the term that describes the relationship between these two sugars? *enantiomers ?*

2. Cellulose is created from β-D-glucopyranose, while glycogen is created from α-D-glucopyranose. Human digestive enzymes cannot break down cellulose while glycogen is readily degraded to release glucose. What accounts for this difference?

3. Identify the pairs of epimers and their relationships in the set of molecules below:

D-fructose   D-glucose   D-galactose   D-mannose

epi 1   *epi 2*   *epi 1*

epi 2

Key Concepts

Biochemistry Chapter 5

Saponification
Triacylglycerols
Enzymatic cleavage
Anions and cations

Lipid Saponification

Inflammation of the pancreas, or pancreatitis, occurs due to premature activation of digestive enzymes in the pancreas. Hypocalcemia, or lowered blood calcium concentration, may result from lipase hydrolysis of triacylglycerols in areas surrounding the pancreas. What is the most likely mechanism by which this hypocalcemia occurs?

PTH & callitonin
↑Ca²⁺   ↓Ca²⁺

 Simplify the question.

Some questions on Test Day may appear very complex, and it may even seem that there is not enough information provided. However, simplifying and rewording the question may turn a difficult-appearing question into a much simpler one. The question stem states that *lipase* cleaves triacylglycerols, resulting in a lowered calcium concentration in the blood. A simpler form of this question might be: *What are the products of triacylglycerol hydrolysis and why do these products lower blood calcium?*

2 **Determine the products of triacylglycerol hydrolysis by lipase.**

Enzyme names are one of the many areas of biochemistry in which nomenclature is helpful. Enzymes are generally named after their substrates or main functions. In this case, the name *lipase* implies that the substrate is fat (*lip–*); *–ase* is a suffix identifying the entity as an enzyme.

Human *pancreatic lipase* digests triacylglycerols to form two free fatty acid molecules and one molecule of 2-monoacylglycerol. Like the pancreatic proteases (*trypsin*, *chymotrypsin*, and *carboxypeptidases A* and *B*), pancreatic lipase is secreted as a zymogen—a proenzyme that must be activated to carry out its function. This is mostly a protective function; digestive enzymes cannot differentiate between self and nonself, thus pancreatic lipase is only activated once it reaches the duodenum, preventing autodigestion of the pancreas. Not all of these details are absolutely necessary to answer the question. The most important thing to note about lipase is its main function: that it causes the release of free fatty acids from dietary triacylglycerols.

③ Identify what product is capable of binding to calcium.

Calcium is a Group IIA (Group 2) alkaline earth metal; as such, it normally exists in compounds or as a +2 cation. If calcium is being pulled from the bloodstream, it is most likely forming an ionic bond with one of the products of saponification. Therefore, let's determine if one of the products is negatively charged.

Water is required in the hydrolysis of triacylglycerols by pancreatic lipase. The water can protonate the hydroxyl groups of glycerol once the free fatty acids are released, as well as the hydroxyl group within the carboxyl moiety of the free fatty acid itself. However, this reaction takes place within the alkaline environment of the pancreas (pH ≈ 8.5), which normally releases bicarbonate to neutralize the acidic chyme dumped into the duodenum by the stomach. Thus, this reaction does not take place in an environment that favors the protonation of these compounds. The stronger acid between glycerol and the free fatty acids will be more easily deprotonated, and will exist in a negatively charged form.

Fatty acids contain a carboxylic acid group, the pK_a of which is usually around 4. Glycerol contains alcohols, the pK_a values of which are usually around 17. While it is not necessary to have memorized the various pK_a values of the different functional groups, you should recognize that a carboxylic acid is generally much more acidic than an alcohol.

Therefore, we would expect that most of the free fatty acid molecules would exist in a negatively charged state. Calcium ions are positively charged and will react with fatty acids to form a chalky white substance. This is an example of saponification, which is essentially the hydrolysis of triacylglycerols followed by binding of a cation to the free fatty acids.

glycerol: (handwritten structure) OH with OH and OH groups

Takeaways

Saponification does not always involve sodium hydroxide, although NaOH and KOH are frequently used for this reaction. Saponification is a general term for soap-making, in which an amphipathic carboxylate group is bound to cations after hydrolyzing a lipid ester to form a polyol and free fatty acids.

Things to Watch Out For

Many questions are interdisciplinary and require diverse knowledge in multiple areas. In this particular example, it is necessary to understand biochemistry (lipid structure), biology (the digestive system), general chemistry (group trends), and organic chemistry (functional groups' pKa values). Expect that the MCAT will ask some questions asking you to bring together multiple content areas.

Related Questions

1. Common household soap is produced by reacting a fat or oil with a base to form sodium or potassium salts of long-chain fatty acids. When used in hard water, which contains high concentrations of mineral salts, a precipitate may form that is difficult to remove. What is this precipitate, and what other conditions might reduce the effectiveness of soap?

   (handwritten) FAs that bond to other cations ↓ solubility in water

2. Adipocere, or grave wax, will form on a dead body buried in cold, humid, and low-oxygen conditions. What is likely to account for the formation of adipocere?

   (handwritten) from anaerobic bacteria doing saponification

3. What would result following treatment of a triacylglycerol with a strong acid rather than a base? Could this result in saponification?

Key Concepts

Biochemistry Chapter 6
Semiconservative replication
DNA
DNA replication
Polymerase chain reaction

DNA Replication

The following molecule of DNA is replicated using two cycles of PCR in the presence of ^{15}N-labeled guanine. What percentage of the DNA strands will contain the labeled guanine in both strands (sense and antisense strands)?

5′—CATACTGATCATCTAGCGTATGCGT—3′

3′—GTATGACTAGTAGATCGCATACGCA—5′

1 Determine what happens after the first round of replication.

DNA replication is semiconservative, which means that for each of the two original strands of DNA, one new strand of DNA is synthesized as its complement.

Our templates for this first round of replication are these strands:

5′—CATACTGATCATCTAGCGTATGCGT—3′

3′—GTATGACTAGTAGATCGCATACGCA—5′

Neither of these original strands contains the labeled guanine. Hence, the first round of replication gives us these two DNA molecules:

5′—CATACTGATCATCTAGCGTATGCGT—3′

3′—GTATGACTAGTAGATCGCATACGCA—5′

and

5′—CATACTGATCATCTAGCGTATGCGT—3′

3′—GTATGACTAGTAGATCGCATACGCA—5′

where G represents ^{15}N-labeled guanine.

The original strand with the 5′ to 3′ polarity at the site of replication will be the lagging strand because nucleotides can only be added in the 5′ to 3′ direction. *Primase* lays down a short RNA primer to which *DNA polymerase* can bind; as the replication fork moves down the DNA molecule, more single-stranded DNA is exposed and additional primers are laid down to fill in the opened space. Thus, the lagging strand is synthesized in short fragments (called Okazaki fragments). The RNA primers are subsequently replaced with DNA before *ligase* joins the short fragments together. This process allows the lagging strand's production to follow the replication fork. This is not a concern for the leading strand, which can synthesize a continuous strand of DNA after one primer is laid down.

2 Determine what happens after the second round of replication.

Our templates for the second round of replication are as follows:

5′—CATACTGATCATCTAGCGTATGCGT—3′

3′—GTATGACTAGTAGATCGCATACGCA—5′

and

5′—CATACTGATCATCTAGCGTATGCGT—3′

3′—GTATGACTAGTAGATCGCATACGCA—5′

Hence, the second round of replication gives us these four DNA molecules:

5′—CATACTGATCATCTAGCGTATGCGT—3′

3′—GTATGACTAGTAGATCGCATACGCA—5′

and

5′—CATACTGATCATCTAGCGTATGCGT—3′

3′—GTATGACTAGTAGATCGCATACGCA—5′

and

5′—CATACTGATCATCTAGCGTATGCGT—3′

3′—GTATGACTAGTAGATCGCATACGCA—5′

and

5′—CATACTGATCATCTAGCGTATGCGT—3′

3′—GTATGACTAGTAGATCGCATACGCA—5′

where G again represents ^{15}N-labeled guanine.

In the second round of replication, the strands resulting from the first round of replication are used as templates to create new DNA strands.

3 Determine the percentage of DNA molecules that only have ^{15}N-labeled guanine.

After two rounds of replication, two double-stranded DNA molecules have both strands labeled with the ^{15}N-labeled guanine, whereas the other two double strands of DNA still maintain one original strand. Thus, of the double-stranded DNA molecules, 50 percent will have both strands with the ^{15}N-labeled guanine.

Takeaways

DNA replication is semiconservative. The newly synthesized strand of DNA will be identical to the old complementary strand, provided that there are no mutations.

Things to Watch Out For

Be careful in noting the polarity of the strands. Remember that DNA is always synthesized in the 5′ to 3′ direction.

Related Questions

1. Polymerase chain reaction, or PCR, may be performed to amplify small samples of DNA for analysis. In PCR, a sample is denatured with heat, replicated, and then cooled to reanneal the strands. The strands undergo this process several times to rapidly increase the amount of sample available for biochemical testing. The DNA polymerase used for this process is *not* generally human DNA polymerase, but that of *T. aquaticus*, a bacterium. Why is human DNA polymerase NOT used for PCR?

   human polymerase can't w/stand heat

2. Which strand is more prone to mutations, the leading strand or the lagging strand?

   lagging strand

3. A molecule of DNA is replicated using three cycles of PCR in the presence of ^{15}N-labeled adenine. How many of the newly formed DNA molecules will contain at least one unlabeled strand?

High-Yield Problem-Solving Guide questions continue on the next page. ▶ ▶ ▶

Key Concepts

Biochemistry Chapter 7

Operons
Gene expression in prokaryotes
Inducible systems
Repressible systems

Operons

Prokaryotes often use operons to control gene expression. The *lac* operon, present in prokaryotes, has been studied extensively. In the presence of lactose and the absence of glucose, how are the appropriate genes induced? What happens when lactose levels fall and glucose levels rise?

1 Identify the role of the *lac* operon.

Operons are functional units found in bacterial chromosomes and include structural genes that can code for cellular proteins such as enzymes. In addition, a typical operon also contains a promoter, an operator region, and a regulatory gene. The promoter is the site at which *RNA polymerase* binds. The operator serves as the binding site for the repressor protein encoded by the regulatory gene. All of the genes within the operon are controlled by this unique mechanism. When the repressor binds to the operator region, the polymerase is blocked and transcription does not occur.

The *lac* operon is a prototypical inducible system. The genes in the *lac* operon regulate enzymes needed to break down lactose in prokaryotes. Gene transcription is a significant energy cost for an organism. In order to prevent wasteful use of energy, inducible systems allow for the transcription of genes only when they are beneficial in the current environment. The *lac* operon, in particular, allows for transcription of genes essential to the digestion of lactose when glucose is not present.

2 Recall the function of the *lac* operon.

As mentioned above, the *lac* operon is an inducible system that encodes genes used in the digestion of lactose. The repressor protein is normally bound to the operator region, preventing transcription. When the disaccharide lactose enters the cell, it binds to the repressor. This binding is considered a form of allosteric regulation. The binding of lactose causes a conformational change, resulting in dissociation of the repressor from the operator DNA sequence, making those genes available for transcription. However, this is not the end of the story—there has to be something that attracts RNA polymerase to the site to transcribe those genes.

Determine the process by which these genes are transcribed.

Once the repressor has been unbound from the operator region, the normal process of gene transcription can occur. However, it is important to recognize that transcription of the genes for lactose digestion require both the presence of lactose *and* the absence of glucose.

If the promoter sequence varies from the consensus sequence, then RNA polymerase will not bind tightly without help. The solution to this problem is the catabolite activator protein (CAP), which is present when glucose levels are low. In the absence of glucose, *adenylate cyclase* is also active and produces cAMP. CAP binds cAMP, and this complex binds to the CAP-binding site located just before the promoter region. Once bound, the complex helps recruit RNA polymerase, which can then start transcribing the genes for lactose digestion.

It is not necessary to know all of these details to answer this question; the important point to note is that the transcription of the genes for lactose digestion requires not only that lactose is *present*, but also that glucose is *absent*.

Predict what happens when lactose levels fall and glucose levels rise.

As lactose levels fall, lactose will dissociate from the repressor, which then binds to the operator region. The presence or absence of glucose also affects the intracellular concentration of cyclic AMP (cAMP) because catabolites of glucose will inhibit adenylate cyclase and inhibit the production of cAMP. Without cAMP, the cell cannot transcribe the genes needed to metabolize lactose, even when lactose is present. This results in the preferential use of glucose. Both of these conditions help to decrease the production of the enzymes required for lactose digestion.

Related Questions

1. What happens to the *lac* operon in the presence of both lactose and glucose?

2. What is the difference between an inducible system and a repressible system?

3. The *trp* operon governs the synthesis of tryptophan by prokaryotes. In a tryptophan-poor medium, what is the process by which the genes for tryptophan synthesis can be turned on?

Takeaways
Operons are complex systems used to control gene transcription. Inducible systems allow for the transcription of genes as needed for survival.

Things to Watch Out For
Avoid making the question more complicated than it is. While we covered additional details about the *lac* operon in this explanation, the key point is that operons have multiple parts that each serves a specific function. Operons are complex, but can be broken down into simpler pieces.

Key Concepts

Biochemistry Chapter 8

Tonicity
Concentration gradients
Sodium–potassium pump
Osmosis

[handwritten notes:]
- moved to ↑ solutes
= water would go to that
enviro
= water would pushout more
, so ↓ ⧸ ATP consumption?

Membrane Traffic

The sodium–potassium pump is an ATPase that pumps 3 Na^+ out of the cell and 2 K^+ into the cell for each ATP hydrolyzed. Cells can use the pump to help maintain cell volume. What would most likely happen to the rate of ATP consumption if a cell were moved to a hypertonic environment?

1 Determine the relationship between the two solutions to predict the flow of water.

When an environment is described as hypertonic, it means that the environment is more concentrated than the cell is. Note that you can also express this condition by stating that the cell is hypotonic to the environment. A hypotonic solution is one that is less concentrated than the solution to which it is being compared:

The cell is being moved into a hypertonic environment, which means that the environment is more concentrated with solutes than the interior of the cell is. Water will naturally flow from the hypotonic environment to the hypertonic environment across a semipermeable membrane; thus, we can predict that water will flow out of the cell.

2 Given the flow of water, determine how the cell might regulate the sodium–potassium pump to maintain homeostasis.

Without any compensation, water will flow out of the cell, decreasing cell volume. The sodium–potassium pump moves two potassium ions into the cell as it moves three sodium ions out of the cell. The net effect of the pump is to decrease cell solute concentration by one ion per ATP hydrolyzed. Therefore, to counter the efflux of water from the cell, the sodium–potassium pump can be downregulated. This would decrease the number of ions leaving the cell; because water follows dissolved solutes, less water would leave the cell accordingly:

Thus, when brought into a hypertonic environment, we would expect that the cell would decrease the rate of ATP consumption to maintain a constant volume. If the cell were brought into a hypotonic environment, the opposite trend would be observed.

Related Questions

1. Antidiuretic hormone (ADH) directly increases the ability of the blood to reabsorb water from the nephron. If an individual's blood becomes <u>hypotonic</u> with respect to the filtrate, would ADH secretion increase or decrease? ↑

2. The reabsorption of water from the filtrate increases as the concentration of the interstitial fluid increases. Using the terms *hypertonic* and *hypo-osmotic*, describe the relationship between the interstitial fluid and the filtrate as well as the relationship between the filtrate and the interstitial fluid.

3. Alcohol and caffeine block the activity of ADH, a hormone that increases the ability of the blood to reabsorb water from the filtrate. An individual drinks a large cup of coffee in the morning and, when he goes to the restroom, finds that his urine is <u>nearly colorless.</u> Was the urine produced hypotonic, isotonic, or hypertonic to the blood?

— no solutes → hypotonic

Key Concepts

Biochemistry Chapter 9

Glycolysis

Substrate-level phosphorylation

Red blood cells

ATP

Glycolysis

> Pyruvate kinase deficiency is a partial enzyme defect that often results in anemia caused by a decrease in the integrity of red blood cells. What is the purpose of this enzyme and why does a deficiency in its activity cause anemia?

1 **Identify the reaction catalyzed by pyruvate kinase.**

Pyruvate kinase (PK) catalyzes the final reaction of glycolysis. While the focus in this question is on PK, remember that the other high-yield glycolytic enzymes to remember for Test Day are *hexokinase/glucokinase, phosphofructokinase-1* and *-2, glyceraldehyde-3-phosphate dehydrogenase*, and *3-phosphoglycerate kinase.*

Pyruvate kinase is a notable enzyme for three reasons. First, it catalyzes the formation of pyruvate from phosphoenolpyruvate (PEP) during the final reaction of glycolysis. Second, this reaction is one of the substrate-level phosphorylation steps during glycolysis, generating ATP from ADP and an inorganic phosphate. Because glucose is split into two three-carbon molecules during glycolysis, the conversion of PEP to pyruvate occurs twice for every glucose molecule and results in 2 ATP. Finally, this reaction catalyzed by pyruvate kinase is one of the irreversible reactions of glycolysis. Thus, pyruvate kinase cannot be used to generate PEP from pyruvate—this conversion requires *pyruvate carboxylase* and *phosphoenolpyruvate carboxykinase* (PEPCK) during gluconeogenesis.

2 **Determine the effect of the inability to form pyruvate.**

If an individual has a partial enzyme defect of pyruvate kinase, then significantly less pyruvate will be generated during glycolysis. Pyruvate kinase deficiency is the only common partial enzyme defect of glycolysis and is caused by a mutation in the *PKLR* gene. A variety of mutations in this gene can all cause reduced function of the pyruvate kinase enzyme. The *PKLR* gene produces an isoform of pyruvate kinase in various body tissues—most notably, the liver and red blood cells. Logically, these cells with reduced pyruvate kinase activity produce less pyruvate. In addition, because one of the substrate-level phosphorylation steps is lost, the net production of ATP per molecule of glucose drops from two to zero. In most cell types, this would mean that glucose could not be processed, but there would be little impact on the β-oxidation of fatty acids and other energy-producing pathways.

3 **Consider why the lack of pyruvate kinase would be so detrimental to red blood cells in particular.**

The question tells us that a person with pyruvate kinase deficiency often has anemia due to a decrease in the integrity of red blood cells. Why might this be? Mature erythrocytes lack mitochondria and rely solely on glycolysis for ATP production. In the absence of pyruvate kinase, red blood cells have little energy available for necessary processes such as membrane maintenance, leading to changes in cell shape. Ultimately, these misshapen cells are phagocytized by macrophages in the spleen. This premature destruction of red blood cells results in a shortage of red blood cells, or anemia. This anemia is exacerbated by the fact that some red blood cells may lyse within the vasculature because they cannot use the sodium–potassium pump to maintain cell volume effectively. Chronic hemolytic anemia also results in splenomegaly, or an enlarged spleen, excess iron in the bloodstream, and reduced oxygen transport.

Takeaways

Pyruvate kinase is an essential enzyme for red blood cells in particular. Biochemical pathways do not occur in isolation; each aberration in a pathway may have far-reaching consequences for the organism as a whole.

Things to Watch Out For

Many students, upon seeing this question, will recognize the red blood cell will have difficulty making pyruvate; however, it is important to go one step further to determine the real reason why this is uniquely such a problem for the red blood cell.

Related Questions

1. Which step(s) in glycolysis require an *input* of ATP? 1st & 3rd

2. Which step(s) in glycolysis *produce* ATP? last & 6th

3. Which step(s) in glycolysis catalyze the reduction of NAD⁺?
   5th
   glyceraldehyde 3-P → 1,3 phosphoglycerate

Key Concepts

Biochemistry Chapter 10

Electron transport chain
Oxidative phosphorylation
Respiratory complexes
Mitochondrial membranes

Electron Transport Chain and Oxidative Phosphorylation

Cyanide is a deadly poison that binds irreversibly to cytochrome a/a_3. What are the most likely immediate consequences of this disturbance?

 Identify where in the electron transport chain cytochrome a/a_3 is located.

The electron transport chain consists of a set of four complexes distributed within the inner mitochondrial membrane that are sequentially reduced and oxidized by the passage of electrons. In this question, knowledge of the order of the complexes is helpful. In complex I, electrons are transferred from NADH to coenzyme Q. This is not a direct transfer as flavin mononucleotide (FMN) and an iron–sulfur cluster are used as intermediates. In complex II, electrons are transferred from succinate to coenzyme Q, using FAD and an iron–sulfur cluster as intermediates. In complex III, electrons are transferred from coenzyme Q to cytochrome c. Finally, in complex IV, electrons are transferred from cytochrome c to oxygen, using cytochrome a/a_3—the target of cyanide—as an intermediate.

2 **Recall the function of the electron transport chain.**

Energy-rich molecules, such as glucose or fatty acids, are metabolized in a series of oxidation reactions that donate electrons to coenzymes, including nicotinamide adenine dinucleotide (NAD^+) and flavin adenine dinucleotide (FAD). In their reduced forms, NADH and $FADH_2$ each donate electron pairs to the specialized carriers in the electron transport chain. While shuttling electrons to oxygen, the electron transport chain generates a proton gradient by pumping protons from the mitochondrial matrix to the intermembrane space, across the inner mitochondrial membrane. More specifically, complexes I, III, and IV are all involved in creating this proton-motive force, a concentration gradient that is subsequently used to power ATP synthase. As protons flow down the concentration gradient back into the mitochondrial matrix, energy is released; this energy is used to phosphorylate ADP with an inorganic phosphate (P_i), producing ATP.

3 Determine the effects of cyanide.

Now that we have identified the location of cytochrome a/a_3 within the electron transport chain and described the overall function of the chain—in particular, the generation of the proton-motive force—we can predict the toxic effects of cyanide in the mitochondrion. Cytochrome a/a_3 is the only electron carrier that contains a heme iron with a free ligand that can react with oxygen. The cyanide anion inhibits cytochrome a/a_3 by binding to the iron moiety, essentially blocking the transport of electrons from cytochrome c to oxygen. This disruption means that electrons cannot be passed to oxygen, the final electron acceptor of the chain. Thus, oxygen will not be reduced to water. It is important to note that electron transport is tightly coupled to oxidative phosphorylation through the proton-motive force, so this site-specific inhibition of the electron transport chain will also prevent ATP synthesis. Halting the electron transport chain will eventually result in a buildup of NADH, an important regulator of a number of metabolic enzymes. A buildup of NADH would inhibit *citrate synthase, isocitrate dehydrogenase*, and the α-*ketoglutarate dehydrogenase complex* in the citric acid cycle. In an effort to continue glycolysis, lactate would be formed in order to regenerate NAD^+.

Related Questions

1. Certain compounds, such as 2,3-dinitrophenol, serve to uncouple the proton gradient and ATP production. Besides a decrease in ATP production, what other effects would be likely to occur if an individual was administered one of these uncoupling agents?

2. If a toxin were administered that inhibited the electron transport chain at complex I, would the amount of ATP produced be more or less than if cyanide were administered?

    ↑ ATP, still produced from FADH₂

3. What is one possible explanation why $FADH_2$ produces less ATP than NADH? comes in later

Takeaways

It is not sufficient to memorize the electron transport chain. Fundamental understanding of the electron transport chain and how a toxin may change its function is necessary to answer questions like these on Test Day.

Things to Watch Out For

The electron transport chain is nothing more than a series of oxidation–reduction reactions in which each complex has a higher reduction potential than the one that preceded it. This allows for a flow of electrons down the chain. Remember that oxidation is a loss of electrons, and reduction is a gain.

Key Concepts

Biochemistry Chapter 11

β-Oxidation

Electron carriers

ATP

NADH

FADH$_2$

β-Oxidation

How many <u>NADH and FADH$_2$</u> will be formed by the oxidation of one molecule of palmitate (16:0) to form acetyl-CoA?

(handwritten) $\frac{16}{2} - 1 = 7$ divisions

8 acetyl CoA → 4 NADH / FADH$_2$

1 Determine how many acetyl-CoAs will be made from one molecule of palmitate.

Palmitate is one of the most common saturated fatty acids found in humans—*saturated* meaning that the fatty acid does not contain multiple-order bonds. Palmitate also contains an even number of carbons and thus can be metabolized completely to acetyl-CoA. (If a fatty acid with an odd number of carbons is oxidized, a three-carbon propionyl-CoA will also be produced.) The β-oxidation of a fatty acid occurs by successively removing two-carbon fragments from the carboxyl end of the fatty acyl-CoA molecule. These two-carbon units are acetyl-CoA molecules. Thus, dividing the total number of carbons in the chain by two will give the number of acetyl-CoA molecules produced from one palmitate molecule. That is, $16 \div 2 = 8$ units of acetyl-CoA will be released from one molecule of palmitoyl-CoA.

(handwritten)
① 2x bond = 1 FADH
② hydrate
③ hydroxyl ox = NADH

2 Recall the number of NADH and FADH$_2$ molecules produced in each oxidation step.

The energy yield from the β-oxidation pathway is high, which explains why fatty acids are considered a desirable energy source. Each cycle in the β-oxidation pathway results in the removal of two-carbon molecules of acetyl-CoA and consists of a sequence of <u>four reactions</u>. In the first reaction, the fatty acid is oxidized to form a double bond. This oxidation step is coupled to the reduction of a molecule of flavin adenine dinucleotide (FAD) to its energy-carrying form, FADH$_2$. The second reaction features hydration of this double bond, forming a hydroxyl group. Third, the hydroxyl group is oxidized to form a carbonyl; this reaction is coupled to the reduction of nicotinamide adenine dinucleotide (NAD$^+$) to its energy-carrying form, NADH. Finally, the fatty acid is cleaved into a shorter acyl-CoA and acetyl-CoA. Thus, for each cycle of β-oxidation, one molecule of NADH and one molecule of FADH$_2$ are generated.

3 **Determine how many rounds of oxidation must occur to split palmitate into 8 acetyl-CoA molecules.**

The steps that lead to the release of acetyl-CoA are repeated in an even number fatty-acid chain $\frac{n}{2} - 1$ times, where n is the number of carbons in the chain. Note that the final thiolytic cleavage will result in two acetyl groups; only one molecule of NADH and one molecule of FADH$_2$ are produced during the generation of *both* of the final acetyl-CoA molecules. Palmitate consists of 16 carbons and yields 8 molecules of acetyl-CoA. Thus, there are $\frac{16}{2} - 1 = 7$ rounds of oxidation during the metabolism of palmitate. The image below illustrates these cleavage steps, where a vertical line indicates each oxidation step:

Takeaways

Calculations of yields should be carried out methodically. If you are unsure of how many oxidations will occur by simply glancing at the description of the molecule, given here as (16:0), then draw it out to ensure a correct answer.

7   6   5   4   3   2   1

4 **Calculate the yield of NADH and FADH$_2$.**

Because there will be seven oxidations, and each oxidation yields one molecule each of NADH and FADH$_2$, then seven molecules of NADH and seven molecules of FADH$_2$ will result from the oxidation of palmitate.

Things to Watch Out For

Remember that oxidation and reduction reactions are always paired with one another. Therefore, if there are two oxidation steps during a round of β-oxidation, then two molecules must be reduced in the process. In this case, one molecule each of NADH and FADH$_2$ are produced via the reduction of their oxidized forms.

Related Questions

1. β-Oxidation of a fatty acid yields nine molecules of NADH and nine molecules of FADH$_2$. How many carbons were initially present in the fatty acid, assuming it was saturated?   *20*

2. How many molecules of ATP would be generated by the complete oxidation of one molecule of palmitate (16:0)?   NADH= 3 ATP , FADH$_2$ = 1 ATP
   2.5   1.5

   28 ATP
   1 krebs = 3 NADH, 1 FADH$_2$
   acetyl   4 1 GTP = 1 ATP
   CoA
            X 8

3. How many molecules of ATP would be generated by the complete oxidation of one molecule of arachidic acid (20:0)?

Key Concepts

Biochemistry Chapter 12

Postprandial (absorptive or well-fed) state
Postabsorptive (fasting) state
Insulin
Glucagon

Hormonal Regulation of Metabolism

Shortly after ingesting a high-carbohydrate meal, hormones are released that stimulate the body to utilize and store this fuel. What is the most significant of these hormones? What are the effects of this hormone on its target tissues?

 insulin↑

1 Identify the hormone released in response to carbohydrates.

Insulin secretion by the *β-cells* of the islets of Langerhans in the pancreas occurs when the cells sense a rise in blood glucose concentration. This rise in blood glucose concentration, which takes place after a carbohydrate-rich meal, is the trigger for insulin release from the pancreas. Together, the GLUT 2 glucose transporter and the glycolytic enzyme *glucokinase* act as a glucose sensor, detecting the relative concentration of glucose and releasing insulin appropriately.

2 Determine the target tissues and effects of insulin.

If insulin is released in response to the high blood glucose concentrations that occur during the postprandial state, then it makes sense that the functions of insulin can be grouped into two themes: utilization of fuel and storing of fuel energy in more compact forms for later use.

The three main target tissues for insulin are liver, muscle, and adipose tissues. In the liver, insulin inhibits gluconeogenesis, which decreases *de novo* production of glucose. Insulin also stimulates *glucokinase* and *glycogen synthase*—and inhibits *glucose-6-phosphatase* and *glycogen phosphorylase*, thereby initiating storage of excess glucose as glycogen. In muscle and adipose tissue, insulin increases the uptake of glucose into the cell by increasing the number of GLUT 4 transporters found in the cell membrane. This decreases blood glucose levels by increasing the uptake of glucose by these tissues. In adipose tissue, insulin also promotes the conversion of excess glucose into fatty acids and triacylglycerols. In muscle, insulin also promotes protein synthesis. Interestingly, the brain, renal tubules, intestinal mucosa, red blood cells, and *β*-cells are not sensitive to insulin. Thus, circulating glucose is oxidized to CO_2 and water in these tissues (or to pyruvate in red blood cells) during both the well-fed and postabsorptive states.

③ Determine the effects of increased blood glucose and insulin on other pathways.

When blood glucose concentration and insulin levels are elevated, certain pathways are inhibited to prevent futile cycling. For example, regulatory enzymes in glycogenolysis and gluconeogenesis (like glucose-6-phosphatase and glycogen phosphorylase, mentioned earlier), are inhibited by insulin. This prevents the production or release of extra glucose when glucose concentrations are already relatively high. In addition, ketone body formation will also be inhibited (unless insulin is completely absent, as is the case in an individual with type 1 diabetes mellitus). Protein breakdown in muscle will also be inhibited and insulin can stimulate the uptake of amino acids and protein synthesis in muscle cells.

Related Questions

1. Identify the hormonal changes that occur during the postabsorptive state.

2. An insulinoma is a tumor that secretes high levels of insulin. What would be likely symptoms of this condition?

3. A glucagonoma is a tumor that secretes high levels of glucagon. What would be likely symptoms of this condition?

Takeaways

Hormonal regulation of metabolism is a commonly tested topic. Insulin, glucagon, and blood glucose levels all play a large role in regulation of various metabolic pathways.

Things to Watch Out For

While the MCAT can certainly test particular details of a given pathway, it behooves you to understand the main purpose of a given pathway to predict its regulation. Given that insulin is released when blood glucose concentrations are high, it only makes sense that insulin would be an activator of glycogen production (glycogenesis) and an inhibitor of glycogen breakdown (glycogenolysis).

Solutions to Related Questions

1: Elements of Peptide Structure

1. Cysteine residues contain sulfhydryl groups that form disulfide bonds, a type of tertiary structure. Disulfide bonds can also stabilize local secondary and other tertiary structures as well. In addition, disulfide bonds help form a hydrophobic core within proteins, facilitating hydrophobic interactions. A change in a single cysteine residue may interrupt a key disulfide bridge, resulting in the inability of a protein to maintain its secondary and tertiary structures or its hydrophobic core. Ultimately, this may also disrupt quaternary structure by changing interactions between multiple peptides. Thus, this single change can cause disruption of protein structure and function.

2. 6 *M* HCl is concentrated solution of a strong acid. In fact, the pH of this solution is approximately –0.78. For comparison, gastric acid has a pH of 2 and a concentration of approximately 0.01 *M* HCl. Treatment of a protein with a strong acid will result in denaturation of the protein, or loss of elements of secondary, tertiary, and quaternary structure. Concentrated strong acid may also permit hydrolysis of the peptide bond, interrupting primary structure.

3. This question combines concepts from both amino acid structure and peptide function. A G protein-coupled receptor contains a transmembrane domain that consists mainly of hydrophobic residues. Because this mutation is not in the binding site of the receptor, it is unlikely to affect substrate binding. The specific mutation described substitutes one hydrophobic amino acid for another, which should cause minimal changes in the secondary and tertiary structures of the protein. Therefore, this mutation is unlikely to affect the structure or function of the peptide.

2: Lineweaver–Burk Plots

1. A noncompetitive inhibitor binds to an allosteric site, rather than the active site. Binding of the inhibitor to an allosteric site changes the conformation of the active site, leading to a decrease in the efficiency of enzyme catalysis, which results in a decrease in v_{max}. However, K_m will not change due to noncompetitive inhibition because any copies of the enzyme still in the active conformation can bind the substrate with the same affinity. Therefore, compared to the line without inhibitor, the line with a noncompetitive inhibitor will have the same *x*-intercept, but a higher *y*-intercept. This is shown in the diagram below:

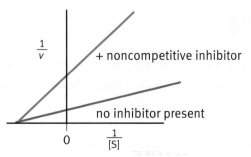

2. An uncompetitive inhibitor binds to an allosteric site, but only when the substrate is already bound to the enzyme. This results in an increased affinity for substrate bound to enzyme and decreased dissociation of the enzyme–substrate complex. Therefore, uncompetitive inhibition results in a decrease in both v_{max} and K_m. Compared to the line without an inhibitor, the line with an uncompetitive inhibitor will have a more negative x-intercept and higher y-intercept—a shift upwards and to the left, which is shown in the diagram below:

3. Michaelis–Menten plots contain the same information as Lineweaver–Burk plots, but have different axes. The y-axis in a Michaelis–Menten plot is reaction rate or velocity, v, and the x-axis is substrate concentration, [S]. Monomeric enzymes will result in a hyperbolic shape in the graph, reaching a plateau at v_{max}. A competitive inhibitor will not affect v_{max}; however, the curve will be stretched to the right because K_m increases, as shown in the diagram below:

3: Isoelectric Focusing

1. If a polypeptide is in an environment with a lower pH than its pI, then this implies that it is in a relatively acidic environment compared to its pI and the polypeptide will be more protonated than at its pI. This means that it will take on a positive charge. Cations always migrate toward the cathode in any type of electrochemical cell.

2. When an amino acid reaches its pI, it takes on a net charge of zero. As such, the species overall no longer has an electrostatic force acting on it $\left(F_e = \dfrac{kQq}{r^2} \right)$. Even if we considered the force on each charge within the zwitterion separately, we could say that the species is in translational equilibrium: the negatively charged carboxylate group (or deprotonated R group) is attracted to the anode and the positively charged amino group (or protonated R group) is attracted to the cathode.

3. If the pH gradient were reversed, then the samples would run off of the gel. A negatively charged sample would migrate toward the anode. In a standard isoelectric focusing setup, this would mean that the sample would move into a more acidic environment, pick up protons to achieve an overall charge of zero, and then stop moving. The opposite would occur for cations, which would move to a more alkaline environment, become deprotonated to achieve an overall charge of zero, and then stop moving. If the gel were reversed, however, then anions would move into more alkaline environments and cations would move into more acidic environments. In both cases, the zwitterionic form would not be achieved and the samples would continue migrating until they reached the end of the cell.

4: Isomerism in Carbohydrates

1. Anomers are cyclic epimers that differ in chirality at the anomeric carbon. Mutarotation occurs about the anomeric carbon, which arises when a hydroxyl group in the sugar attacks the carbonyl carbon, leading to ring closure through a nucleophilic addition reaction. The position of the –H and –OH groups on C-1 relative to the free –CH$_2$OH group in the sugar dictates whether the sugar is α or β. The molecules shown below are the two anomers of D-glucose.

α-D-glucopyranose β-D-glucopyranose

2. Cellulose, or dietary fiber, cannot be digested by humans and acts as a bulking agent in feces. Monosaccharides can traverse the walls of the intestine to enter the cells of the epithelium that lines the digestive tract. Polysaccharides must be enzymatically broken down into monosaccharides to enter the digestive tract. Cellulose is a large polysaccharide and humans lack the enzymes required to break the β-1,4 bonds that hold the compound together. This is reflective of enzyme specificity of the active site: human enzymes can break down α-1,4 bonds, but not β-1,4 bonds.

3. Epimers are sugar diastereomers that differ in configuration at <u>exactly one chiral carbon</u>. The first structure, fructose, contains a carbonyl group at C-2. None of the other structures contain a carbonyl on C-2, so fructose has no epimers in this group. Next, compare D-glucose and D-galactose. These two sugars differ only at C-4; therefore, D-glucose and D-galactose are C-4 epimers. Next, a comparison of D-glucose and D-mannose reveals inverted configuration at C-2, making them C-2 epimers. Finally, comparison of D-galactose and D-mannose reveals inverted configuration at C-2 and C-4, which means that these molecules are diastereomers of each other, but not epimers.

5: Lipid Saponification

1. Soap is a carboxylate salt of a fatty acid ionically bonded to a cation. Soap consists of two parts: a hydrophilic, negatively charged carboxylate group with a high affinity for water, and a nonpolar, hydrophobic alkyl tail that interacts with organic materials, such as soil and grease. The buildup is likely composed of fatty acids that are bonded to other cations that reduce its solubility in water, such as calcium (like the example with pancreatitis) or magnesium. In addition to hard water decreasing the solubility of soap, water that is acidic can reduce the effectiveness of soap. Acidic solutions contain large quantities of protons and will rapidly protonate the negatively charged carboxylate groups of the fatty acids. This reduces the hydrophilicity of these groups, reducing the effectiveness and solubility of soap.

2. The question stem states that adipocere or grave wax occurs in a cold, humid, low-oxygen environment. Bodies quickly begin decomposing after death as bacteria begin to digest the corpse. A low-oxygen environment favors anaerobic bacterial species. These anaerobes carry out saponification of fatty tissues in the body, leading to the formation of a chalky substance in and around fatty tissues.

3. Treating a triacylglycerol molecule with an acid instead of a base could still result in hydrolysis of the ester bonds; however, the carboxylate ions would undergo rapid protonation to form carboxylic acids, resulting in diminished interactions between the polar heads and water. This would decrease the solubility of the resulting carboxylic acids relative to the carboxylate anions. These compounds could not be considered soap. Soap, by definition, is composed of carboxylate salts—not carboxylic acids.

6: DNA Replication

1. Human DNA polymerase is not used for PCR because of the heating and cooling processes involved. PCR requires enough heat to be transferred to the DNA molecules to cause them to denature and separate into two single strands. This amount of thermal energy would also likely denature human DNA polymerase, rendering it unable to carry out replication. The genus name of *T. aquaticus*, *Thermus*, is reflective of the fact that this bacterium's DNA polymerase is active at very high temperatures and is able to carry out replication even under the harsh conditions required in PCR.

2. The lagging strand is significantly more likely to acquire mutations than the leading strand. The lagging strand is synthesized in a discontinuous manner as Okazaki fragments, which must subsequently be coupled together by DNA ligase. This means that the lagging strand contains many more RNA primers, which must be removed and substituted for by DNA. This stop-and-start synthesis pattern and the fact that the lagging strand requires more postreplicatory modifications means that the lagging strand is more prone to mutations.

3. While the ^{15}N-labeled guanine question given in this chapter showed each of the daughter strands individually, there is another way to approach this question. Each of the two original unlabeled strands will end up in only one of the resulting DNA molecules; thus, only two of the eight resulting DNA molecules will contain an unlabeled strand.

7: Operons

1. Glucose is the preferred fuel for most organisms. As such, even in the presence of lactose, there is no need to process this disaccharide if glucose is plentiful. When there is glucose present, adenylate cyclase is inactive, which means that cAMP is not available to bind to CAP. Without the cAMP–CAP complex, RNA polymerase cannot bind strongly to the DNA. By extension, transcription of the genes for lactose digestion will not occur.

2. Inducible genes require the presence of a compound known as an inducer. In other words, the genes of the operon are only transcribed in the presence of a particular substrate—in the example in the question, this substrate is lactose. Repressible systems are repressed in the presence of a specific substrate and allow for certain genes to be turned off under particular conditions. Repressible systems are examples of negative feedback, in which the presence of the product of a pathway suppresses the pathway itself. This mechanism helps prevent wasteful energy use by the cell.

3. The *trp* operon is a repressible system. In the absence of the amino acid tryptophan, the repressor is unable to bind to the regulator sequence. Because there is no repressor, the genes required for tryptophan synthesis are available for transcription. In repressible systems, the default setting for the gene is *on*. When tryptophan is present, it binds to the repressor and the tryptophan–repressor complex binds to the operator region, halting transcription of the genes required for tryptophan synthesis.

8: Membrane Traffic

1. If an individual's blood becomes hypotonic with respect to the filtrate, then the body would aim to increase free water excretion to regain homeostasis. This means that the kidney would decrease the amount of water reabsorbed from the filtrate into the blood. This could be accomplished by decreasing the secretion of ADH, which would promote the loss of more water in the urine, increasing the blood concentration.

2. If the concentration of the interstitial fluid is higher than that of the filtrate, then the interstitial fluid is hypertonic (or hyperosmotic) relative to the filtrate. The filtrate, then, is hypotonic (or hypo-osmotic) to the interstitial fluid.

3. If the activity of ADH is blocked, then it is unable to carry out its function—concentrating the urine by promoting the reabsorption of water from the filtrate into the interstitial fluid. Thus, after drinking coffee, an individual would excrete larger volumes of water. The fact that the urine is clear is indicative of its low concentration. When water cannot be reabsorbed from the collecting duct, the urine will be less concentrated (hypotonic) relative to the blood.

9: Glycolysis

1. ATP is consumed during two steps in glycolysis. The first is the conversion of glucose to glucose 6-phosphate by hexokinase or glucokinase. The second ATP-requiring step occurs during the conversion of fructose 6-phosphate to fructose 1,6-bisphosphate by phosphofructokinase-1 (PFK-1). Both of these steps involve the phosphorylation of sugars; ATP provides the phosphate required for these reactions.

2. ATP is produced through substrate-level phosphorylation in two different reactions. The first occurs during the conversion of 1,3-bisphophoglycerate to 3-phosphoglycerate by phosphoglycerate kinase. The second is the conversion of phospho-enolpyruvate to pyruvate by pyruvate kinase. Notice that each of these steps involves the removal of a phosphate from an intermediate of glycolysis. It is important to remember that 2 ATP are produced in each of these reactions for every glucose that enters glycolysis. This is because fructose 1,6-bisphosphate is cleaved into dihydroxyacetone phosphate and glyceraldehyde 3-phosphate.

3. The conversion of glyceraldehyde 3-phosphate to 1,3-bisphosphoglycerate by glyceraldehyde-3-phosphate dehydrogenase results in the reduction of NAD^+ to NADH. Like the substrate-level phosphorylation reactions described previously, 2 NADH are generated for every glucose that enters glycolysis. NADH can then feed into the electron transport chain to be used in oxidative phosphorylation.

10: Electron Transport Chain and Oxidative Phosphorylation

1. Uncoupling often occurs because the inner mitochondrial membrane has been made "leaky" by increasing its permeability. This dissipates the proton gradient, reducing the amount of ATP produced. In a futile attempt to restore the proton gradient and regain the necessary level of ATP production, more NADH is oxidized and more oxygen is consumed as the electron transport chain increases its activity. Many of the reactions in respiration release heat. Thus, use of 2,3-dinitrophenol can result in (potentially fatal) hyperthermia.

2. The amount of ATP produced if the electron transport chain were inhibited at complex I is, perhaps counterintuitively, greater than if the chain were inhibited at complex IV (such as by cyanide). Complex I is responsible for the oxidation of NADH and the pumping of some protons into the intermembrane space. While inhibition of complex I would stop this electron carrier from feeding electrons into the chain, $FADH_2$ could still provide electrons because it transfers them to Complex II, after the point of inhibition. This would still allow creation of a proton-motive force using Complexes III and IV, with no buildup of electrons at the end of the chain. Thus, ATP could still be produced from $FADH_2$, even if it cannot be made from NADH.

3. As described previously, $FADH_2$ donates electrons to the electron transport chain at Complex II, while NADH donates electrons at Complex I. Assuming no inhibition occurs, protons are pumped into the intermembrane space, thereby increasing the proton-motive force. The proton-motive force is directly proportional to the energy stored in the concentration gradient; therefore, the larger the proton-motive force is, the more energy available for generating ATP.

11: β-Oxidation

1. In order to yield nine molecules of NADH and nine molecules of FADH$_2$, there must be nine rounds of oxidation. Using the same equation given in this question to determine the number of cycles (or mathematical deduction), the number of carbons can be found:

$$\frac{n}{2} - 1 = 9$$
$$n = 20$$

Thus, the original fatty acid must contain 20 carbons. This is arachidic acid (20:0).

2. β-Oxidation of palmitate would yield 7 NADH and 7 FADH$_2$, as described in the question. Each NADH can generate 2.5 ATP, whereas each FADH$_2$ can result in 1.5 ATP. Thus, there are $7 \times 2.5 + 7 \times 1.5 = 28$ ATP generated from the molecules of NADH and FADH$_2$. In addition, each molecule of acetyl-CoA can generate 3 NADH, 1 FADH$_2$, and 1 molecule of GTP (which is easily converted to ATP) during the citric acid cycle, resulting in an additional $3 \times 2.5 + 1 \times 1.5 + 1 = 10$ ATP per acetyl-CoA. β-Oxidation of palmitate yields 8 acetyl-CoA molecules, which results in 80 molecules of ATP. Therefore, in total, $28 + 80 = 108$ molecules of ATP will be created by complete oxidation of one molecule of palmitate. However, one molecule of ATP was required at the beginning to activate palmitate to palmitoyl-CoA. Therefore, the final yield is $108 - 1 = 107$ ATP.

3. First, the number of oxidation cycles, acetyl-CoA molecules, and NADH and FADH$_2$ molecules produced must be determined. Using the same logic as in the previous questions, β-oxidation of arachidic acid will result in nine NADH (22.5 ATP) and nine FADH$_2$ (13.5 ATP), for a total of 36 ATP. Because there are 20 carbons in arachidic acid, 10 acetyl-CoA molecules will result. Each acetyl-CoA molecule will yield 10 ATP, resulting in 100 ATP. The total quantity of ATP produced from complete oxidation of arachidic acid is 136 ATP. However, one molecule of ATP as required for activation of arachidic acid, making the total yield 135 ATP.

12: Hormonal Regulation of Metabolism

1. The postabsorptive (fasting) state occurs when blood glucose concentrations start to drop following a meal. Glucagon and epinephrine levels rise. In the liver, glycogen is broken down and the resulting glucose is released into the bloodstream. Gluconeogensis is also upregulated in response to glucagon, but this response is much slower. Amino acids are released from skeletal muscle, and free fatty acids are released from adipose tissue in response to increased epinephrine and decreased blood glucose. Amino acids and free fatty acids are taken up by the liver, where the amino acids provide the carbon skeletons and the oxidation of fatty acids provides the ATP required for gluconeogenesis. Concomitantly, pathways such as glycogenesis and lipid synthesis are inhibited.

2. An insulinoma releases excess insulin. This excess release of insulin results in low blood glucose levels (hypoglycemia). Because the brain cannot function properly at low blood glucose concentrations, altered mental status may occur. In addition, low blood glucose levels affect the nervous system, which can result in headache, fatigue, double vision, and blurring of vision. It is also important to note that as blood glucose levels fall, epinephrine is released, which can lead to tremors, palpitations, sweating, hunger, anxiety, and nausea.

3. A glucagonoma releases excess glucagon, causing elevated blood glucose levels (hyperglycemia). Normally, insulin has a suppressive effect on the secretion of glucagon. The marked increase in glucagon will cause breakdown of triacylglycerols in adipose tissue, resulting in the release of into the bloodstream, which can ultimately result in weight loss. Patients with this condition often present with diabetes mellitus because of lipids the body's inability to manage blood glucose levels, despite a compensatory increase in insulin secretion.

Biology

Key Concepts

Biology Chapter 1

Prokaryotic genetics
Antibiotic resistance
Transformation
Conjugation
Transduction

Prokaryotic Genetics

Bacterial genetic recombination can result in enhanced resistance to antibiotics. What bacterial genetic recombination process(es) is/are most likely to quickly convert entire bacterial colonies from being sensitive to a given antibiotic to being resistant to that antibiotic?

1 Formulate a plan for answering the question.

This question is asking for identification of various methods used by bacteria for genetic recombination, and which of these processes may be most suited to the widespread acquisition of genes that confer antibiotic resistance in a colony. This indicates that this question requires two levels of thought. First, we need content knowledge regarding bacterial genetic recombination. Then, we must think critically about these processes with an eye toward recognizing what processes are most favorable for the rapid and widespread acquisition of antibiotic resistance.

Note that while there are two prokaryotic kingdoms—Archaea and Bacteria—our focus in this question is on bacteria, specifically.

2 Recall and define each bacterial genetic recombination process.

Overall, there are three main methods of exchanging genetic information between prokaryotic cells: transformation, conjugation, and transduction.

Transformation occurs when a prokaryote picks up a piece of foreign DNA from the environment and integrates this DNA into its genome. Once integrated, this foreign DNA will be replicated in all subsequent rounds of binary fission and will thus be passed on to all daughter cells of this prokaryote. Transformation is a particularly common method of genetic recombination in gram-negative bacilli.

Conjugation is a prokaryotic form of sexual reproduction in which a conjugation bridge is formed between two cells. One cell, called a donor male (+), forms a sex pilus that can attach to a recipient female (−) cell. Once the sex pilus has fused with the recipient cell, genetic material can be passed through the conjugation bridge. This transfer is unidirectional, from the donor male to the recipient female. To form the sex pilus, a cell requires a sex factor, the best studied of which is the fertility (F) factor. During conjugation, a plasmid may be passed through the conjugation bridge; the

F factor is commonly transferred, turning the recipient female into a donor male cell as well. Other times, the donor male can attempt to donate its entire genome to the recipient female.

Finally, transduction is the transfer of genetic material from one prokaryote to another using a bacteriophage as an intermediate. This is an accidental method of genetic recombination because it arises from improper packaging of genetic material during the formation of new virions within a bacterium. First, a bacteriophage infects a bacterium, and its genetic material is replicated as new virions are assembled within the cell. As these viral genomes are packaged into capsids, small segments of bacterial DNA may accidentally be trapped within the capsid. The bacterium ultimately lyses, releasing these virions. When the virion carrying bacterial genetic information infects another bacterium, the transfer is completed; the second bacterium receives genetic material from the first via the bacteriophage vector.

③ Determine which of these processes is most favorable for the transferral of antibiotic resistance.

Which of these methods can transfer genetic material for antibiotic resistance? In short: all of them. Each process can transfer genetic material that codes for antibiotic resistance mechanisms. However, two of these processes are fairly random: transformation and transduction. Transformation requires the bacterium to encounter the genetic material for antibiotic resistance in its environment. While it is entirely possible for this to occur for individual bacteria, it is unlikely to convert an entire established bacterial colony from being antibiotic sensitive to being antibiotic resistant. Similarly, transduction requires the accidental removal of bacterial genetic information followed by packaging into phages. While this may convert individual bacteria from being antibiotic sensitive to being antibiotic resistant, it is unlikely to convert an entire colony.

Conjugation, on the other hand, is a deliberate and specific transferal of genetic material from one bacterium to another. Further, in many cases of conjugation, the recipient cell acquires the necessary sex factor to carry out conjugation with other cells; that is, the recipient is converted into a donor. This would allow rapid, exponential spread of genetic material between bacterial organisms. If the sex factor were located on the same plasmid as an antibiotic resistance gene, then this would allow the rapid conversion of an entire preexisting colony from being antibiotic sensitive to being antibiotic resistant.

Takeaways

Antibiotic resistance may be acquired through any of the three major prokaryotic genetic recombination processes, but the rate and ubiquity of the acquisition varies between the three processes. Transformation and transduction both occur on the individual level, whereas conjugation can convert entire colonies.

Things to Watch Out For

The wording of this question is important—it implies that the bacterial colonies acquiring antibiotic resistance in this question already exist. Transformation and transduction could result in whole colonies with antibiotic resistance—but these colonies would have to be descended from an individual cell that underwent recombination.

Related Questions

1. A pharmaceutical company would like to induce the production of a target protein by a particular strain of *E. coli*. What would be the required characteristics of the plasmid in order to create large colonies of *E. coli* that produce the target protein?

2. A researcher discovers that a type of bacteriophage removes the exact same sequence of DNA from each bacterium infected. What does this information likely indicate about the bacteriophage's ability to feed into either the lytic or lysogenic cycle?

3. It is noted by a researcher that a certain colony of bacteria has developed an extremely high rate of recombination, acquiring multiple phenotypic changes in a very short period of time. What mechanism related to conjugation would most likely explain this finding?

High-Yield Problem-Solving Guide questions continue on the next page. ▶ ▶ ▶

Key Concepts

Biology Chapter 2
Menstrual cycle
FSH
LH
Estrogen
Progesterone
Positive and negative feedback

Menstrual Cycle

During the follicular phase of the menstrual cycle, a dominant follicle is produced that secretes estrogen. If this follicle produces normal amounts of estrogen during the early days of its maturity but declines in estrogen production by day 10 of the menstrual cycle, what would be the result?

1 Visualize the menstrual cycle, focusing on the follicular phase.

During the follicular phase, the hypothalamus secretes gonadotropin-releasing hormone (GnRH), which acts on the anterior pituitary to promote the release of follicle-stimulating hormone (FSH). FSH acts on the ovary and promotes the development of several ovarian follicles. The mature follicle begins secreting estrogen. Together, the hypothalamus, anterior pituitary, and ovary form one of the many endocrine axes (often called the hypothalamic–pituitary–ovarian or HPO axis):

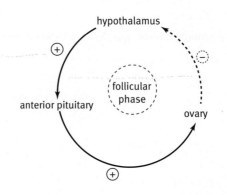

2 Determine the normal role of estrogen up until day 10.

Estrogen has both positive and negative feedback effects in the menstrual cycle. Early in the follicular phase, estrogen acts on the uterus, causing vascularization of the endometrium. It also acts in a negative feedback loop to inhibit the release of FSH from the anterior pituitary in order to prevent the development of multiple eggs:

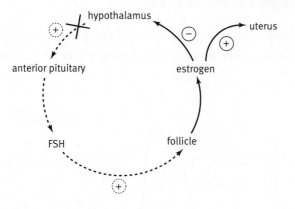

Because the question stem states that early levels of estrogen are normal, vascularization of the uterus and inhibition of FSH will both occur normally.

3 Determine the normal role of estrogen after day 10.

The question also states that estrogen levels decline after day 10. Start by considering the normal role of estrogen after this point. Estrogen levels increase rapidly around day 12 of the cycle, and this burst of estrogen surpasses a threshold to begin having a positive feedback effect on the secretion of FSH and luteinizing hormone (LH). This results in the LH surge. The LH surge is responsible for ovulation, or the release of an egg:

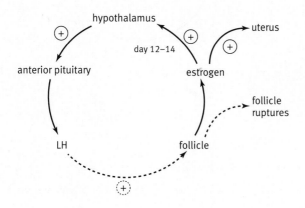

Takeaways

It is important to have a good understanding of the normal way that systems such as the menstrual cycle function. Using that knowledge, different variables, such as disease or dysfunction, can be applied to the system, and the results of that dysfunction can be found in a methodical way.

Things to Watch Out For

Estrogen has both negative and positive feedback effects on FSH and LH at different times in the menstrual cycle. Remember that estrogen levels fall dramatically after the LH surge but rise again during the luteal phase. During this phase, however, both estrogen and progesterone are now produced by the corpus luteum, and both have a negative feedback effect.

4 Examine the consequences of a decrease in estrogen after day 10.

Based on the information in the previous step, if estrogen levels decrease after day 10 rather than increase as they normally should, there will be no ovulation:

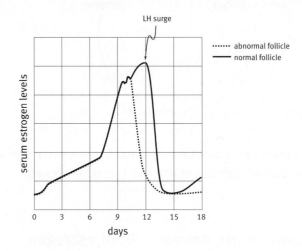

Related Questions

1. At what point in the follicular phase is FSH inhibited?

2. How do the levels of progesterone change during the menstrual cycle? What is the function of progesterone?

3. How could ovulation be prevented during the menstrual cycle through biochemical means?

High-Yield Problem-Solving Guide questions continue on the next page. ▶ ▶ ▶

Key Concepts

Biology Chapter 3
Neurulation
Gastrulation
Implantation
Cleavage

Stages of Embryogenesis

Hirschsprung's disease is a congenital disorder that occurs when neural crest cells fail to complete their migration to the digestive tract. That is, the neural crest cells that should migrate the farthest under normal circumstances never reach their final location. How might this affect function?

1   Recall the functions of neural crest cells.

Neural crest cells arise from the tips of the neural folds. As the neural folds fuse in the midline, they form the neural tube; the neural crest cells are displaced from the tube and migrate to various sites in the body. These cells differentiate into the peripheral nervous system (including the sensory ganglia, autonomic ganglia, adrenal medulla, and Schwann cells), as well as specific cell types in other tissues (such as calcitonin-producing cells of the thyroid, melanocytes in the skin, and others).

2   Identify the pattern of neural crest cell migration.

Neural crest cells migrate outward from the tip of each neural fold. They enter the walls of the digestive tract in a cranial-to-caudal fashion, meaning that they innervate the portions of the tract closest to the mouth first, and the portions of the tract closest to the anus last.

Takeaways

Neural crest cells originate from the tips of the neural folds and migrate to form a diverse group of tissues, including the peripheral nervous system, calcitonin-producing cells of the thyroid, melanocytes, and others.

Things to Watch Out For

Neural crest cells migrate into the wall of the digestive system in a cranial-to-caudal (mouth-to-anus) fashion. Note that this is the opposite direction as the formation of the gut tube itself, which grows from anus to mouth in deuterostomes, such as humans.

3   Determine the effect of a lack of neural crest cells on function in the digestive tract.

In Hirschsprung's disease, the neural crest cells destined for the distal portions of the digestive tract never reach their location, and thus cannot form the parts of the enteric nervous system that would normally exist in these parts of the gut tube. Hirschsprung's disease can affect a variable length of the gut tube starting from the anus and including some length of the large intestine.

Because the neural crest cells ultimately form both sensory and autonomic ganglia, both of these modalities would be lost. This means that there would be reduced sympathetic and parasympathetic responses in the digestive tract (slowed or absent peristalsis, reduced secretion) as well as a loss of visceral sensation, making it difficult for a person with this diagnosis to sense when he or she needs to defecate.

Related Questions

1. Gestational trophoblastic neoplasms include choriocarcinoma, a highly invasive cancer that has often widely metastasized by the time of diagnosis. Why might choriocarcinoma have a propensity to invade and metastasize?

2. A mutation occurs in the mesoderm very early in gastrulation. This mutation is then propagated through many cell divisions. What organ systems are likely to be affected by such a mutation?

3. A zygote undergoes indeterminate cleavage to form two separate zygotes. What is a possible outcome of this division?

Key Concepts

Biology Chapter 4

Action potentials
Depolarization
Refractory periods
Nervous stimuli

Action Potential

A neuron's action potential is depicted below. If during the action potential a stimulus was applied at the time point indicated by the arrow, what would be the result?

1 Identify the parts of the action potential.

The action potential can be broken down into four portions:

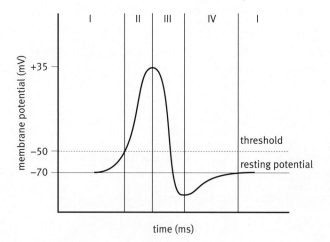

- **Region I:** The cell is at rest and all gates are closed.
- **Region II:** Depolarization—The sodium channels open and sodium flows into the cell, moving the membrane toward the sodium equilibrium potential.
- **Region III:** Repolarization—The sodium channels inactivate and potassium channels open, moving the cell closer to the potassium equilibrium potential.

- **Region IV:** Hyperpolarization—The sodium channels are deinactivated but closed and the potassium channels are closed. The cell is ready to undergo another action potential, but the distance to the threshold is greater so it is harder to stimulate the cell. This is known as the relative refractory period.

2 Review the characteristics of the action potential.

Action potentials propagate by the spread of charge to adjacent segments of membrane. They are considered *all-or-nothing* phenomena because once threshold is reached, an action potential will continue through the same stereotyped pattern of electrical potential changes, regardless of the identity or magnitude of the initiating stimulus. During the depolarization and repolarization phases of the action potential (regions II and III), no other action potential can be elicited, no matter how large the stimulus. This is known as the absolute refractory period.

3 Evaluate the region in which the new stimulus is being applied.

The new stimulus is applied during repolarization. This is part of the absolute refractory period, a time during which no new action potentials can be elicited—no matter how strong the stimulus. Therefore, the new stimulus will *not* produce a new action potential. Instead, the action potential will continue through the rest of its electrical potential changes unchanged.

Related Questions

1. At what point during the action potential is sodium closest to its electrochemical equilibrium?

2. How does a neuron encode the magnitude of a stimulus?

3. How could an action potential be inhibited?

Takeaways

While the potassium channels involved in the action potential can be open or closed, the sodium channels have three possibilities: open, closed, or inactivated. Inactivation occurs at positive potentials and the channel must be brought down below threshold to be deinactivated. Note that when the channel is deinactivated, it is still closed, not open; the membrane potential will have to be brought to threshold again for this channel to be opened.

Things to Watch Out For

This question is an example of one with which many students have difficulty: the "nothing changes" question. It may seem anticlimactic that the answer to this question is that the action potential continues unaltered, but the MCAT sometimes includes scenarios where a new piece of information has no effect. This can be seen in *any* section—including CARS.

Key Concepts

Biology Chapter 5
Anterior pituitary
Hypothalamus
Thyroid
Negative feedback

Endocrine Organs

Thyroid function is often measured by blood levels of thyroid-stimulating hormone. Why is this an effective measure of thyroid function?

1 Identify the function of thyroid-stimulating hormone.

Thyroid-stimulating hormone, or TSH, triggers the uptake of iodine by the thyroid and the production and secretion of triiodothyronine (T_3) and thyroxine (T_4) from the gland. These thyroid hormones regulate the basal metabolic rate of the body by making energy production more or less efficient, as well as altering the utilization of glucose and fatty acids. Increased amounts of T_3 and T_4 will lead to increased cellular respiration. This leads to a greater amount of protein and fatty acid turnover by speeding up both synthesis and degradation of these compounds.

2 Recall the axis in which TSH plays a role.

Many of the endocrine pathways start with the hypothalamus signaling to the pituitary. This establishes a number of axes, the relevant one here being the hypothalamic–pituitary–thyroid or HPT axis. The hypothalamus secretes thyroid-releasing hormone, or TRH. TRH travels through the hypophyseal portal system directly to the anterior thyroid, which releases TSH in response. TSH then acts on the thyroid to stimulate the release of thyroid hormones, which can act on target tissues.

3 Recall how the pathway is regulated.

In addition to acting on target tissues, the thyroid hormones also act as inhibitors of the hypothalamus and anterior pituitary. When levels of T_3 and T_4 are adequate, they suppress synthesis and secretion of TRH and TSH. This paradigm, known as negative feedback, is common throughout the body, and is likely to show up in some form on Test Day.

4 Draw a conclusion.

TSH levels give an indication of the cause of thyroid dysfunction. If an individual presents with symptoms of hyperthyroidism, simply taking a measure of the concentrations of thyroid hormones is insufficient to determine the cause of the symptoms. Is the problem in the thyroid itself, leading to excessive secretion of thyroid hormones despite a lack of signaling from the endocrine tissues in the brain? Is the problem in the central nervous system, leading to excessive secretion through the release of high levels of TSH? This can only be determined by measuring an accurate level of TRH or TSH. TRH is hard to measure because it is in high concentrations within the hypophyseal portal system, but not in the systemic circulation. TSH, however, can easily be measured from a peripheral blood sample.

If an individual has hyperthyroid symptoms, a high level of TSH in the blood would indicate that the problem originates within the brain (or that TSH is being secreted from a tumor somewhere in the body). The high levels of TSH cause the thyroid gland to produce more thyroid hormones, leading to the symptoms. On the other hand, if an individual has hyperthyroid symptoms with a low level of TSH, this would indicate that the problem is at the level of the thyroid (or that thyroid hormones are being secreted from a tumor somewhere in the body). These thyroid hormones cause negative feedback on the hypothalamus and anterior pituitary, leading to a low level of TSH (and TRH, if one measured its concentration in the hypophyseal portal system).

If an individual has hypothyroid symptoms, the same delineation could be made by measuring TSH. A low level of TSH with hypothyroid symptoms implies that the problem is at the level of the hypothalamus or anterior pituitary, whereas a high level of TSH with hypothyroid symptoms implies that the problem is at the level of the thyroid.

Takeaways

Negative feedback systems are common throughout the endocrine system. Many of these systems can be organized into axes, including the hypothalamic–pituitary–adrenal, hypothalamic–pituiary–thyroid, and hypothalamic–pituitary–ovarian, –testicular, or –gonadal axes.

Things to Watch Out For

Proper diagnosis of an endocrinopathy usually requires measurement of at least two different hormones or analysis of at least two different organs. This allows determination of the site of the problem. In this question, a high concentration of thyroid hormone could be due to a problem in the brain or the thyroid; measurement of TSH would distinguish between these two sites of pathology.

Related Questions

1. A pituitary tumor compresses the stalk and causes a cessation of ACTH secretion. What effects would this lack of ACTH secretion have?

2. The posterior pituitary gland is also known as the neurohypophysis. Based on the relationship to other brain structures, why does this name make sense?

3. The pancreas is said to have both exocrine and endocrine functions. What is the difference between an exocrine and an endocrine organ?

Key Concepts

Biology Chapter 6
The respiratory system
Alveoli
Gas exchange
Dead space

The Respiratory System

The volume of the lungs that does not participate in gas exchange is considered physiological dead space. There are two types of dead space that are seen at rest: anatomical and alveolar. Anatomical dead space includes the conducting areas, such as the mouth and trachea, where oxygen enters the respiratory system but does not contact alveoli. Alveolar dead space is the area in the alveoli that does contact air but lacks sufficient circulation to participate in gas exchange. How can physiological dead space be reduced?

1 Examine each type of dead space separately.

Anatomical dead space refers to the air that remains in the conducting pathways—the mouth and trachea—with every breath. Because the size and length of the mouth and trachea are set and relatively unchangeable for a given individual, it is unlikely that physiological dead space can be decreased much through changes in the anatomical dead space.

Alveolar dead space consists of alveoli that contact air but do not participate in gas exchange. Because the alveoli are normal, they are capable of participating in gas exchange under the right conditions; therefore, alveolar dead space can be reduced.

2 Review the method of gas exchange at the tissues and in the lungs.

In the normal lung, oxygen will diffuse from alveolar air into the pulmonary capillaries. When the partial pressure of O_2 in the alveolar air and capillary blood equilibrate, the diffusion stops. Normally, this occurs before the blood in the pulmonary capillary exits the lungs and is considered perfusion-limited gas exchange. This O_2 is bound to hemoglobin and is taken and released to the tissues. CO_2 is produced by the tissues and diffuses into capillary blood, where it is carried to the lungs primarily as HCO_3^-. At the lungs, the reaction is reversed and CO_2 is exhaled:

3 Determine why some alveoli do not participate in gas exchange.

There is not sufficient bloodflow through the capillaries of these dead space alveoli to induce them to participate in gas exchange. There must be bloodflow to a given alveolus for gas exchange to occur in that alveolus.

4 Determine how to increase bloodflow through the lungs.

If pulmonary bloodflow were increased, then more alveoli would be perfused with blood and would therefore participate in gas exchange. Increasing pulmonary bloodflow would require increasing the output of the right ventricle. Cardiac output increases during exercise because there is an increased heart rate and increased venous return due to skeletal muscle activity. Therefore, exercise would increase the amount of pulmonary bloodflow. This increased flow of blood through the lungs would recruit more alveoli for gas exchange and, therefore, reduce alveolar and physiological dead space.

Pulmonary bloodflow could also be increased through the administration of vasodilators, which open the blood vessels, lowering vascular resistance and increasing flow. Certain vasodilators are particularly active in the lungs.

Takeaways

The respiratory system is intimately linked to the circulatory system. Oxygen is delivered to tissues, and CO_2 is removed from tissues and ultimately removed from the body through exchange from the pulmonary capillaries into the alveolar space.

Things to Watch Out For

Under resting conditions, alveolar oxygen equilibrates with the blood in the pulmonary capillaries. This is considered a perfusion-limited exchange. Under conditions of exercise, the partial pressures of oxygen do not necessarily equilibrate along the length of the pulmonary capillary and a partial pressure gradient is maintained even at the venous end of the capillary.

Related Questions

1. What is the result if bloodflow to the left lung is completely blocked by a pulmonary embolus?

2. If an area of the lung is not ventilated due to an obstruction of the airways, what is the partial pressure of oxygen (P_aO_2) in the pulmonary capillaries of that area?

3. At what point will the diffusion of oxygen from the alveolus to the capillary stop?

Key Concepts

Biology Chapter 7
Oxyhemoglobin dissociation curve
Carbon monoxide
Hemoglobin
Left and right shifts

Oxyhemoglobin Dissociation Curve

Carbon monoxide (CO) binding to hemoglobin occurs in competition with oxygen (O_2) binding to hemoglobin; hemoglobin's affinity for CO is over 200 times its affinity for O_2. However, the binding of CO at one site increases the affinity for O_2 at the remaining sites. Draw the oxyhemoglobin dissociation curve for CO poisoning, measuring hemoglobin oxygen content (in units of % hemoglobin saturation) on the vertical axis.

1 Visualize the normal oxyhemoglobin dissociation curve.

The oxyhemoglobin dissociation curve shows the percent saturation of hemoglobin as a function of the partial pressure of oxygen (PO_2). At a PO_2 of 100 mmHg (the partial pressure of oxygen in the lungs), hemoglobin saturation is 100 percent, which means that four oxygen molecules are bound to nearly every hemoglobin molecule. At a PO_2 of 40 mmHg (the partial pressure of oxygen in resting tissues), hemoglobin is 80 percent saturated. At a PO_2 of 20 mmHg (the partial pressure of oxygen in exercising tissues), hemoglobin is 30 percent saturated with oxygen molecules. Oxygen binds cooperatively to hemoglobin, meaning that the binding of the first oxygen molecule facilitates the binding of the next, and so on. This results in a sigmoidal, or S-shaped, curve:

② Examine the effect that carbon monoxide binding has on oxygen binding.

The question stem states that CO competes with O_2 when binding hemoglobin. Because hemoglobin's affinity for CO is 200 times greater than O_2, hemoglobin will preferentially bind CO first. This will decrease the amount of O_2 that can bind to hemoglobin and, therefore, decrease the amount of O_2 that is in the blood.

③ Determine the effect that carbon monoxide binding will have on the oxyhemoglobin dissociation curve.

The question stem also states that the binding of CO increases hemoglobin's affinity for O_2 at the remaining sites. Any physiological factor that increases the affinity of hemoglobin for oxygen (such as decreased PCO_2, increased pH, or decreased temperature) has the effect of shifting the curve to the left. Any physiological factor that decreases the affinity of hemoglobin for oxygen (such as increased PCO_2, decreased pH, or increased temperature) has the effect of shifting the curve to the right. The right shift is known as the Bohr effect. However, in this case, the affinity of hemoglobin for oxygen is increased, and so there will be a left shift in the oxyhemoglobin dissociation curve. It is this left shift that makes CO poisoning so deadly; with CO bound to hemoglobin, the O_2 molecules are bound so tightly that they cannot be off-loaded at the tissues, and tissue hypoxia occurs:

Takeaways

Be familiar with the concepts of PO_2 and PCO_2, what factors change their values, and how they are represented graphically.

Things to Watch Out For

Right shifts in the dissociation curve (Bohr effect) are more commonly seen, but be prepared for the factors that can cause the curve to shift to the left, including decreased PCO_2, increased pH, decreased temperature, fetal hemoglobin, and certain pathological states—such as carbon monoxide poisoning.

Related Questions

1. How would exercise affect the oxyhemoglobin dissociation curve?

2. What type of compensatory reactions would a high PCO_2 cause?

3. What would the oxyhemoglobin dissociation curve look like in a patient with metabolic alkalosis?

High-Yield Problem-Solving Guide questions continue on the next page. ▶ ▶ ▶

Key Concepts

Biology Chapter 8
Immunoglobulins
Active immunity
Passive immunity
Innate immunity
Adaptive immunity

Immune Function

X-linked severe combined immunodeficiency (SCID) occurs due to a mutation in a protein necessary for the receptors for interleukins IL-2, IL-4, IL-7, IL-9, and IL-15. This results in the absence or near absence of T-cells and natural killer (NK) cells. B-cells are present but are nonfunctioning in these individuals. Why, despite their presence, are B-cells nonfunctional in those with SCID?

1 Summarize and simplify the question.

The question stem states that severe combined immunodeficiency (SCID) results when there is a mutation in a protein required for the receptors for various interleukins. This results in a lack of T-cells and natural killer (NK) cells. B-cells are still present but are nonfunctional. Given this information, this question is really asking about how a receptor mutation will cause a lack of some cell types (T-cells and NK cells), while producing nonfunctional B-cells.

2 Identify the normal purpose of interleukins.

Interleukins are the language of communication in the immune system. Interleukins direct the proliferation and maturation of lymphocytes including T-cells and B-cells. In addition, portions of the innate immune system are also coordinated by interactions with interleukins. Interleukins are known to activate macrophages, NK cells, and B-cells.

3 Determine how a mutation in an interleukin receptor may affect immune system signaling.

Communication between cells often requires interactions between some soluble molecule and a receptor. Lack of a functioning receptor often has the same effect as a lack of the effector molecule.

The question stem states that there is a mutation in a protein required for interleukin receptors. This mutation affects the function of multiple interleukins. The dysfunction of this interleukin receptor results in defective immune system signaling. If the immune system cannot signal between cells properly, then numerous processes may be affected. Interleukins are part of the system that induces proliferation of T-cells and NK cells. In addition, without effective interleukin signaling, T-cells that are produced may not be able to migrate to the thymus for maturation. A lack of mature T-cells will result in the inability of T-cells to signal to B-cells. If there is no signaling to B-cells, then plasma and memory cells will not form, and antibody production will not occur. Therefore, there will be little to no humoral protection against antigens in these individuals.

 Using the information discussed, propose a hypothesis.

To summarize the information previously considered, lack of a functioning interleukin receptor results in a near complete loss of function of the adaptive immune system. T-cells and NK cells do not mature, and B-cells are not able to function. If the same protein is involved in multiple receptor types, then mutations of this protein will affect multiple interleukin receptors. The resulting phenotype is a nonfunctioning adaptive immune system. T-cells and NK cells are unable to proliferate, and signaling to B-cells is severely limited.

Related Questions

1. During pregnancy, some immunoglobulins are transferred across the placenta. After birth, breast milk also contains antibodies that provide the infant with reduced susceptibility to infection. What is a potential disadvantage of this type of immunity?

2. Allergic reactions, such as seasonal allergies, rely on the cross-linking of immunoglobulins that are already on the surface on mast cells. Why does the first exposure to an allergen rarely result in an immune response?

3. Respiratory droplets, created during sneezing or coughing, can carry bacteria and viruses. What type of immunity is represented by the cilia of the respiratory passages that carry these viruses toward the oropharynx to be swallowed or expelled?

Takeaways

Because of the interdependencies of the immune system, dysfunction of one arm of the immune system may cause dysfunction of other arms of the immune system. In this example, a lack of functional T-cells leads to a lack of functional B-cells.

Things to Watch Out For

Many of the questions focusing on the immune system on the MCAT focus on the crosstalk of this system. Most important among these forms of communication are those between the innate and adaptive immune systems and those between T- and B-cells.

Key Concepts
Biology Chapter 9
Digestive enzymes
Pancreatic enzymes
Pancreas
Duodenum
Gastric acid

The Digestive System

During the gastric phase of digestion, the presence of food in the stomach, particularly amino acids and peptides, causes G cells to secrete gastrin, which in turn stimulates parietal cells. Gastrin secretion is normally inhibited once acidic chyme, with a pH less than 3, reaches the duodenum. What would occur if a tumor secreted excess gastrin in an unregulated fashion?

1 Determine the role of gastrin in the stomach.

According to the question stem, gastrin stimulates parietal cells when food is present in the stomach. Parietal cells secrete hydrochloric acid, and therefore gastrin is a physiological agonist of HCl secretion. Once the chyme reaches a certain acidity (pH < 3) and moves into the small intestine, gastrin secretion is inhibited and therefore HCl secretion is decreased.

2 Determine the role of hydrochloric acid in the stomach.

In the stomach, HCl is necessary for the proper function of *pepsin* because low pH promotes activation of *pepsinogen* to pepsin; this enzyme is also most active in the pH range of 1–3.

3 Examine what occurs when acidic chyme reaches the small intestine.

Once the chyme moves into the small intestine, the pH needs to be increased to reach the optimal pH for pancreatic proteases and lipases (around 8.5). Therefore, gastrin release is inhibited, and the pancreas is stimulated to secrete bicarbonate into the duodenum to neutralize the acid. The pancreas also releases hydrolytic enzymes, such as *amylase, trypsinogen, chymotrypsinogen, carboxypeptidases A and B,* and pancreatic lipase.

4 Examine the effect of a gastrin-secreting tumor.

A gastrin-secreting tumor will secrete gastrin at all times and will not be inhibited by normal feedback mechanisms, such as the presence of chyme in the small intestine.

This gastrin will continually stimulate parietal cells to produce HCl. This excess of acid will move with the chyme into the small intestine. Normal amounts of bicarbonate will be released; however, this is not enough to neutralize such an excess of HCl.

This condition—caused by a gastrin-secreting tumor—is called *Zollinger–Ellison syndrome*. The tumor is usually located in the pancreatic islets of Langerhans.

5 Determine the effects of an acidic environment in the small intestine.

Pancreatic enzymes require a more alkaline environment than gastric enzymes for optimal activity. If the environment in the small intestine is too acidic, then pancreatic enzymes will be unable to function normally. While proteins and carbohydrates are partially digested before they reach the small intestine, fats have very little digestion until they reach the duodenum. If *pancreatic lipase* is unable to function due to an excessively acidic environment, it will not be able to digest lipids. This will result in the malabsorption of lipids, which leads to excretion of fats in the feces, also known as *steatorrhea*. The excess acid can also cause gastric and duodenal ulcers, in which the mucosal lining is worn away and acid can damage the underlying epithelial cells.

Related Questions

1. A patient with a peptic ulcer takes a large dose of antacid. This would primarily reduce the activity of which digestive enzyme?

2. Pancreatic ductal cells secrete bicarbonate, which is moved into the intestinal lumen. What would be the physiological results if these ductal cells were destroyed by an autoimmune disorder?

3. Pancreatitis is a disease that prevents the pancreas from being able to produce adequate amounts of lipase. What will be the physiological result of this component of the disease?

Takeaways

The effects of excess acid on the digestive system include the direct effects of acid on the tissues (gastric and duodenal ulcers) as well as biochemical effects on the digestive enzymes (denaturation and decreased activity).

Things to Watch Out For

An acidic duodenal pH will affect the function of all of the pancreatic enzymes, but some protein absorption can still occur because proteins are partially digested in the stomach. Carbohydrate digestion does not rely heavily on pancreatic secretions; absorption of some carbohydrates can still occur because they begin digestion in the mouth and continue to be broken down by disaccharidases in the intestinal brush border.

Key Concepts

Biology Chapter 10

Plasma osmolarity

Filtrate osmolarity

Antidiuretic hormone

Aldosterone

Water reabsorption

Kidney Function

A student discovers that drinking diet caffeinated soda results in a significant increase in urine volume and frequency. What are the physiological factors driving this phenomenon?

1 Identify the relevant kidney functions affected: filtration, secretion, and/or reabsorption.

Excessive urine output means that there is a failure to reabsorb water from the nephron. Thus, the problem is at the level of reabsorption.

Renal failure relating to filtration usually results in irregular plasma osmolarity (for example, the urea concentration may be too high, or the albumin concentration may be too low). Secretion plays a critical role in maintaining blood pH, potassium concentrations in blood, and nitrogenous waste concentrations in the filtrate. Reabsorption also affects filtrate concentration, as essential substances such as glucose, amino acids, vitamins, and salts are returned to the blood.

2 Identify the roles of plasma osmolarity and antidiuretic hormone.

Caffeine (as well as alcohol) inhibits either the secretion or activity of antidiuretic hormone (ADH or vasopressin), thus decreasing water reabsorption from the collecting duct.

ADH works directly on the collecting duct by increasing its permeability to water; thus, a decrease in ADH levels will lead to a decrease in water reabsorption. ADH secretion is normally triggered by a sustained increase in plasma osmolarity. The reabsorption of water from the filtrate into the blood dilutes the blood, lowering the plasma osmolarity. Thus, if ADH is not released or cannot activate its receptor, water will not be reabsorbed and the plasma osmolarity will remain high. If the water remains in the urine, it increases urinary volume and frequency.

Identify the roles of blood pressure, renin, and aldosterone.

Ingestion of a large volume of soda increases arterial pressure, leading to a decrease in renin and aldosterone secretion and, therefore, a decrease in water reabsorption.

Recall that renin is released in response to low blood pressure in the kidneys. Renin activates angiotensinogen to angiotensin I, which is converted to angiotensin II by angiotensin-converting enzyme in the lungs. Angiotensin II promotes secretion of aldosterone from the adrenal cortex. Recall that aldosterone increases sodium reabsorption in the distal convoluted tubule and collecting duct, and because water follows sodium from the filtrate into the blood, aldosterone also increases water reabsorption.

If renin and aldosterone secretion is reduced, then sodium and water will not be reabsorbed in the distal convoluted tubule and collecting duct, and are excreted in the urine. The increase in water increases urinary volume and frequency.

4 Identify the role of filtrate osmolarity.

An abnormally high filtrate osmolarity will decrease the osmotic gradient between the tubule and the interstitial fluid, causing a drop in water reabsorption.

Diet sodas substitute aspartame for sugar, but unlike glucose, the aspartame cannot be reabsorbed back into the blood from the nephron—hence the high filtrate osmolarity. Even if you did not know that aspartame cannot be reabsorbed from the nephron, it is imperative to recognize the role that filtrate osmolarity can play in water reabsorption. Recall that in diabetes mellitus, a similar mechanism is at play: due to the high glucose concentration, not all of the sugar can be reabsorbed from the nephron, leading to an abnormally high filtrate concentration, less water reabsorption, and ultimately the excretion of a larger volume of urine that also contains glucose.

Related Questions

1. A patient has been found to have insufficient levels of antidiuretic hormone. What symptoms would this individual have?

2. Diabetics who fail to take insulin experience dehydration. What are the physiological factors driving this phenomenon?

3. A patient with renal failure has nephrons that lack the ability to actively secrete or reabsorb any substances. What functions might the kidney still be able to perform?

Takeaways

Questions related to the nephron appear in varying contexts. The key is to isolate the relevant component of kidney function being tested (filtration, secretion, and/or reabsorption) and then to tease apart which particular components of that function (such as filtrate osmolarity or hormonal control) are being affected.

Things to Watch Out For

Under most circumstances, the kidney produces urine that is hypertonic to the blood, but in the situation described here, the urine produced is likely to be hypotonic to the blood. Alcohol consumption produces similar physiological effects. However, frequent urination does not always mean that the urine is hypotonic to the blood. Patients who excrete protein in their urine (filtration failure) have low blood osmolarities, and thus have a low level of water reabsorption. Therefore, the urine produced may still be hypertonic to the blood.

Key Concepts

Biology Chapter 11
Muscle contraction
Parathyroid hormone
Calcium homeostasis
The sarcomere
Cardiac muscle

Muscle Contraction

What process during muscle contraction is likely to be affected by a deficiency of parathyroid hormone?

1 Identify the function of parathyroid hormone.

Parathyroid hormone (PTH) is involved in calcium homeostasis. Release of para-thyroid hormone results in an increased calcium concentration in the blood. Specifi-cally, PTH decreases excretion of calcium by the kidneys, increases absorption of calcium in the gut (via vitamin D), and increases bone resorption, thereby freeing up calcium. PTH is subject to feedback inhibition—as levels of plasma calcium rise, PTH secretion is decreased.

PTH also affects phosphorus homeostasis by resorbing phosphate from bone and reducing reabsorption of phosphate in the kidney (thus promoting its excretion in the urine). PTH also promotes the activation of vitamin D, which is required for the absorption of calcium and phosphate in the gut. For this question, we will focus primarily on the role of PTH in calcium homeostasis.

2 Predict the effect of a deficiency of parathyroid hormone.

If parathyroid hormone is not released, then all of these mechanisms will be down-regulated. Calcium excretion in the kidneys will be decreased, less calcium would be absorbed from the gut, and bone resorption would decrease. This could lead to hypocalcemia, or low concentrations of calcium in the blood.

3 Recall the role of calcium in muscle contraction.

During muscle contraction, depolarization of the muscle cells results in the opening of calcium channels in the sarcolemma. Calcium then binds to troponin, causing a conformational change in tropomyosin, which exposes the myosin-binding sites on actin.

4 Identify the process affected by low calcium levels.

If prolonged enough, low calcium levels in the blood can lead to low calcium levels within the sarcoplasmic reticulum of muscle cells. When stimulated, these muscle cells will have a smaller efflux of calcium from the sarcoplasmic reticulum, which will affect the binding of calcium to troponin.

Under normal circumstances, it is the binding of calcium to troponin that causes a conformational change in tropomyosin, exposing the myosin-binding sites on actin and permitting cross-bridge formation for muscle contraction. Therefore, a decreased calcium concentration in the muscle cell will lead to less cross-bridge formation and a weaker muscle contraction. Because each muscle fiber contains numerous molecules of troponin, this may also result in an inability to recruit all of the muscle fibers in an organized, efficient fashion.

Related Questions

1. An autoimmune disease produces antibodies against the acetylcholine receptor at the neuromuscular junction. Which step in muscle contraction is likely to be affected most directly by this disease?

2. Which division of the sarcomere does not change in size during muscle contraction?

3. A student is attempting to identify types of muscle tissue by microscopic examination. A sample contains cells with one or two nuclei and intercalated discs between the cells. The overall appearance is striated. What muscle type is likely included in this sample?

Takeaways

The intracellular environment of the muscle cell can be impacted by its extracellular environment. Prolonged changes in blood concentrations of various electrolytes can impact the internal environment of muscle (and other) cells, leading to changes in their physiology.

Things to Watch Out For

This question was very specific. You may know that one of the symptoms of hypocalcemia is tetany, but that phenomenon is related to changes in permeability of neurons, rather than muscle contraction itself. When a question is very specific, provide a specific answer related to the theme of the question stem.

Key Concepts

Biology Chapter 12

Hardy–Weinberg equilibrium

$p^2 + 2pq + q^2 = 1$

Allele frequencies

Genotype frequencies

Hardy–Weinberg Equilibrium

Gigantism is coded for by a recessive allele. The dominant allele for the same gene codes for the normal phenotype. In an isolated geographic area, 9 people out of a sample of 10,000 were found to have gigantism, whereas the rest had normal phenotypes. Assuming Hardy–Weinberg equilibrium, calculate the frequency of the recessive and dominant alleles as well as the number of heterozygotes in the population.

① Solve for the frequency of the recessive allele.

Because gigantism will only emerge with a homozygous recessive genotype, it will be represented as gg. In the Hardy–Weinberg equation, the recessive genotype frequency is depicted as q^2. By taking the square root of q^2, we get the frequency of the recessive gigantism allele, q, which is 0.03:

$$\text{gigantism} = \text{homozygous recessive} = \text{gg} = q^2$$

$$q^2 = \frac{9}{10,000} = 0.0009$$

$$q = 0.03$$

recessive allele frequency = 3%

② Solve for the frequency of the dominant allele.

The frequency of the dominant allele, p, plus the frequency of the recessive allele, q, equals 1. To solve for the frequency of the dominant allele, simply subtract the recessive allele frequency from 1:

$$p + q = 1$$
$$p = 1 - q$$
$$= 1 - 0.03$$
$$= 0.97$$

dominant allele frequency = 97%

3 **Solve for the number of heterozygotes.**

To find the number of heterozygotes, we need to recall which part of the Hardy–Weinberg equation corresponds to the frequency of heterozygotes in the population. This is the expression $2pq$:

$$2pq = \text{frequency of heterozygotes}$$

$$Gg = 2pq = 2 \times 0.97 \times 0.03$$

$$= 0.058 \ (5.8\%)$$

To find the size of the heterozygous population, multiply the frequency by the total size of the population:

$$0.058 \times 10{,}000 = 580 \text{ people}$$

Related Questions

1. Suppose a similar survey was done in another area. This time, 90 people with gigantism were found from a survey of 200,000 people. Calculate the same parameters with the new survey.

2. An allele f occurs with a frequency of 0.8 in a wolfpack population. Determine the frequencies of the genotypes FF, Ff, and ff.

3. If the frequency of homozygous recessive individuals for a certain autosomal recessive disease is 16 percent, determine the percentage of phenotypically normal individuals.

Takeaways

Remember both Hardy–Weinberg equations: $p + q = 1$ and $p^2 + 2pq + q^2 = 1$. p is the frequency of the dominant allele; q is the frequency of the recessive allele. p^2 is the frequency of the homozygous dominant genotype, $2pq$ is the frequency of the heterozygous genotype, and q^2 is the frequency of the homozygous recessive genotype.

Things to Watch Out For

There are five circumstances in which the Hardy–Weinberg equations may fail to apply. These are: mutations, migration, genetic drift, nonrandom mating, and natural selection. The Hardy–Weinberg equations refer to populations that are stable and *not* evolving.

Solutions to Related Questions

1. Prokaryotic Genetics

1. In this question, we must think about the characteristics required to induce the transcription of the DNA encoded on the plasmid. First, in order for bacteria to transcribe the genetic sequence, an appropriate promoter must be present. In addition, the genetic material to be transcribed must be close enough to the promoter to facilitate effective transcription. In order to ensure efficient conversion of all of the bacteria in a colony to bacteria able to produce this protein, the plasmid should also encode a sex factor so that the plasmid can be efficiently transferred between cells.

2. The fact that the same bacterial genetic sequence is transferred each time this bacteriophage infects a bacterium implies that the process of transduction is not random in this case. This is likely the case if the phage genome integrates into the bacterial genome and, when the phage genome is later released from the bacterial genome, it takes a small segment of bacterial DNA with it. This implies that the bacteriophage must enter the lysogenic cycle. To replicate and subsequently infect other bacteria, the bacteriophage will also have to reenter the lytic cycle at some point.

3. Sometimes, the sex factor becomes incorporated into the bacterial genome. This information is generally carried on a plasmid, but, by the process of transformation, it may become part of the bacterial genome itself. When this occurs, the entire genome will be replicated and the bacterium will attempt to transfer the entire genome during conjugation. The conjugation bridge is usually not stable enough to permit transfer of the entire bacterial genome, but sizable portions of it are often still transferred. This results in high frequency recombination. Cells that have undergone this particular change are known as Hfr or high frequency of recombination cells.

2. Menstrual Cycle

1. FSH is inhibited early in the follicular phase to prevent the development of multiple follicles. While some FSH is necessary for the development of a follicle at all, the body prevents the formation of many follicles by negative feedback of estrogen on the hypothalamus and anterior pituitary. Later in the follicular phase, FSH levels rise in parallel with LH levels as estrogen's feedback mechanism switches from negative feedback to positive feedback.

2. Progesterone levels are very low during the follicular phase of the menstrual cycle, and do not begin to rise until the luteal phase. The corpus luteum, which does not exist until the secondary oocyte has been released from the ovary, secretes progesterone to develop and maintain the endometrium. Thus, progesterone levels rise during the luteal phase. It is the drop in the level of progesterone that ultimately stimulates menses, which—by definition—begins on day 0 of the cycle.

3. Ovulation can be prevented biochemically by manipulating the hormones involved in the menstrual cycle. Birth control pills, or oral contraceptive pills (OCPs), keep estrogen and progesterone levels elevated so that FSH and LH are constantly inhibited. Because of this inhibition, a follicle does not develop and the LH surge does not occur, thereby preventing ovulation.

3. Stages of Embryogenesis

1. Trophoblasts are the cells that form the placenta. In formation of the placenta, these cells must invade the endometrium to create the interface between the mother and the developing embryo. This means that this cell type is particularly inclined toward rapid division and invasion of foreign tissues. Thus, if a malignancy develops, the ability of this cell to invade blood vessels and spread (metastasize) is often more pronounced than with other cell types.

2. The mesoderm is the middle germ layer within the gastrula. The mesoderm gives rise to the musculoskeletal system, the circulatory system, much of the excretory system, the gonads, the muscular and connective tissue layers of the digestive and respiratory systems, and the adrenal cortex. Thus, a mutation that occurs early in the process of development will have far-reaching consequences, affecting each of these organ systems.

3. Indeterminate cleavage means that the cells are still capable of developing into any cell type, and could even develop into entire organisms. If a zygote undergoes indeterminate cleavage, and the cells actually separate from each other, then twinning may occur. Because these twins arose from the same zygote, they would be considered monozygotic or identical twins. Depending on when during development the organisms split from each other, the resulting twins could be dichorionic/diamniotic, monochorionic/diamniotic, or monochorionic/monoamniotic.

4. Action Potential

1. The opening of the sodium channel brings the membrane potential closer to sodium's electrochemical equilibrium potential. The longer the channel is open, the closer the membrane potential will get to this equilibrium potential. Therefore, sodium is closest to its electrochemical equilibrium right before the sodium channels are inactivated. This corresponds to the highest point of the action potential in the graph—the point right between regions II and III, around +35 mV (the actual equilibrium potential for sodium is close to +60 mV).

2. An action potential is an all-or-nothing response, so the speed and magnitude of an individual action potential cannot be altered. Rather, the magnitude of a stimulus is encoded by the frequency of action potential firing. A lower-magnitude stimulus elicits a lower firing frequency; a higher-magnitude stimulus elicits a higher firing frequency.

3. When a membrane is hyperpolarized, it is further from the threshold potential and would require a larger stimulus to create an action potential. Therefore, hyperpolarizing a membrane would be a way to inhibit an action potential. Action potentials are also inhibited during the absolute refractory period, which occurs during the action potential itself. Finally, blockage or inactivation of the sodium channel will prevent the depolarization phase of the action potential, thereby inhibiting the rest of the action potential from occurring.

5. Endocrine Organs

1. ACTH, or adrenocorticotropic hormone, is one of the tropic hormones released by the anterior pituitary. The hypothalamus releases corticotropin-releasing factor (CRF), which triggers the release of ACTH from the anterior pituitary. Then, ACTH stimulates cortisol secretion from the adrenal cortex. Cortisol is one of the hormones that aids in wakefulness as well as aiding in the maintenance of blood pressure. Lack of cortisol is likely to result in fatigue and low blood pressure.

2. The posterior pituitary is best thought of as an extension of the hypothalamus. The bodies of the nerves of the posterior pituitary are actually located in the hypothalamus, which sends axons down the length of the pituitary stalk into the region of the posterior pituitary. The two main hormones released from the posterior pituitary, antidiuretic hormone (ADH or vasopressin) and oxytocin, are made in the hypothalamus and stored in the nerve terminals of the posterior pituitary. Thus, *neurohypophysis* is an appropriate name for the posterior pituitary as this organ is simply an extension of certain hypothalamic neurons.

3. An exocrine organ is one that secretes its products into ducts, which empty onto an epithelial surface. Examples of exocrine organs include lacrimal glands, sweat glands, salivary glands, mammary glands, and the digestive portions of the pancreas. Endocrine organs secrete hormones into the bloodstream, where the hormones travel to distant target tissues. Examples of endocrine organs include the hypothalamus, pituitary gland, thyroid, parathyroid glands, pancreas, adrenal glands, and gonads.

6. Respiratory System

1. If respiration is occurring normally but there is no bloodflow to the left lung, then there is no gas exchange occurring in the left lung. If no oxygen is being diffused from the air into the blood and no CO_2 is being released, then the P_AO_2 of the alveoli will equal the PO_2 of inspired air, around 100 mmHg O_2.

2. If there is an airway obstruction but bloodflow to the lung is normal, then there is no gas exchange. The blood that flows into the lung will have the same PO_2 and PCO_2 as systemic venous blood. Because no gas exchange occurs, this value will remain the same for blood that exits the lung and throughout the pulmonary capillaries in that area. P_VO_2 is approximately 40 mmHg and P_VCO_2 is approximately 47 mmHg.

3. When the P_AO_2 of inspired air equals the P_aO_2 of capillary blood, then diffusion of oxygen from the alveolus to the capillary will stop. Note that in physiology, A stands for alveolar, whereas a stands for arterial.

7. Oxyhemoglobin Dissociation Curve

1. Exercise will lead to an increase in body temperature as well as an increase in CO_2 production by the tissues. Through the bicarbonate buffer system, the excess CO_2 generates protons, lowering the pH. The pH may be further lowered if anaerobic metabolism is occurring, generating lactic acid. These factors cause the Bohr effect—a shift in the oxyhemoglobin dissociation curve to the right.

2. A high PCO_2 will lead to an increase in ventilation rate. This allows the body to exhale additional carbon dioxide, bringing the body back to a normal PCO_2. In prolonged cases of hypercarbia (high concentrations of carbon dioxide in the blood), the kidney may begin excreting additional acid, shifting the bicarbonate buffer system to lower the concentration of carbon dioxide in the blood.

3. In metabolic alkalosis, blood pH will be increased due to the loss of H^+ ions (or production of bicarbonate ions). Increased pH shifts the oxygen dissociation curve to the left, increasing the affinity of hemoglobin for oxygen.

8. Immune Function

1. Infants can receive antibodies from their mothers across the placenta and through breast milk. This type of immunization is known as passive immunity. The infant receives IgG antibodies while *in utero*, and then receives IgA antibodies while breast-feeding. This provides some protection from immunity while the child is very young. However, this form of immunity is not permanent and wanes rapidly when exposure to these antibodies ceases. The only way to maintain ongoing protection against a particular antigen is through the creation of memory cells. Without memory cells, the infant will be susceptible to the antigen as soon as the passive immunity wanes. Thus, the primary disadvantage of this type of immunity is that it is not permanent.

2. The question stem states that the immunoglobulins required for an allergic reaction are already attached to mast cells. This means that the immunoglobulins must already be present in the body. During the first exposure, the immunoglobulins required for allergic reactions have not yet been synthesized. During the creation of immunoglobulins, the first ones created are of the IgM class. After exposure to the antigen, isotype switching occurs, which allows for the production of IgE—the main form of antibody involved in allergic reactions. It is these IgE molecules on mast cells that must cross-link in order to cause degranulation of the mast cell and the release of the inflammatory mediators that cause an allergic reaction. Thus, the reason that the first exposure does not result in an allergic reaction is that IgE is formed *after* and *in response to* this first exposure.

3. Cilia, along with mucus, line the respiratory tract. The mucus is able to entrap an offending substance, and the cilia are able to move this mucus up to the oropharynx, where it can be swallowed or expelled. Because this type of immunity is not specific to a particular antigen, it is known as innate immunity.

9. The Digestive System

1. A large dose of antacid would increase the pH of the stomach and therefore inactivate pepsin. The optimum pH for pepsin is between 1 and 3; pepsin is denatured and inactivated at pH values greater than 5.

2. If the ductal cells were destroyed and the pancreas could not secrete bicarbonate, the acidic chyme that moves into the duodenum would not be neutralized and pancreatic lipase would not be able to function. This would result in the malabsorption of lipids and steatorrhea (fatty stools). This may also leave the duodenum susceptible to ulceration.

3. Inadequate amounts of pancreatic lipase will lead to steatorrhea. If lipids are not broken down by lipase, they cannot be absorbed by the small intestine and will be excreted in the feces. Steatorrhea is often described as the formation of greasy or oily stool, which is often foul-smelling due to partial breakdown by gut bacteria. These stools often float because of their high concentration of fat.

10. Kidney Function

1. If a patient has insufficient levels of antidiuretic hormone (ADH or vasopressin), he or she would suffer symptoms of diabetes insipidus, a disease characterized by ADH deficiency or lack of response by the kidneys to ADH secretion. These symptoms include excess urine production because of the inability to reabsorb water in the collecting ducts, extreme thirst due to fluid loss, and a hyperosmolar blood plasma concentration.

2. The reason why diabetics who fail to take insulin experience dehydration is linked to their excess blood glucose. Having a higher concentration of glucose in the blood means that there will be more glucose filtered into the urine—more than can be reabsorbed in the proximal convoluted tubule. With this system overloaded, glucose continues to pass through the nephron and pulls water with it. The more water that is pulled into the nephron, the more will get excreted in the urine, thus causing dehydration.

3. Just because this patient's nephrons have lost the ability to actively secrete or reabsorb substances does not mean that they cannot passively move substances. Therefore, the passive flow of ions and water will still occur. The kidney may also be able to filter blood effectively, permitting the passage of water, ions, and dissolved biomolecules while retaining cells and proteins in the vasculature. The kidney may also be able to carry out its nonurinary functions as well, such as vitamin D activation and production of erythropoietin.

11. Muscle Contraction

1. This condition, called *myasthenia gravis*, renders acetylcholine receptors nonfunctional. Acetylcholine is the neurotransmitter used at the neuromuscular junction; thus, if acetylcholine is unable to bind, then the muscle cell will not be depolarized. If depolarization does not occur, then the sarcoplasmic reticulum will not open, and calcium release will not occur. Myasthenia gravis is characterized by muscle weakness, especially after repeated stimulation of the same skeletal muscle tissue.

2. The sarcomere is divided into segments (bands or zones) depending on the filaments within that segment. The Z-lines define the boundaries of each sarcomere, and the M-line defines its middle. Because a sarcomere shortens during contraction, the Z-lines and M-lines must become closer to each other. The I-band consists only of thin filaments, whereas the H-zone consists only of thick filaments. During contraction, the thin filaments slide along the thick filaments, resulting in smaller I-bands and H-zones. The A-band contains the entire length of the thick filaments. This band remains constant in size during contraction; the actin and myosin filaments slide over one another but do not change length themselves.

3. There are two types of striated muscle: cardiac and skeletal muscle. Skeletal muscle has numerous nuclei, whereas cardiac muscle contains one or two nuclei per cell. In addition, intercalated discs contain many gap junctions that allow for rapid conduction of charge between adjacent cardiac muscle cells. Therefore, it is cardiac muscle that is described in the question stem.

12. Hardy–Weinberg Equilibrium

1. If a similar survey found 90 people with gigantism out of 200,000 people, then the frequency of the recessive allele is $\sqrt{\dfrac{90}{200,000}} = \sqrt{\dfrac{9}{20,000}} = \sqrt{\dfrac{4.5}{10,000}} \approx \dfrac{2.1}{100} = 0.021$. The frequency of the dominant allele is $1 - 0.021 = 0.979$. The number of heterozygotes in the population is $(2 \times 0.979 \times 0.021) \times 200,000 \approx 2 \times 1 \times 21 \times 200 = 8400$ people (actual = 8305).

2. If allele f occurs with a frequency of 0.8, then allele F occurs with a frequency of 0.2. Thus, the frequency of FF = $0.2 \times 0.2 = 0.04$ (4%), the frequency of Ff = $2 \times 0.2 \times 0.8 = 0.32$ (32%), and the frequency of ff = $0.8 \times 0.8 = 0.64$ (64%).

3. If the frequency of homozygous recessive individuals is 0.16 (16%), then $1 - 0.16 = 0.84$ (84%) of individuals are phenotypically normal, assuming that the phenotype coded for by the dominant allele is "normal."

4

General Chemistry

Key Concepts

General Chemistry Chapter 1

Atomic mass
Atomic weight
Mass number
Isotopes

Atomic Mass and Weight

Following an experiment, an unknown element has several isotopes with the following abundances:

$$^{64}X = 48.89\%, 63.929 \text{ amu}$$
$$^{66}X = 27.81\%, 65.926 \text{ amu}$$
$$^{67}X = 4.11\%, 66.927 \text{ amu}$$
$$^{68}X = 18.57\%, 67.925 \text{ amu}$$
$$^{70}X = 0.62\%, 69.925 \text{ amu}$$

What is the atomic weight of the unknown element? What is the element's identity? How many protons, neutrons, and electrons does $^{70}X^+$ have?

 Determine the atomic weight of the element.

The atomic weight is the weighted average of the different atomic masses. To find a weighted average, we start by multiplying the atomic mass of each isotope by its relative abundance, given as a decimal. In this example, we are precise with the calculations, but on Test Day, you would want to round these values to simplify the arithmetic and arrive at the answer more quickly:

$$63.929 \text{ amu} \times 0.4889 = 31.2549 \text{ amu}$$
$$65.926 \text{ amu} \times 0.2781 = 18.3340 \text{ amu}$$
$$66.927 \text{ amu} \times 0.0411 = 2.7507 \text{ amu}$$
$$67.925 \text{ amu} \times 0.1857 = 12.6137 \text{ amu}$$
$$69.925 \text{ amu} \times 0.0062 = 0.4335 \text{ amu}$$

Now, add together the values. Unlike average calculations in arithmetic, we have already taken into account the relative abundances and therefore do not need to divide by n, the number of samples:

$$31.2549 + 18.3340 + 2.7507 + 12.6137 + 0.4335 = 65.3868 \text{ amu}$$

Thus, the atomic weight of this element is $65.3868 \frac{\text{amu}}{\text{atom}}$; its molar mass would be $65.3868 \frac{\text{g}}{\text{mol}}$.

2 **To determine the unknown element, look in the Periodic Table and find the element with the atomic weight closest to your estimated value.**

By definition, the weighted average of the atomic masses is the atomic weight. This is the value listed in the Periodic Table for that element's weight. The value we calculated, $65.3868 \frac{amu}{atom}$, is closest to the atomic weight of zinc (Zn), which is listed in our Periodic Table as $65.4 \frac{amu}{atom}$.

3 **Determine the number of protons, neutrons, and electrons in a zinc-70 +1 cation.**

Looking at the Periodic Table, the atomic number of zinc is 30. The atomic number, Z, represents the number of protons in an element and actually defines the element's identity; that is, all atoms of zinc contain 30 protons.

The mass number, A, represents the number of protons plus the number of neutrons in a given atom. The various isotopes of zinc in this question have the same number of protons, but vary in their numbers of neutrons. For zinc-70, there are $70 - 30 = 40$ neutrons.

There are equal numbers of protons and electrons in a neutral atom. In the zinc-70 cation, there will be one fewer electron, giving the atom a charge of +1. Therefore, there are $30 - 1 = 29$ electrons in the zinc-70 +1 cation.

Takeaways

The atomic number is the number of protons in an element; if the element is neutral, it is also the number of electrons. The mass number is the number of protons and neutrons combined. The atomic weight is reported on the Periodic Table and is the weighted average of the atomic masses of each isotope.

Things to Watch Out For

One of the biggest traps with math-heavy general chemistry questions is trying to make calculations precise. On the MCAT, answer choices are usually far enough apart that you can round and still get sufficiently close to identify the right answer. Avoid holding onto four decimal places, as we did here, because it will greatly increase the amount of time it takes to answer the question.

Related Questions

1. Which has a larger number of molecules—a mole of carbon dioxide, or a mole of water? Which one has a larger mass?

2. The atomic weight of silicon is 28.086 amu. If the isotopes in a sample are silicon-23, 24, 25, 26, and 29, which isotope is the most abundant?

3. A nuclear detector finds 80 atoms of oxygen-16 (15.999 amu), 60 atoms of oxygen-14 (13.999 amu), and 60 atoms of oxygen-18 (17.999 amu). What is the molar mass of this sample?

Key Concepts

General Chemistry Chapter 2

Periodic trends
Ionization energy
Atomic radius
Electron affinity
Electronegativity

Periodic Trends

Arrange the following elements in ascending order in terms of the following periodic properties: (a) electronegativity, (b) ionization energy, and (c) atomic radius.

Rb, Fr, Mg, Ca, P, Fe, Sb, O, Cl, F

1 **Assess the trends.**

This first step just requires us to think about how periodic trends work. For all trends, there is a general direction of increasing value. Electronegativity and first ionization energy increase as one moves up and to the right in the Periodic Table (with some exceptions). Atomic radius, on the other hand, decreases in value in that direction.

2 **Order the elements from bottom left to top right.**

We'll use electronegativity as our trend of choice while ordering these elements. Begin with the least electronegative element, francium (Fr), and the most electronegative element, fluorine (F), at the ends of the spectrum:

$$Fr < \_\_ < \_\_ < \_\_ < \_\_ < \_\_ < \_\_ < \_\_ < \_\_ < F$$

Let's compare oxygen (O) and chlorine (Cl), which are next to F. To determine which is more electronegative, consider the hypochlorite ion (ClO^-). The hypochlorite ion has a charge of −1. Recall that chlorine typically attains a charge of −1 in compounds, and oxygen typically attains a charge of −2, to complete their respective octet configurations. This cannot be the case in ClO^- because adding these oxidation states gives us −1 + (−2) = −3, when the ion's charge is −1.

Oxygen and chlorine do not have the same electronegativity, so there must be a polar covalent bond between them. If chlorine were more electronegative, then it would take on charge of −1. To maintain the overall −1 charge of the ion, oxygen's charge would have to be 0. This cannot be the case—a polar covalent bond requires that one side be slightly positive and the other slightly negative. However, if oxygen were more electronegative, then it would take on a charge of −2. To maintain the ion's overall −1 charge, chlorine's charge would have to be +1. This makes sense—there is a polar covalent bond between the two atoms, giving oxygen a slightly negative (−2) charge and chlorine a slightly positive (+1) charge. Therefore, oxygen must be more electronegative, and we can put these two elements into the list:

$$Fr < \_\_ < \_\_ < \_\_ < \_\_ < \_\_ < \_\_ < Cl < O < F$$

The next closest atoms to the top right corner of the Periodic Table are phosphorus (P) and antimony (Sb). Phosphorus is closer to F, O, and Cl than antimony and is more electronegative:

$$Fr < \_\_ < \_\_ < \_\_ < \_\_ < Sb < P < Cl < O < F$$

Iron (Fe) is a transition metal and is the next closest to the top right corner, so it comes next:

$$Fr < \_\_ < \_\_ < \_\_ < Fe < Sb < P < Cl < O < F$$

Finally, the remaining metals can be ranked based on their proximity to Fr. Rubidium (Rb) is just two periods above Fr so it will be just slightly more electronegative than Fr. Calcium (Ca) is the next highest, and finally magnesium (Mg). Thus, the trend for electronegativity is:

$$Fr < Rb < Ca < Mg < Fe < Sb < P < Cl < O < F$$

Recognize that ionization energy should roughly parallel the order for electronegativity. For reference, the electronegativities and ionization energies of these elements are tabulated below:

Element	Fr	Rb	Ca	Mg	Fe	Sb	P	Cl	O	F
Electronegativity (Pauling Scale)	0.7	0.82	1.00	1.31	1.83	2.05	2.19	3.16	3.44	3.98
Ionization Energy $\left(\frac{kJ}{mol}\right)$	380	403	590	738	763	834	1012	1251	1314	1681

 3 **Reverse the trend to get the ranking for atomic radius.**

Unlike electronegativity and first ionization energy, which increase as one moves up and to the right on the Periodic Table, atomic radius *decreases* as one moves up and to the right.

Thus if,

$$Fr < Rb < Ca < Mg < Fe < Sb < P < Cl < O < F$$

is the order of increasing electronegativity and first ionization energy, the reverse order is the one in which the atomic radii increase:

$$F < O < Cl < P < Sb < Fe < Mg < Ca < Rb < Fr$$

Note that there are different definitions for atomic radius; most scientists use empirical or calculated atomic radii to make predictions about periodic trends.

Takeaways

Electronegativity, ionization energy, and electron affinity generally increase as one moves up and to the right in the Periodic Table. Atomic radius generally decreases in the same direction.

Things to Watch Out For

Remember that these are only trends, and are not absolute. There are many exceptions to the periodic trends, especially in the transition metals. Usually, if the MCAT asks for analysis of a particular periodic trend, the question will involve elements that follow that trend as expected.

 KAPLAN 119

Related Questions

1. Rank the following elements or ions from smallest to largest radius: B^{3+}, C, Be, O^{2-}

2. Which element—phosphorus or selenium—would you expect to have a higher ionization energy?

3. The first ionization energy of an element is $549.5 \frac{kJ}{mol}$, its second ionization energy is $1064.2 \frac{kJ}{mol}$, and its third ionization energy is $4138 \frac{kJ}{mol}$. To which group does this element most likely belong?

High-Yield Problem-Solving Guide questions continue on the next page. ▶ ▶ ▶

Key Concepts

General Chemistry Chapter 3

VSEPR theory
Coordinate covalent bonds
Covalent bond notation
Geometry and polarity

VSEPR Theory and Geometry

A student attempts to form an amminated vanadium complex using a concentrated aqueous ammonia solution. During the reaction, the solvated vanadium ions undergo a side-reaction to produce the hydrated coordination complex $[V(H_2O)_6]^{4+}$. Assuming the complex ion structure is solely based on the ligands and central ion, what is the geometry of this complex?

The student attempts to decompose this complex with heat to reform solid vanadium. The complex changes color but does not yield pure vanadium. The student performs thermochemical analysis and determines the reaction to be:

$$[V(H_2O)_6]^{4+} \rightarrow [VO(H_2O)_5]^{2+} + 2\ H^+$$

What is the geometry of the decomposed complex ion?

During the decomposition process, the student notices that the aqueous ammonia remaining in solution forms ammonium cations. Crystallizing the solution and measuring the bond angles using X-ray diffraction spectrometry, the student notices that there is a mixture of compounds with bond angles of 104.5°, 107°, and 109.5°. What molecules do these bond angles likely belong to?

1 **Count the number of bonds and lone pairs in the first vanadium complex.**

As written, the complex is composed of six ligands and a central metal ion. The metal ion does not have lone pairs, so it must organize six groups of electrons around itself. This can be represented with the shorthand AX_6, which corresponds to octahedral geometry:

Note that even though the water molecules have lone pairs, we can ignore them because they will not alter the structure around the central cation.

2 **Determine the number of bonds and lone pairs in the second vanadium complex.**

The decomposed molecule has one fewer aqua ligand, but now has an oxygen atom. Oxygen will create a double bond with the vanadium to complete its octet, while the other five water molecules will serve as ligands around the central vanadium cation. Thus, vanadium still must organize six groups of electrons around itself (AX_6). The geometry remains octahedral:

Note that this would be a slightly distorted octahedral geometry because the V=O double bond creates slightly more repulsion than the single bonds with the aqua ligands.

3 **Determine the compounds remaining in solution.**

We are told that the ammonia in solution forms ammonium cations. The solution is aqueous and thus also contains water molecules. Therefore, there are three molecules: water, ammonia, and ammonium:

4 **Analyze the structures for their molecular and electronic geometries.**

Count the number of bonds and lone pairs in each molecule to identify their geometries. All three of these molecules have four groups around the central atom, which means that they all have tetrahedral electronic geometries. The angles that we are given, however, refer to molecular geometries. Remember that molecular geometry considers only the positions of the various nuclei, and not of the lone pairs. Water has two bonds and two lone pairs, and therefore takes on bent molecular geometry. Ammonia has three bonds and one lone pair, and therefore takes on trigonal pyramidal molecular geometry. Ammonium has four bonds and no lone pairs, and therefore takes on tetrahedral molecular geometry.

5 Determine which compound has each of the bond angles based on their numbers of lone pairs.

As the number of lone pairs increases, the bond angle decreases because lone pairs can sit closer to the central nucleus and exert a greater degree of repulsion. Therefore, water, with its two lone pairs, should have the smallest bond angle ($104.5°$). Ammonia, with one lone pair, should have the intermediate bond angle ($107°$). Finally, ammonium, with no lone pairs, should have the largest bond angle ($109.5°$).

Related Questions

1. Why is the geometry of aluminum chloride different from that of phosphorus tribromide?

2. Why is the maximum bond angle between adjacent groups in a bent molecule greater than that of an octahedral molecule?

3. Why is the geometry of the sulfate anion the same as that of a sulfuric acid molecule?

High-Yield Problem-Solving Guide questions continue on the next page. ▶ ▶ ▶

Key Concepts
General Chemistry Chapter 4
Gram equivalent weight
The mole
Molar mass
Balancing equations

Stoichiometry

During the course of the disproportionation reaction

$$H_2PO_4^- \rightleftharpoons HPO_4^{2-} + H_3PO_4$$

how many grams and molecules of phosphoric acid could be created from 242.5 grams of dihydrogen phosphate? If this amount of phosphoric acid were dissolved in enough water to create one liter of solution, what would the normality of this solution be (with respect to protons)?

1 Balance the formula.

The given formula is unbalanced. To balance it, we simply need to double the number of dihydrogen phosphate molecules:

$$2\,H_2PO_4^- \rightleftharpoons HPO_4^{2-} + H_3PO_4$$

2 Convert the given units to moles.

Stoichiometry is nothing more than an extended application of dimensional analysis. There are four major conversion factors that can be used to convert from the given units to moles (or vice-versa):

- **Molar mass**, **molecular weight**, or **formula weight** (from the Periodic Table): convert from mass (in grams or amu) to moles
- **Avogadro's number** (6.02×10^{23} mol^{-1}): converts from a number of particles to moles
- **Molarity**, **molality**, **normality**, or other **measures of concentration**: convert from volume or mass of solution to moles
- **Ideal gases at STP** ($22.4\,\frac{L}{mol}$): converts from volume of gas to moles

In this question, we are given a mass (242.5 g), which must be converted to moles. To do this, we need to know the molar mass of dihydrogen phosphate, which can be determined using the Periodic Table. The molar mass is $2 \times 1\,\frac{g}{mol} + 1 \times 31\,\frac{g}{mol} + 4 \times 16\,\frac{g}{mol} = 97\,\frac{g}{mol}$.

Now, dividing the given mass by the molar mass gives us the number of moles:

$$\frac{242.5\,g}{97\,\frac{g}{mol}} = 2.5\,mol$$

Multiply by the mole ratio.

The next step requires us to use the balanced chemical equation to shift from calculations for dihydrogen phosphate to calculations for phosphoric acid. The mole ratio is simply the stoichiometric coefficient of the desired compound (phosphoric acid) divided by the stoichiometric coefficient of the compound we are given information about (dihydrogen phosphate):

$$2.5 \text{ mol } H_2PO_4^- \times \left[\frac{1 \text{ mol } H_3PO_4}{2 \text{ mol } H_2PO_4^-} \right] = 1.25 \text{ mol } H_3PO_4$$

In other words, reacting 2.5 moles of dihydrogen phosphate will result in 1.25 moles of phosphoric acid.

 Convert from moles to the desired units in the answer choice.

We are asked for two different units: mass and number of molecules. Starting with mass, we use the molar mass to convert from moles to grams:

$$1.25 \text{ mol } H_3PO_4 \times \left[\frac{98 \text{ g } H_3PO_4}{1 \text{ mol } H_3PO_4} \right] = 122.5 \text{ g } H_3PO_4$$

This first example points out the utility of setting up all of the conversion factors before multiplying. Consider if Steps 2 through 4 were done in one large multiplication problem:

$$242.5 \text{ g } H_2PO_4^- \times \left[\frac{1 \text{ mol } H_2PO_4^-}{97 \text{ g } H_2PO_4^-} \right]\left[\frac{1 \text{ mol } H_3PO_4}{2 \text{ mol } H_2PO_4^-} \right]\left[\frac{98 \text{ g } H_3PO_4}{1 \text{ mol } H_3PO_4} \right] \approx \frac{240}{2} = 120 \text{ g } H_3PO_4$$

Even with rounding, the answer obtained is still very close to the actual answer.

For the number of molecules, we use Avogadro's number:

$$1.25 \text{ mol } H_3PO_4 \times \left[\frac{6.02 \times 10^{23} \text{ molecules}}{1 \text{ mol } H_3PO_4} \right] = 7.53 \times 10^{23} \text{ molecules}$$

5 **Determine the normality of a one liter solution containing 1.25 moles of phosphoric acid.**

The normality is the molarity of a given molecule multiplied by the number of equivalents of interest given off by one mole of the molecule. For this question, the equivalent of interest is protons. Thus, we simply need to multiply the molarity of the solution by the number of protons that can be given off by phosphoric acid.

Takeaways

Stoichiometry is an extended version of dimensional analysis that can be answered with a consistent three-step method:

1. Convert from the given units to moles
2. Use the mole ratio
3. Convert from moles to the desired units in the answer choices

Things to Watch Out For

Stoichiometry problems can take up a lot of time if you do each step individually. Writing out all of the conversion factors before doing the math may work to your advantage, as the MCAT tends to use numbers that cancel out "nicely."

The molarity is equal to the moles of solute divided by liters of solution:

$$\frac{1.25 \text{ mol } H_3PO_4}{1 \text{ L}} = 1.25 \text{ } M \text{ } H_3PO_4$$

Because phosphoric acid can give off three protons, the normality is:

$$1.25 \text{ } M \text{ } H_3PO_4 \times 3 = 3.75 \text{ } N \text{ } H_3PO_4$$

Related Questions

1. In the formation of water from diatomic hydrogen and oxygen gases, how many grams and molecules of water are produced when 26 g of hydrogen gas react in the presence of excess oxygen?

2. If butane is combusted in the presence of excess oxygen, resulting in the production of 179.2 L CO_2 at STP, what mass of butane was present at the beginning of the reaction?

3. If 44.8 L of heptane react with 1.204×10^{24} molecules of oxygen in a combustion reaction, how many grams of water are produced?

High-Yield Problem-Solving Guide questions continue on the next page. ▶ ▶ ▶

Key Concepts

General Chemistry Chapter 5

Reaction kinetics

Reaction mechanisms

Rate laws

Rate tables

Rate Laws

Consider the nitration reaction of benzene:

The rate data below were collected with the nitration of benzene carried out at 298 K. From this information, determine the rate law for this reaction.

Trial	$[C_6H_6]$ (M)	$[HNO_2]$ (M)	Initial Rate $\left(\dfrac{M}{s}\right)$
1	1.01×10^{-3}	2.00×10^{-2}	5.96×10^{-6}
2	4.05×10^{-3}	2.00×10^{-2}	5.96×10^{-6}
3	3.02×10^{-3}	6.01×10^{-2}	5.40×10^{-5}

1 **Write down the general form of the rate law.**

The general form of the rate law includes a rate constant, k, multiplied by the concentrations of each of the reactants raised to a certain power:

$$\text{rate} = k[C_6H_6]^x[HNO_2]^y$$

2 **Determine the order of the reaction with respect to benzene.**

Choose two trials in which the concentration of benzene changes while the concentration of nitrous acid remains constant. When we do this, we can set up a proportionality between the rate and the concentration of benzene:

$$\text{rate} = k[C_6H_6]^x[HNO_2]^y$$

If k and $[HNO_2]$ are constant, then:

$$\text{rate} \propto [C_6H_6]^x$$

Let's use trials 1 and 2. Here, the concentration of benzene quadruples while the concentration of nitrous acid remains constant. The rate does not change. Putting this information into the proportionality, we get:

$$\frac{\text{rate}_2}{\text{rate}_1} = \left[\frac{[C_6H_6]_2}{[C_6H_6]_1} \right]^x$$

$$1 = 4^x$$

$$x = 0$$

Thus, the reaction is zero-order with respect to benzene.

3. Determine the order of the reaction with respect to nitrous acid.

The fact that the reaction is zero-order with respect to benzene is great news because it means that the rate law must be:

$$\text{rate} = k[HNO_2]^y$$

We can ignore the concentration of benzene in our calculations because its concentration will have no effect on the rate. So, let's compare trials 1 and 3 to determine the order with respect to nitrous acid. From trial 1 to trial 3, the concentration of nitrous acid tripled, and the rate went up by a factor of 9. Plugging this in, we get:

$$\frac{\text{rate}_3}{\text{rate}_1} = \left[\frac{[HNO_2]_3}{[HNO_2]_1} \right]^y$$

$$9 = 3^y$$

$$y = 2$$

Thus, the reaction is second-order with respect to nitrous acid.

4. Write down the rate law with the correct orders.

Taking this information together, the rate law must be:

$$\text{rate} = k[C_6H_6]^0[HNO_2]^2 = k[HNO_2]^2$$

Takeaways

To determine the order with respect to a particular reactant, use the equation: change in rate = (proportional change in concentration)^x, where x = the order with respect to that reactant.

Things to Watch Out For

Make sure that you select two trials where one reactant's concentration changes but all other concentrations are constant. If there are no two trials where one of the reactants changes, create a new trial using the information you've gleaned about the reaction orders with respect to the *other* reactants.

Related Questions

1. What is the value of the rate constant k for the nitration of benzene? What are its units?

2. Given the data below, determine the rate law for the reaction of pyridine with methyl iodide. Find the rate constant k for this reaction and its units.

Trial	$[C_5H_5N]$ (M)	$[MeI]$ (M)	Initial Rate $\left(\dfrac{M}{s}\right)$
1	1.00×10^{-4}	1.00×10^{-4}	7.50×10^{-7}
2	2.00×10^{-4}	2.00×10^{-4}	3.00×10^{-6}
3	2.00×10^{-4}	4.00×10^{-4}	6.00×10^{-6}

3. Cerium(IV) is a common inorganic oxidant. Determine the rate law for the following reaction and compute the value of the rate constant k along with its units:

$$Ce^{4+} + Fe^{2+} \rightarrow Ce^{3+} + Fe^{3+}$$

Trial	$[Ce^{4+}]$ (M)	$[Fe^{2+}]$ (M)	Initial Rate $\left(\dfrac{M}{s}\right)$
1	1.10×10^{-5}	1.80×10^{-5}	2.00×10^{-7}
2	1.10×10^{-5}	2.80×10^{-5}	3.10×10^{-7}
3	3.40×10^{-5}	2.80×10^{-5}	9.50×10^{-7}

High-Yield Problem-Solving Guide questions continue on the next page. ▶ ▶ ▶

Key Concepts

General Chemistry Chapter 6

Thermodynamics
Kinetics
Reaction energy profiles
Gibbs free energy

Reaction Energy Profiles

When chalcone (**A**) is subjected to reductive conditions with sodium borohydride, two products can result. The two products are the so-called 1,2-reduction product (**B**), in which the carbonyl is reduced, and the 1,4-reduction product (**C**), in which the conjugated alkene is reduced.

"1,4-reduction"   "1,2-reduction"

C   **A**   **B**

The reaction profiles leading to each reduction product at 298 K are both shown in the plot below:

Based on the plot above, answer the following questions:

1. Which product is more thermodynamically stable? Which one forms faster?

2. Assume that **A** is in equilibrium with **C**. What will the ratio of **C** to **A** be at equilibrium?

3. How could the rate of the reaction of **A** to **C** be made closer to the rate of the reaction of **A** to **B**?

4. Which product would be favored if **A** were subjected to high temperatures for a long time? If **A** were subjected to low temperatures for only a brief period of time? Explain why for each situation.

$$\left(\text{Note: } R = 1.99 \frac{\text{cal}}{\text{mol} \cdot \text{K}}\right)$$

1 **Look at the energy differences between the starting material and the products, as well as the differences between the starting material and the transition state leading to each product.**

Notice that the energy of **C** is lower than that of **B**. Therefore, it is the more thermodynamically stable product.

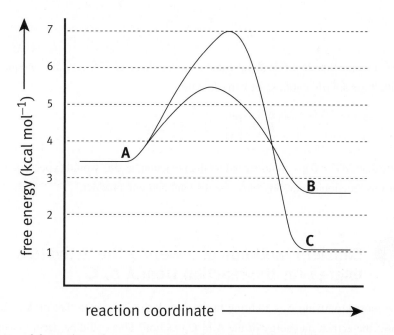

The rate of formation of each product is determined by the difference in energy between the starting material **A** and the top of the hump leading to each product. Because this difference is lower for the formation of **B**, it forms faster.

2 **Note that the difference in energy between the starting material and the products determines the ratio of products (C) to reactants (A) at equilibrium.**

The relevant equation relating the change in free energy to the concentrations of reactants and products at equilibrium is:

$$\Delta G^\circ = -RT \ln K_{eq}$$

We can rearrange it to solve for K_{eq}:

$$\ln K_{eq} = \frac{-\Delta G°}{RT}$$

$$K_{eq} = e^{\frac{-\Delta G°}{RT}}$$

Note from the diagram that $\Delta G° \approx 1000 - 3500 = -2500 \frac{cal}{mol}$. We are told that $R = 1.99 \frac{cal}{mol \cdot K}$ and that $T = 298$ K. Plugging into the equation, we get:

$$K_{eq} \approx e^{\frac{2500 \frac{cal}{mol}}{(2 \frac{cal}{mol \cdot K})(300 \text{ K})}} = e^{\frac{25}{6}}$$

Let's assume that $25 \div 6$ is about equal to 4, and that e (2.718...) is about equal to 3. With these simplifications, we can estimate:

$$K_{eq} = \frac{[\mathbf{C}]}{[\mathbf{A}]} \approx 3^4 = 81 \text{ (actual} = 68)$$

Note that $\Delta G° < 0$ gives more product than reactant, as one would expect for a spontaneous reaction containing only one reactant and one product.

 Consider methods of lowering the activation energy for the reaction from A to C.

The most promising way to bring the rate of **A** to **C** closer to that of **A** to **B** is to lower the activation energy of the **A** to **C** reaction. This could be accomplished by adding a catalyst for the **A** to **C** reaction. Remember: a catalyst speeds up the reaction but is not consumed in the process.

Takeaways

The goal of a reaction profile is to give information about energy *differences*. Make sure to identify the important differences and their significances, as in this problem.

Things to Watch Out For

Be careful to take note of the units of energy on the *y*-axis if there are any necessary computations. The *y*-axis could be given in joules, calories, or Calories (kilocalories).

4 **Consider the effects of temperature on the reactions.**

At high temperatures for a long time, **A** has sufficient energy to keep reacting over and over again to form **B** and **C**, which can then react back to reform **A**. Over time, the lowest energy (thermodynamic) product, **C**, would predominate because it is the most stable.

Between the two products, **B** will form much faster than **C** because its activation energy (the height of the hump) is lower. At low temperatures, there may not be sufficient energy for **B** to revert back to **A**, or for **A** to convert to **C**. Therefore, the faster-forming (kinetic) product, **B**, will predominate.

Related Questions

1. What would be the ratio of **B** to **A** at equilibrium?

2. If a catalyst were added to the reaction of **A** going to **C**, as in Step 3 earlier, would the energies of **A** and **C** be changed as a result? Why or why not?

3. There are actually intermediates involved in the reactions producing both **B** and **C**, which are shown below. Sketch how each reaction profile would look, including the involvement of these intermediates. Be sure to indicate which intermediate is relatively more stable.

Key Concepts

General Chemistry Chapter 7

Hess's law

$\Delta H_{rxn}^{\circ} = \sum \Delta H_{f,products}^{\circ} - \sum \Delta H_{f,reactants}^{\circ}$

Heat of formation

Combustion

Hess's Law

> The standard heat of combustion of glucose ($C_6H_{12}O_6$) is $-2537.3 \frac{kJ}{mol}$. If the ΔH_f° of CO_2 (g) is $-393.5 \frac{kJ}{mol}$ and the ΔH_f° of H_2O (g) is $-241.8 \frac{kJ}{mol}$, then what is the ΔH_f° of glucose?

1 Write a balanced equation for this reaction.

The unbalanced reaction below is typical of all hydrocarbon combustion reactions:

$$C_6H_{12}O_6 + O_2 \rightarrow CO_2 + H_2O$$

(Unless otherwise noted, presume that combustion of a carbohydrate is with oxygen gas.) Begin by balancing the carbon atoms on the right side (6 CO_2), and then balance the hydrogen atoms on the right side (6 H_2O). Finally, balance the oxygen atoms on the left side (6 O_2):

$$C_6H_{12}O_6 + 6\ O_2 \rightarrow 6\ CO_2 + 6\ H_2O$$

2 Apply Hess's law.

To start, let's define a few terms. The standard heat of formation, ΔH_f°, is the amount of thermal energy required to synthesize a compound from its elements in their standard states (the phase in which the element exists at room temperature, 298 K). The heat of reaction, ΔH_{rxn}°, is the amount of thermal energy required to convert the reactants to the products of a reaction. Hess's law states that the difference between the heats of formation of the products and the heats of formation of the reactants is equal to the heat of the reaction:

$$\Delta H_{rxn}^{\circ} = \sum \Delta H_{f,products}^{\circ} - \sum \Delta H_{f,reactants}^{\circ}$$

In this question, we are given the heats of formation for carbon dioxide gas and water vapor, as well as the heat of reaction. What about the standard heat of formation of oxygen? Because oxygen is already in its standard state (a diatomic gas), its standard heat of formation is zero.

With that information, we can plug into Hess's law:

$$\Delta H^{\circ}_{rxn} = \sum \Delta H^{\circ}_{f,products} - \sum \Delta H^{\circ}_{f,reactants}$$

$$-2537.3 \, \frac{kJ}{mol} = \left[6 \times \left(-393.5 \, \frac{kJ}{mol}\right) + 6 \times \left(-241.8 \, \frac{kJ}{mol}\right)\right] - \left[\Delta H^{\circ}_{f,glucose} + 6 \times \left(0 \, \frac{kJ}{mol}\right)\right]$$

$$\Delta H^{\circ}_{f,glucose} = \left[6 \times (-393.5) + 6 \times (-241.8)\right] - (-2537.3)$$

$$\approx 6 \times (-400) + 6 \times (-250) + 2500$$

$$= -2400 - 1500 + 2500 = -1400 \, \frac{kJ}{mol} \left(\text{actual} = -1274.5 \, \frac{kJ}{mol}\right)$$

A negative standard heat of formation means that heat is released to form the compound, whereas a positive standard heat of formation means that heat is required to form the compound. Therefore, forming one mole of glucose from solid carbon, diatomic hydrogen gas, and diatomic oxygen gas releases 1274.5 kilojoules of heat.

Related Questions

1. Given the ΔH°_{f} of carbon dioxide and water, what other piece(s) of information would you need to have to calculate the ΔH°_{comb} of ethane?

2. If the ΔH°_{f} of acetylene is 226.6 $\frac{kJ}{mol}$, what is the ΔH°_{comb} of acetylene?

3. If the ΔH°_{f} of NaBr (s) is −359.9 $\frac{kJ}{mol}$, what is the sum of each ΔH°_{rxn} of the following series of reactions?

$$Na \, (s) \rightarrow Na \, (g) \rightarrow Na^{+} \, (g)$$

$$\frac{1}{2} Br_2 \, (g) \rightarrow Br \, (g) \rightarrow Br^{-} \, (g)$$

$$Na^{+} \, (g) + Br^{-} \, (g) \rightarrow NaBr \, (s)$$

Takeaways

Always determine the balanced equation for the reaction before you begin to apply Hess's law. Recall that enthalpy is a state function, so regardless of the path one takes to get from the reactants to the products, the change in enthalpy will be the same.

Things to Watch Out For

At least one of the wrong answer choices for thermochemistry questions will be the result of carelessness with signs. Carefully organized scratchwork will help you avoid this problem, but perhaps more important is the ability to round judiciously. Only experience (practice) will breed such wisdom.

Key Concepts

General Chemistry Chapter 8

The ideal gas law
Conversion factors
Pressure
Volume
Temperature
Density

The Ideal Gas Law

0.503 m^3 of oxygen gas (density $= 1.43 \frac{\text{kg}}{\text{m}^3}$) is pumped into a rigid 600 mL container. Once inside, the pressure is measured to be 300 atm. What is the temperature of the gas, assuming ideal behavior? $\left(\text{Note: R} = 8.314 \frac{\text{J}}{\text{mol} \cdot \text{K}}\right)$

1 Determine the number of moles of gas.

Let's start with the given volume and density and determine the mass of oxygen gas present:

$$0.503 \text{ m}^3 \text{ O}_2 \times 1.43 \frac{\text{kg}}{\text{m}^3} \approx 0.72 \text{ kg O}_2 = 720 \text{ g O}_2$$

When dealing with gas laws, always carefully hold on to units to make sure the math works out correctly. Now that we have a given mass of oxygen gas, we can determine the number of moles present:

$$720 \text{ g O}_2 \times \left[\frac{1 \text{ mol O}_2}{32 \text{ g O}_2}\right] = 22.5 \text{ mol O}_2$$

2 Convert the remaining variables' units to match those of the given ideal gas constant.

The MCAT frequently makes a simple mathematical problem more challenging by using alternative units and testing your ability to use conversion factors. Here, our pressure will have to be converted to kilopascals:

$$300 \text{ atm} \times \left[\frac{101.325 \text{ kPa}}{1 \text{ atm}}\right] \approx 3 \times 10^4 \text{ kPa}$$

Similarly, our volume will have to be converted to liters:

$$600 \text{ mL} \times \left[\frac{1 \text{ L}}{1000 \text{ mL}}\right] = 0.6 \text{ L}$$

3 Plug the variables into the ideal gas law.

Now that we have the pressure, volume, number of moles of gas, and ideal gas constant in the same units, we can plug into the ideal gas law equation:

Takeaways

Use scientific notation to avoid long multiplication and division problems that eat up time on Test Day. This is especially useful if all of the answer choices vary by powers of ten; you can often omit the coefficient and just focus on the relevant exponents to predict the correct answer choice.

$$PV = nRT \rightarrow T = \frac{PV}{nR}$$

$$T = \frac{\left(3 \times 10^4 \text{ kPa}\right)\left(0.6 \text{ L}\right)}{\left(2.25 \times 10^1 \text{ mol}\right)\left(8.314 \, \frac{J}{\text{mol} \cdot K}\right)}$$

$$\approx \frac{1.8 \times 10^4}{1.8 \times 10^2} = 10^2 \text{ K} = 100 \text{ K (actual} = 97.6 \text{ K)}$$

Related Questions

1. A 22.4 liter vessel contains nitrogen gas at STP. What mass of nitrogen is in the vessel? $\left(\text{Note: R} = 8.314 \, \dfrac{J}{\text{mol} \cdot K}\right)$

2. Humans breathe out a tidal volume of about 0.5 liters of gas at 1.0 atm and 37°C. How many moles of gas are present? (Note: Assume that only carbon dioxide is present in the exhaled gas and that R = 0.0821 $\dfrac{\text{L} \cdot \text{atm}}{\text{mol} \cdot K}$)

3. What is the volume of 2 mol of chlorine gas pressurized to 4000 mmHg at 700°C? $\left(\text{Note: R} = 62.4 \, \dfrac{\text{L} \cdot \text{mmHg}}{\text{mol} \cdot K}\right)$

Things to Watch Out For

Always hold on to units for MCAT calculations, especially when SI and non-SI units are mixed in a question. It is important to make sure that the units cancel correctly to confirm that you have arrived at the correct answer; if the units don't work, the answer cannot be right!

Key Concepts

General Chemistry Chapter 9

pH

Molar solubility

Common ion effect

Le Châtelier's principle

K_{sp}

Molar Solubility

The molar solubility of iron(III) hydroxide in pure water at 25°C is 9.94×10^{-10} M. How would the substance's molar solubility change if placed in an aqueous solution with a pH of 10.0 at 25°C?

1 **Identify the balanced equation for the dissociation reaction.**

The generic dissociation reaction may be expressed as follows:

$$A_x B_y\,(s) \rightleftharpoons x\,A^+\,(aq) + y\,B^-\,(aq)$$

For iron(III) hydroxide, the reaction expression is:

$$Fe(OH)_3\,(s) \rightleftharpoons Fe^{3+}\,(aq) + 3\,OH^-\,(aq)$$

This step allows us to see how many moles of ions are dissolved into the solution per mole of solid dissolved.

2 **Find the K_{sp} expression for the dissociation reaction.**

K_{sp} is an equilibrium constant, just like any other K, and it is given the special name *solubility product* because it is related to the dissolution of a salt into solution. The expression for any K is simply the concentration of each product raised to its stoichiometric coefficient over the concentration of each reactant raised to its stoichiometric coefficient; only gases and aqueous species are included. Remember that the values of all Ks vary only with temperature.

For iron(III) hydroxide, the K_{sp} expression is:

$$K_{sp} = [Fe^{3+}][OH^-]^3$$

3 **Determine the K_{sp} from the molar solubility.**

When solid iron(III) hydroxide is placed into water, some of the salt will dissolve. Based on the balanced chemical equation, if x moles of iron(III) hydroxide dissolve, then x moles of iron(III) and $3x$ moles of hydroxide ions will be dissolved into solution:

$$x\,Fe(OH)_3 \rightleftharpoons x\,Fe^{3+} + 3x\,OH^-$$

The molar solubility is the amount of salt that dissolves to create a saturated solution. If we say that the value of x in this equation is the molar solubility, this implies that—at saturation—there will be x molar Fe^{3+} and $3x$ molar hydroxide ions. From this information, we can determine the K_{sp}:

$$K_{sp} = [Fe^{3+}][OH^-]^3 = (x)(3x)^3 = 27x^4$$

The molar solubility, x, is given as 9.94×10^{-10}. Plugging in, we can find the value of K_{sp}:

$$27 \times (9.94 \times 10^{-10})^4 \approx 27 \times (10^{-9})^4 = 27 \times 10^{-36} = 2.7 \times 10^{-35}$$

 Determine the molar solubility in the solution with a pH of 10.0.

If the pH is 10.0, then the pOH of this solution is $14 - 10 = 4$. This means that the hydroxide ion concentration is 10^{-4}. If x moles of iron(III) hydroxide dissolve, then x moles of iron(III) and $3x$ moles of hydroxide ions will still be dissolved into solution—the difference here is that the hydroxide ion concentration starts at 10^{-4}, not 0. Therefore, the concentration of hydroxide ions at saturation will not be $3x$, but rather $3x + 10^{-4}$. We can include this in the K_{sp} expression:

$$K_{sp} = [Fe^{3+}][OH^-]^3$$
$$2.7 \times 10^{-35} = (x)(3x + 10^{-4})^3$$

On the MCAT, the value of x will almost always be sufficiently small to be considered negligible if we are adding or subtracting x (or, in this case, $3x$):

$$2.7 \times 10^{-35} \approx (x)(10^{-4})^3 = x(10^{-12})$$
$$x \approx 2.7 \times 10^{-23} \; M$$

 Compare the molar solubilities in water and in a solution with a pH of 10.0.

For the solution with a pH of 10.0, the molar solubility is on the order of $10^{-23} \; M$, which represents a significant decrease from its molar solubility in water (around $10^{-9} \; M$). This is due to the common ion effect. If we consider this from the perspective of Le Châtelier's principle, we could point out that the addition of more OH^- will shift the reaction to the left; thus, less iron(III) hydroxide will dissociate.

Takeaways

The value of K_{sp} does not change when a common ion is present; it is a constant that is dependent on temperature only. The molar solubility of the salt, however, does change if a common ion is present.

Things to Watch Out For

Be careful when applying Le Châtelier's principle in cases of precipitation and solvation. For a solution at equilibrium (that is, a saturated solution), adding more solid will not shift the equilibrium to the right. More solid does not dissociate to raise the ion concentrations; it just precipitates to the bottom.

Related Questions

1. Given a substance's K_{sp}, how could you solve for its molar solubility in pure water? What if a common ion were also present in solution?

2. Given a table listing substances and their solubility constants, how could you determine which substance was most soluble in pure water?

3. Given that the sulfate ion can react with acid to form hydrogen sulfate, how would the molar solubility of sulfate salts be affected by varying a solution's pH?

High-Yield Problem-Solving Guide questions continue on the next page. ▶ ▶ ▶

Key Concepts

General Chemistry Chapter 10

Titrations

Acids and bases

Equivalence points

Half-equivalence points

pH

Titrations

Hydrazoic acid, HN_3, is a highly toxic compound that can cause death in minutes if inhaled in a concentrated form. 100 mL of a 0.2 M aqueous solution of HN_3 ($pK_a = 4.72$) is to be titrated with a 0.5 M solution of NaOH. What is the pH of the HN_3 solution before any NaOH is added? How much of the NaOH solution will be needed to reach the equivalence point? What is the pH at this point? How much of the NaOH solution will be needed to reach the half-equivalence point? What is the pH at this point?

 Determine the concentration of H_3O^+ in the hydrazoic acid solution before the titration.

To determine the pH, we need to know the concentration of hydrogen ions in solution. This can be determined from the concentration of dissociated hydrazoic acid, which is the main contributor of hydrogen ions to the solution (there will be a small contribution from the water itself, which autoionizes to produce 10^{-7} M H_3O^+). To determine the hydrogen ion concentration from hydrazoic acid, we will follow the three-step method that can be applied to all K questions:

1. Write out the balanced expression for the reaction

2. Write the expression for K

3. Plug in the values from the question stem or data table

Here, the balanced expression is that for the dissociation of hydrazoic acid in solution:

$$H_2O \ (l) + HN_3 \ (aq) \rightleftharpoons H_3O^+ \ (aq) + N_3^- \ (aq)$$

The K expression is the acid dissociation constant, K_a, which would be written as:

$$K_a = \frac{[H_3O^+][N_3^-]}{[HN_3]}$$

Before any hydrazoic acid has dissociated, its concentration in solution is 0.2 M according to the question stem. At this point, the concentrations of H_3O^+ and N_3^- are negligible. If x moles of hydrazoic acid dissociate to reach equilibrium, then the concentration of hydrazoic acid at equilibrium is $0.2 - x$, and the concentrations of H_3O^+ and N_3^- are each x:

$$K_a = \frac{x^2}{0.2 - x}$$

Remember that the value of x on the MCAT is usually small enough to be considered negligible when added or subtracted. This simplifies our calculations quite a bit:

$$K_a = \frac{x^2}{0.2} = 5x^2$$

We were not given the value of K_a, but we were given pK_a. Remember that "p" is shorthand for $-\log$, so raising 10 to the power of $-pKa$ will give us the K_a:

$$K_a = 10^{-4.72} \approx 10^{-5}$$

Bringing this all together, we can solve for the concentration of H_3O^+:

$$K_a \approx 10^{-5} = 5x^2$$
$$x^2 = 2 \times 10^{-6}$$
$$x = 1.4 \times 10^{-3} = [H_3O^+]$$

2 Find the pH of the hydrazoic acid solution based on the concentration of H_3O^+.

Remember that for a solution with a hydronium ion concentration written in the form $n \times 10^{-m}$, the pH can be approximated as $m - 0.n$, where $0.n$ represents moving the decimal place of the coefficient one position to the left. Therefore, the pH of a solution with a hydronium ion concentration of 1.4×10^{-3} is roughly $3 - 0.14 = 2.86$ (actual = 2.71).

3 Find how much NaOH is needed to reach the equivalence point and the pH at this point.

The equivalence point occurs when the quantity in moles of acid present is equal to the moles of base added. First, calculate the number of moles of hydrazoic acid that we started with:

$$0.1 \text{ L} \times 0.2 \text{ } M = 0.02 \text{ mol HN}_3$$

That means we need to know how much of the NaOH solution is required to obtain 0.02 mol NaOH:

$$\frac{0.02 \text{ mol}}{0.5 \text{ } M} = 0.04 \text{ L NaOH solution}$$

At the equivalence point, all of the HN_3 has been consumed, leaving N_3^- behind. N_3^- is a Brønsted–Lowry base; as such, it will determine the pH at this point. To figure out the pH, we will need to use the K_b of N_3^-, which can be determined from the K_a of hydrazoic acid and the water dissociation constant:

$$K_{a,acid} \times K_{b,conjugate\ base} = K_w$$

The K_b of N_3^- is therefore:

$$\frac{K_w}{K_a} \approx \frac{10^{-14}}{10^{-5}} = 10^{-9}$$

Now we can proceed with the same three-step method. First, we determine the balanced reaction:

$$N_3^- \ (aq) + H_2O \ (l) \rightleftharpoons HN_3 \ (aq) + OH^- \ (aq)$$

Then, the K expression:

$$K_b = \frac{[HN_3][OH^-]}{[N_3^-]}$$

Finally, we put in the relevant values. The concentrations of hydrazoic acid and OH^- are negligible without the reaction of N_3^-, but what is the initial concentration of N_3^- itself? While we would like to say that it's the 0.2 M concentration that hydrazoic acid had at the beginning of the titration, the volume has increased. This dilutes the N_3^-, making its concentration a bit lower:

$$\left[N_3^-\right] = \frac{0.02 \ \text{mol}}{0.1 \ \text{L} + 0.04 \ \text{L}} \approx 0.15 \ M$$

Putting the relevant values into the K_b expression, we can solve for $[OH^-]$:

$$10^{-9} = \frac{[x][x]}{[0.15 - x]} \approx \frac{x^2}{0.15}$$
$$x^2 = 0.15 \times 10^{-9} \approx 10^{-10}$$
$$x = [OH^-] \approx 10^{-5}$$

If $[OH^-]$ is close to 10^{-5}, then the pOH is close to 5. This makes the pH close to 9 (actual = 8.94). Remember to ask yourself whether or not this result makes sense. Here, because we have a basic species (N_3^-), the pH should be above 7, which it is.

 ## Find how much NaOH is needed to reach the half-equivalence point and the pH at this point.

The half-equivalence point will occur when half of the hydrazoic acid has been neutralized. We can simply divide the volume of NaOH needed for the equivalence point by two, which means that 20 mL of the NaOH solution are needed to reach the half-equivalence point.

We could go through the whole three-step method to determine the pH at the half-equivalence point, or we could use a little common sense to avoid computation. At the half-equivalence point, half of the HN_3 has been consumed and converted to N_3^-. Therefore, the HN_3 and N_3^- concentrations are equal:

$$K_a = \frac{[H_3O^+][\cancel{N_3^-}]}{\cancel{[HN_3]}} = [H_3O^+]$$

Taking the negative logarithm of both sides, we get $pH = pK_a = 4.72$.

Related Questions

1. What is the pH after the equivalence point has been exceeded by 5 mL of the NaOH solution in this titration?

2. What would be the pH if the same amount of NaOH solution necessary to get to the half-equivalence point in this titration were diluted into enough pure water to form one liter of solution?

3. If the pK_a of acetic acid is 4.76, then what is the pK_b of acetate?

Things to Watch Out For

Be careful in choosing whether to use K_a or K_b to determine the pH. Make this decision based on whether the dominant species in solution is acidic or basic, respectively.

Key Concepts

General Chemistry Chapter 11

Oxidation
Reduction
Balancing electrochemical
  half-reactions
Conservation of charge

Balancing Oxidation–Reduction Reactions

Balance the following reaction, which takes place in basic solution:

$$ZrO(OH)_2 \, (s) + SO_3^{2-} \, (aq) \rightleftharpoons Zr \, (s) + SO_4^{2-} \, (aq)$$

Separate the two half-reactions.

$$ZrO(OH)_2 \rightleftharpoons Zr$$
$$SO_3^{2-} \rightleftharpoons SO_4^{2-}$$

Break the reactions up by looking at atoms *other* than hydrogen and oxygen.

Balance the atoms of each half-reaction.

First, balance all of the atoms except H and O. Next, in a basic solution, use OH^- and H_2O to balance the O and H atoms (in an acidic solution, use H_2O and H^+):

$$H_2O + ZrO(OH)_2 \rightleftharpoons Zr + 4 \, OH^-$$
$$2 \, OH^- + SO_3^{2-} \rightleftharpoons SO_4^{2-} + H_2O$$

3 Balance the charges of each half-reaction.

Add electrons as necessary to one side of each reaction so that the charges are equal on both sides. The top equation has a total charge of –4 on the right from the 4 hydroxide ions, so 4 electrons need to be added to the left side of the equation. In the bottom equation, there is a total charge of –4 on the left (–2 from the two hydroxide ions and –2 from the sulfite anion) and –2 on the right (from the sulfate anion):

$$4 \, e^- + H_2O + ZrO(OH)_2 \rightleftharpoons Zr + 4 \, OH^-$$
$$2 \, OH^- + SO_3^{2-} \rightleftharpoons SO_4^{2-} + H_2O + 2 \, e^-$$

During this step, be careful to account for all charges, including the charges contributed by molecules other than H^+ and OH^-.

4 **Multiply each reaction by the necessary integer to ensure that equal numbers of electrons are present in each reaction.**

Here, the lowest common multiple between the four electrons in the top reaction and the two in the bottom is four electrons, so we must multiply everything in the bottom reaction by two:

$$4\,e^- + H_2O + ZrO(OH)_2 \rightleftharpoons Zr + 4\,OH^-$$
$$4\,OH^- + 2\,SO_3^{2-} \rightleftharpoons 2\,SO_4^{2-} + 2\,H_2O + 4\,e^-$$

5 **Add the half-reactions, canceling out terms that appear on both sides of the reaction arrow.**

$$ZrO(OH)_2 + 2\,SO_3^{2-} \rightleftharpoons Zr + 2\,SO_4^{2-} + H_2O$$

6 **Confirm that mass and charge are balanced.**

There is a −2 net charge on each side of the reaction equation, and the atoms are stoichiometrically balanced. This last step is extremely important. If mass and charge aren't balanced, then we have made an error in one of the previous steps.

Takeaways

Don't fall into the trap of simply balancing mass in these reactions. If oxidation and reduction are occurring, one must go through this procedure to balance the reaction accurately.

Things to Watch Out For

These kinds of problems can be extremely tedious. Questions that ask you to balance complicated oxidation–reduction reactions are best saved until the end of the section if you have time left over.

Related Questions

1. Which atom is being oxidized in the original equation? Which is being reduced? Identify the oxidizing and reducing agents.

2. A disproportionation reaction is one in which the same species is both oxidized and reduced during the course of the reaction. One such reaction is shown below. Balance the reaction, assuming that it takes place in acidic solution:

$$PbSO_4\,(s) \rightarrow Pb\,(s) + PbO_2\,(s) + SO_4^{2-}\,(aq)$$

3. Dentists may use zinc amalgams to make temporary crowns for their patients. It is absolutely vital that they keep the zinc amalgam dry. The reaction of zinc metal with water is shown below:

$$Zn\,(s) + H_2O\,(l) \rightarrow Zn^{2+}\,(aq) + H_2\,(g)$$

Balance this reaction, assuming that it takes place in basic solution. Why is it so important to keep the amalgam dry?

Key Concepts

General Chemistry Chapter 12

Oxidation–reduction reactions

Electrochemical cells

Stoichiometry

Electromotive force

$\Delta G = -nFE^{\circ}_{cell}$

Electrochemical Cells

A galvanic cell is to be constructed using MnO_4^- | Mn^{2+} ($E^{\circ}_{red} = +1.49$ V) and Zn^{2+} | Zn ($E^{\circ}_{red} = -0.76$ V) half-reactions in acidic solution. Assume that all potentials given are measured against the standard hydrogen electrode at 298 K and that all reagents are present in 1 M concentrations. What is the maximum possible work output of this cell per mole of reactant if it is used to run an electric motor for one hour at room temperature (298 K)? During this amount of time, how much Zn metal would be necessary to run the cell, given a current of 5 A?

 Determine which half-reaction is occurring at the anode and which is occurring at the cathode of the cell.

Compare the standard reduction potentials for both reactions. The standard reduction potential is a measure of how much a particular material "wants" to be reduced. The permanganate reduction potential is greater than that of zinc, so it would "prefer" to be reduced, and zinc would "prefer" to be oxidized. This is a galvanic cell, which houses a spontaneous chemical reaction. Therefore, the zinc will be oxidized at the anode, and the manganese will be reduced at the cathode.

 Write a balanced reaction for the cell.

This can be done using the ion–electron method shown in the previous *Balancing Oxidation–Reduction Reactions* question:

1. $\begin{cases} MnO_4^- \rightarrow Mn^{2+} \\ \quad Zn \rightarrow Zn^{2+} \end{cases}$

2. $\begin{cases} 8\,H^+ + MnO_4^- \rightarrow Mn^{2+} + 4\,H_2O \\ \qquad\qquad Zn \rightarrow Zn^{2+} \end{cases}$

3. $\begin{cases} 8\,H^+ + MnO_4^- + 5\,e^- \rightarrow Mn^{2+} + 4\,H_2O \\ \qquad\qquad Zn \rightarrow Zn^{2+} + 2\,e^- \end{cases}$

4. $\begin{cases} 16\,H^+ + 2\,MnO_4^- + 10\,e^- \rightarrow 2\,Mn^{2+} + 8\,H_2O \\ \qquad\qquad 5\,Zn \rightarrow 5\,Zn^{2+} + 10\,e^- \end{cases}$

5. $16\,H^+ + 2\,MnO_4^- + 5\,Zn \rightarrow 2\,Mn^{2+} + 8\,H_2O + 5\,Zn^{2+}$

3 **Calculate the standard potential for the cell.**

Use the equation $E^\circ_{cell} = E^\circ_{red,cathode} - E^\circ_{red,anode}$:

$$E^\circ_{cell} = +1.49 - (-0.76) = 2.25 \text{ V}$$

The standard potential for the cell is positive, confirming that this is a galvanic (voltaic) cell—once the electrodes are hooked up and immersed in the designated solutions, current will start to flow spontaneously.

4 **Compute $\triangle G^\circ$ for the cell.**

Use the equation $\Delta G^\circ = -nFE^\circ_{cell}$:

$$\Delta G^\circ = (-10 \text{ mol } e^-)\left(10^5 \frac{C}{\text{mol } e^-}\right)(2.25 \text{ V}) = -2.25 \times 10^6 \frac{J}{\text{mol}}$$

$$(\text{actual} = 2.17 \times 10^3 \frac{kJ}{\text{mol}}).$$

The upper limit on the amount of work a reaction can perform is the same thing as ΔG°. Here, the maximum work output per mole of reactant is $2.17 \times 10^3 \frac{kJ}{\text{mol}}$.

5 **Use the Faraday constant to determine the number of moles of electrons transferred and to determine the amount of zinc necessary to run the cell for one hour.**

Remember that current is charge passing though a point per unit of time, and that the Faraday constant indicates how many coulombs of charge make up one mole of electrons. We can use the current and time to determine the amount of charge transferred; we can use the Faraday constant to determine how many electrons are in that amount of charge:

$$n = \frac{It}{F}$$

$$= \frac{(5 \text{ A})(3600 \text{ s})}{10^5 \dfrac{C}{\text{mol } e^-}}$$

$$= 0.18 \text{ mol } e^-$$

Each atom of zinc releases two electrons during oxidation, so 0.09 moles of zinc are necessary to liberate 0.18 moles of electrons. We can then determine the necessary mass of zinc from its molar mass:

$$0.09 \text{ mol Zn} \times 65.4 \ \frac{g}{\text{mol}} \approx 6 \text{ g Zn (actual} = 6.10 \text{ g)}$$

Takeaways

Double-check your work when you balance the cell equations to make sure that you haven't made any arithmetic errors. One small addition or subtraction mistake can have drastic consequences.

Things to Watch Out For

In a galvanic (voltaic) cell, the species with the higher reduction potential will be reduced. In an electrolytic cell, the species with the higher reduction potential will be oxidized.

Related Questions

1. How could one alter the cell setup to reverse the direction of current flow?

2. What would happen to the electromotive force produced by this cell if the amount of zinc present were doubled?

3. Compute the minimum mass of potassium permanganate ($KMnO_4$) necessary to run the cell for the same amount of time as specified above.

Solutions to Related Questions

1. Atomic Mass and Weight

1. A mole of any substance has a quantity of molecules equal to Avogadro's number ($N_A = 6.02 \times 10^{23}$ mol^{-1}). Therefore, while one mole of each substance has the same number of molecules, their masses will be different. Water has a molar mass of $2 \times 1 \frac{\text{g}}{\text{mol}} + 16 \frac{\text{g}}{\text{mol}} = 18 \frac{\text{g}}{\text{mol}}$, whereas carbon dioxide has a molar mass of $12 \frac{\text{g}}{\text{mol}} + 2 \times 16 \frac{\text{g}}{\text{mol}} = 44 \frac{\text{g}}{\text{mol}}$.

2. Given an atomic weight, it is not always possible to tell which isotope is most abundant; for example, bromine has two abundant isotopes: bromine-79 and bromine-81. The atomic weight sits between these two, at 79.9. Bromine-80, which is the closest to this value, is *not* the most abundant isotope. In this case, however, we can tell that silicon-29 must be the most common isotope. For the atomic weight to be 28.086, there must be enough silicon-29 to balance out the other isotopes, which are all less than 28.

3. This question is no different than the one given for zinc; here, let's use rounding to simplify the calculations. There are 200 total atoms, 40% of which are oxygen-16, and 30% of which are oxygen-14 and oxygen-18, respectively. If we multiply the atomic masses by their relative abundances and then add those results together, we get the atomic weight: $0.4 \times 16 \frac{\text{amu}}{\text{atom}} + 0.3 \times 14 \frac{\text{amu}}{\text{atom}} + 0.3 \times 18 \frac{\text{amu}}{\text{atom}} = 6.4 + 4.2 + 5.4 = 16 \frac{\text{amu}}{\text{atom}}$. The question asks for the molar mass, which is the mass of one mole of a substance in grams. This has the same value as the atomic weight, but different units. The molar mass of oxygen is $16 \frac{\text{g}}{\text{mol}}$. Note that we could have actually bypassed all of these calculations—the value reported in the Periodic Table *is* the atomic weight for an element.

2. Periodic Trends

1. In the neutral state, we would expect atomic radii to increase as we move from the upper right corner of the Periodic Table to the lower left: O < C < B < Be. When an atom gains electrons, its size increases significantly; in fact, we would predict that the divalent oxygen anion would be the largest. The opposite is true for cations; we would expect that boron, having lost three electrons, would be the smallest species. Therefore, we could rank these species from smallest to largest as follows:

$$B^{3+} < C < Be < O^{2-}$$

2. Both phosphorus and selenium are equidistant from the upper right corner of the Periodic Table. However, the element with the higher effective nuclear charge (Z_{eff}) will have the higher ionization energy. Selenium has more electrons that shield valence electrons from the nucleus, reducing its Z_{eff}. Therefore, we would expect phosphorus to have a higher first ionization energy than selenium.

3. The second ionization energy of an element will always be higher than the first ionization energy, and the third ionization energy will always be higher still. Thus, this trend is expected. However, note that the increase from second to third ionization energy is much higher than the increase from first to second ionization energy. This implies that it requires some energy to remove one electron from the element, more energy to remove a second electron, and then much, much more energy to remove a third. In other words, this element seems to gain some stability after losing two electrons that is greatly disturbed by removing a third. Elements in Group IIA (Group 2) best fit this description; specifically, these are the ionization energies for strontium (Sr).

3. VSEPR Theory and Geometry

1. The formula for aluminum trichloride is $AlCl_3$, and that for phosphorus tribromide is PBr_3. Based solely on the number of bonds, we might expect that both will have trigonal planar geometry. We must analyze the Lewis structure to determine if there are lone pairs. Aluminum is in Group IIIA (Group 13), so it has three valence electrons. Because it has already formed three single bonds, it has no electrons left to form a lone pair and will have the expected trigonal planar geometry. Phosphorus is in Group VA (Group 15), so it has five valence electrons. Because it has formed three single bonds, it must have one lone pair remaining; it therefore has trigonal pyramidal geometry. These two molecules vary in geometry because phosphorus has a lone pair, while aluminum does not.

2. A molecule with octahedral geometry has six groups organized around a central atom. In order to maximize the distance between any two groups, four of the groups occupy a square plane around the atom, and two are axial (up and down). This makes the maximum angle between two adjacent groups 90°. In a bent molecule, there are four groups (two of which are lone pairs). With fewer groups to arrange in three-dimensional space, each group can spread farther away from the others to minimize the amount of repulsion between adjacent groups. In bent molecules, this angle is around 104.5°. In other words, the angle is larger in a bent molecule than an octahedral molecule because fewer groups are sharing the same space.

3. The sulfate anion (SO_4^{2-}) has a tetrahedral structure because it has four groups arranged around a central atom (AX_4 geometry). The negative charges do not influence its overall geometry because the electrons are delocalized due to resonance. Thus, the charge is distributed around the whole molecule. Sulfuric acid (H_2SO_4) has two hydroxyl groups and two S=O bonds. While there are slight deviations in the angles between sulfate and sulfuric acid, the fact that both molecules arrange four groups around the central sulfur atom means that the geometry is tetrahedral for both.

4. Stoichiometry

1. Water is formed from hydrogen and oxygen gases through the reaction $2\ H_2 + O_2 \rightarrow 2\ H_2O$. 26 g of hydrogen gas corresponds to 13 moles of H_2 (molar mass = $2\ \frac{g}{mol}$), which will produce 13 moles of water. 13 moles of water can then be converted to the various desired units to obtain 234 g H_2O (molar mass = $18\ \frac{g}{mol}$) and 7.83×10^{24} molecules H_2O (using Avogadro's number). Note that the phrase *excess oxygen* implies that no limiting reagent calculation is required.

2. Let's start by balancing the reaction for the combustion of butane. The balanced reaction is:

$$2 \, C_4H_{10} + 13 \, O_2 \rightarrow 8 \, CO_2 + 10 \, H_2O$$

For this calculation, we are given the units of liters of gas at STP, which can be converted to moles using the equivalence factor $22.4 \, \frac{L}{mol}$. Then, we'll use the mole ratio from the balanced equation above. Finally, we'll convert to a mass of butane using its molar mass ($4 \times 12 \, \frac{g}{mol} + 10 \times 1 \, \frac{g}{mol} = 58 \, \frac{g}{mol}$). The calculations are:

$$179.2 \, L \, CO_2 \times \left[\frac{1 \, mol \, CO_2}{22.4 \, L \, CO_2}\right]\left[\frac{2 \, mol \, C_4H_{10}}{8 \, mol \, CO_2}\right]\left[\frac{58 \, g \, C_4H_{10}}{1 \, mol \, C_4H_{10}}\right]$$

$$\approx \frac{180 \times 2 \times 60}{20 \times 8} = 9 \times 15 = 135 \, g \, C_4H_{10} \, (\text{actual} = 116 \, g)$$

3. This question is similar to those from before, but also introduces a limiting reagent. Start by balancing the equation. The balanced equation for the combustion of heptane is:

$$C_7H_{16} + 11 \, O_2 \rightarrow 7 \, CO_2 + 8 \, H_2O$$

To determine the limiting reagent, convert each of the units given to moles: 44.8 L of heptane represents 2 moles of heptane; 1.204×10^{24} molecules of oxygen represents 2 moles of oxygen. Now, think logically. To react to completion, 2 moles of heptane would require 22 moles of oxygen based on the balanced chemical equation. Because we have only 2 moles of oxygen, this must be the limiting reagent. Now, we proceed as with any other stoichiometry calculation, using the 2 moles of oxygen as our given:

$$2 \, mol \, O_2 \left[\frac{8 \, mol \, H_2O}{11 \, mol \, O_2}\right]\left[\frac{18 \, g \, H_2O}{1 \, mol \, H_2O}\right]$$

$$= \frac{288}{11} \approx \frac{286}{11} = 26 \, g \, H_2O \, (\text{actual} = 26.2 \, g)$$

5. Rate Laws

1. The value of the rate constant can be determined by plugging the values from any of the trials into the rate law:

$$\text{rate} = k[HNO_2]^2$$
$$5.96 \times 10^{-6} = k[2.00 \times 10^{-2}]^2$$
$$5.96 \times 10^{-6} = k[4.00 \times 10^{-4}]$$
$$1.49 \times 10^{-2} = k$$

Its units can be determined by considering the other units in the rate law. The rate is measured in $\frac{M}{s}$, whereas $[HNO_2]$ is measured in M. Thus, the units of k must be $\frac{1}{M \cdot s}$.

2. If we compare trials 2 and 3, we can quickly determine that doubling the concentration of MeI while holding the concentration of pyridine constant resulted in a doubling of the rate. This means the exponent on MeI must be 1 ($2^1 = 2$). Determining the rate with respect to pyridine is a bit more challenging. Let's invent another trial based on what we know about MeI. If we hold the concentration of pyridine constant while *halving* the concentration of MeI, the rate should get cut in half:

Trial	$[C_5H_5N]$ (M)	$[MeI]$ (M)	Initial Rate $\left(\dfrac{M}{s}\right)$
1	1.00×10^{-4}	1.00×10^{-4}	7.50×10^{-7}
2	2.00×10^{-4}	2.00×10^{-4}	3.00×10^{-6}
2a	2.00×10^{-4}	1.00×10^{-4}	1.50×10^{-6}
3	2.00×10^{-4}	4.00×10^{-4}	6.00×10^{-6}

Now we can compare trials 1 and 2a. The concentration of pyridine doubles while the concentration of MeI remains constant. The rate also doubles. Therefore, the exponent on pyridine must also be 1 ($2^1 = 2$). The rate law is rate = $k[C_5H_5N][MeI]$. The rate constant could be calculated from trial 1:

$$\text{rate} = k[C_5H_5N][MeI]$$

$$7.5 \times 10^{-7} \frac{M}{s} = k[1.00 \times 10^{-4}\ M][1.00 \times 10^{-4}\ M]$$

$$75\ M^{-1}\,s^{-1} = k$$

3. The same steps can be used here, even though the numbers do not work quite "cleanly." Between trials 1 and 2, the concentration of cerium(IV) is constant while the concentration of iron(II) gets multiplied by just a bit more than 1.5. The rate also gets multiplied by just a bit more than 1.5. Therefore, the order with respect to iron(II) is 1 ($1.55^1 = 1.55$). Comparing trials 2 and 3, the concentration of cerium(IV) is multiplied by a bit more than 3, while the concentration of iron(II) is constant. The rate also gets multiplied by a bit more than 3. Therefore, the order with respect to cerium(IV) is also 1 ($3.1^1 = 3.1$). The rate law for the reaction of cerium(IV) and iron(II) is therefore rate = $k[Ce^{4+}][Fe^{2+}]$. The rate constant can be determined using trial 1:

$$\text{rate} = k[Ce^{4+}][Fe^{2+}]$$

$$2.00 \times 10^{-7} \frac{M}{s} = k[1.10 \times 10^{-5}\ M][1.80 \times 10^{-5}\ M]$$

$$2.00 \times 10^{-7} \frac{M}{s} \approx k[2 \times 10^{-10}\ M^2]$$

$$10^3\ M^{-1}\,s^{-1} \approx k\ (\text{actual} = 1.01 \times 10^3\ M^{-1}\,s^{-1})$$

6. Reaction Energy Profiles

1. The ratio of **B** to **A** at equilibrium can be determined using the equation $\Delta G° = -RT \ln K_{eq}$:

$$K_{eq} = \frac{[B]}{[A]} = e^{\frac{-\Delta G°}{RT}} = e^{\frac{900\ \frac{cal}{mol}}{(2\ \frac{cal}{mol\,\cdot\,K})(300\ K)}} \approx e^{1.5} \approx \text{between 3 and 9 (actual} = 4.56)$$

2. If a catalyst were added to the reaction of **A** forming **C**, the energies of **A** and **C** would not be changed. A catalyst only lowers the activation energy by lowering the energy of the transition state, and does not affect the energies of the reactants or products.

3. The complete reaction profiles for the reactions producing **B** and **C** from **A** are shown below. The intermediate leading to **C** is relatively more stable because the electrons in the double bond and in the lone pair on the oxygen atom can be delocalized. This can be seen in the plot from its lower energy.

7. Hess's Law

1. An ideal hydrocarbon combustion reaction has two reactants (the hydrocarbon and oxygen) and two products (carbon dioxide and water). To determine the heat of reaction—which is combustion in this case—we will need the heats of formation for all of the reactants and products. We know that the heat of formation of diatomic oxygen gas is zero, so if we are given the heats of formation for carbon dioxide and water, we also need to know the heat of formation of ethane to determine the heat of combustion.

2. First, we must balance the chemical equation for the combustion of acetylene:

$$C_2H_2 + \frac{5}{2} O_2 \rightarrow 2\ CO_2 + H_2O$$

Note that the fractional stoichiometric coefficient in front of oxygen is not a concern because we'll be multiplying that coefficient by the heat of formation of oxygen gas, which is zero. We can apply Hess's law to answer this question. The heats of formation of all of the reactants and products are given, so we can solve for the heat of combustion:

$$\Delta H^{\circ}_{rxn} = \sum \Delta H^{\circ}_{f,products} - \sum \Delta H^{\circ}_{f,reactants}$$

$$\Delta H^{\circ}_{comb} = \left[2 \times \left(-393.5\ \frac{kJ}{mol}\right) + 1 \times \left(-241.8\ \frac{kJ}{mol}\right)\right] - \left[1 \times \left(226.6\ \frac{kJ}{mol}\right) + \frac{5}{2} \times \left(0\ \frac{kJ}{mol}\right)\right]$$

$$\approx 2 \times (-400) - 250 - 225$$

$$= -800 - 475 = -1275\ \frac{kJ}{mol} \left(actual = -1255.4\ \frac{kJ}{mol}\right)$$

3. Enthalpy is a state function; therefore, the path taken to get from the reactants to the products does not matter in determining the enthalpy change. If we add these five reactions together, the net reaction is:

$$Na\ (s) + \frac{1}{2} Br_2\ (g) \rightarrow NaBr\ (s)$$

This is equivalent to synthesizing sodium bromide from its elements in their standard states, which is, by definition, the standard heat of formation. Thus, the sum of the heats of reaction for these five reactions is $-359.9\ \frac{kJ}{mol}$.

5

Organic Chemistry

Key Concepts

Organic Chemistry Chapter 1

Nomenclature

Functional group priority

Nomenclature

What is the IUPAC name for the following compound?

 Identify the longest carbon chain containing the highest-order functional group.

In this case, the highest-priority functional group is the ester. Therefore, we will name everything attached to the ester as a substituent, including the cyclohexyl ring on the left. The longest continuous chain containing the ester is three carbons long.

oxocyclohexyl

longest continuous chain and ester group

methoxy

2 Number the chain.

As mentioned in Step 1, the longest continuous chain containing the ester is three carbons long. Carbon 1 will be the carbonyl carbon because the ester is the highest-priority functional group. Because the ester has three carbons, this will be a *propanoate* ester.

Name the substituents.

The first substituent is the ethyl group on the ester, which we will identify by placing the word *ethyl* in front of the ester name. Next, there is a methyl group attached to an oxygen, which will be named as a *methoxy–* group. Finally, there is a cyclohexane containing a ketone, the naming of which will be discussed in the next step.

④ **Assign a number to each substituent.**

The ethyl group is the esterifying group and is not assigned a number, but rather is listed as an adjective before the rest of the molecule's name.

The methoxy group is on carbon 2.

How do we handle the ring attached to carbon 3? If there were nothing attached to the ring, we would simply name the ring as a *cyclohexyl* substituent. However, there is a ketone in the ring. Recall that when aldehydes or ketones are named as substituents, they are named with the prefix *oxo–*. The numbering works, as shown, by assigning the number 1 to the carbon attached to the parent carbon chain. Therefore, the ketone on the ring will be at carbon 2. We'll name the whole ring as a *(2-oxocyclohexyl)–* substituent and put it in parentheses to indicate that it follows a numbering system *within* a substituent.

⑤ **Complete the name.**

The name of our compound will be ethyl 2-methoxy-3-(2-oxocyclohexyl) propanoate.

Takeaways

The key to the nomenclature problems is to be as systematic as possible. Don't try to do everything at once, or you risk confusing yourself.

Things to Watch Out For

Don't forget to include parentheses if a substituent is further substituted so that you don't confuse the two numbering systems.

Related Questions

1. How would the name be altered if the alkyl group attached to the ester oxygen contained substituents?

2. Upon reduction with sodium borohydride, followed by dilute acid workup, the molecule below gave two products in unequal yield. Draw them and provide the correct IUPAC name for each.

3. What are the two possible products of the reaction shown below? Draw and provide IUPAC names for both.

High-Yield Problem-Solving Guide questions continue on the next page. ▶ ▶ ▶

Key Concepts

Organic Chemistry Chapter 2

Stereochemistry
Fischer projections
Oxidation–reduction reactions
meso compounds

Stereoisomers

A student wanted to prepare chiral polyols by taking sugars and reacting them with sodium borohydride. She took D-xylose, shown below, and treated it with sodium borohydride, followed by a dilute aqueous acid workup. On purifying and isolating the product, she found that it did not rotate plane-polarized light. What was the structure of the product, and why didn't it rotate light?

1 Convert the molecule from a Natta projection to a Fischer projection.

Natta (wedge-and-dash) projections are frequently used in organic chemistry, but are more challenging to use for absolute configuration determinations than Fischer projections. This is especially true when the highest-priority group for Cahn–Ingold–Prelog nomenclature (–OH, in this case) is in the "back." Converting to a Fischer projection may enable you to see stereochemical relationships more clearly. Note that the center carbon atom is drawn in reverse because the rules of Fischer projections require that the horizontal bonds always project forward, not backward.

2 Draw the product of the initial reaction.

Sodium borohydride is a reducing agent and will reduce the aldehyde to a primary alcohol.

③ Look for planes of symmetry in the product.

There are two major ways that optical activity could be lost in a previously optically active solution: the formation of a racemic mixture, or the generation of an achiral compound. In the latter case, the molecule could have zero chiral centers or could be a *meso* compound—one that has stereocenters but also contains a plane of symmetry. It is easiest to check for a *meso* compound because all we need to do is identify a plane of symmetry. To check for a racemic mixture, we would have to assign (*R*) and (*S*) designations to every chiral carbon in the molecules. In this case, there is a plane of symmetry in the product running through C-3:

Takeaways

Any time optical activity is lost in a reaction, either a racemic mixture or an achiral compound has been formed.

Things to Watch Out For

With molecules that contain multiple stereocenters, consider drawing them as Fischer projections to be able to spot planes of symmetry or assign (*R*) and (*S*) nomenclature easily.

Related Questions

1. The specific rotation of a certain D-carbohydrate is +140°. What is the specific rotation of its L-isomer? What would be the observed rotation in a solution containing 1 *M* of each isomer?

2. Which of these three D-aldopentoses (shown below) would result in achiral polyols when subjected to borohydride reduction?

3. A *meso* compound contains chiral centers but is overall achiral. Is the reverse true? That is, can a molecule that does *not* contain chiral centers be overall *chiral*?

Key Concepts

Organic Chemistry Chapter 3

Hybridized orbitals
Covalent bonding
s- and p-orbitals
pK$_a$
Bond dissociation energy

Hybridized Orbitals

Orbital hybridization affects more than just the shape of molecules. In fact, *sp* hybrid orbitals can have quite different properties than *sp*³ orbitals, even on atoms of the same element. The compounds below differ only in the hybridization of the carbon atom highlighted. First, arrange them in order of increasing pK$_a$ for the highlighted protons. Then, arrange them by increasing bond dissociation energy between the two carbons.

1 Order the compounds by pK$_a$.

The K_a (acid dissociation constant) of a molecule measures its acidity; the higher the K_a, the more acidic the compound. The term "p" is shorthand for −log, so pK$_a$ = −log K_a. This mathematical relationship means that the *lower* the pK$_a$, the more acidic the compound. In each of these three compounds, the proton to be lost differs only by the hybridization of the carbon to which it is attached. The C–H bond in compound **1** is *sp*³-hybridized, the C–H bond in **2** is *sp*²-hybridized, and the C–H bond in **3** is *sp*-hybridized.

To understand the acidity trend in this group, we need to consider not only the neutral molecules but their anions as well. Each anion in this case has a lone pair of electrons where the proton was once bound. In the case of compound **1**, the electrons are in an *sp*³ orbital; in **2**, in an *sp*² orbital; and in **3**, in an *sp* orbital.

It's useful to say that these lone pairs are in different hybrid orbitals, but how does that actually affect the relative stabilities of their anions? The anions' stabilities are dependent on the energies of the two electrons in the lone pair; these energies are in turn based on the energies of the orbitals in which they are located. Each of these orbitals is a hybrid of *s*- and *p*-orbitals. Remember that *s*-orbitals are much lower in energy than their *p* counterparts, and hybrid orbitals have energies that are weighted averages of their constituent orbitals. Therefore, the anion with the most *s* character should be the most stable, and the anion with the most *p* character should be the least stable. The order of anion stability is:

1 < 2 < 3

This isn't the whole picture, though. We were asked to arrange the compounds in order of increasing pK_a, not anion stability—and the less stable the anion is, the less acidic its conjugate acid will be. The less acidic the conjugate acid, the higher the pK_a. Putting it all together, the molecules can be arranged in order of increasing pK_a:

3 < 2 < 1

 Order the compounds by bond dissociation energy between the two carbons.

Bond dissociation energy is the energy required to break a bond, leaving one electron with each fragment, which forms two radicals. It is the standard measure of bond strength in organic chemistry. In general, bond strength and bond energy are related: as bond strength increases, so does bond dissociation energy. Also, the shorter the bond, the stronger it is. For instance, triple bonds are stronger and shorter than double bonds between the same atoms; these, in turn, are shorter and stronger than single bonds. Thus, the C≡C bond in the *sp*-hybridized compound (**3**) should be the shortest and strongest. The weakest will be the one between two *sp*³-hybridized carbons (**1**). Thus, the order should be:

1 < 2 < 3

Related Questions

1. Which will lose a hydrogen more easily, a compound with a higher or lower pK_b?

2. What is the hybridization of the carbon atom in carbon dioxide?

3. What is the highest bond order in 5-hydroxy-2,6-dimethyl-3-heptanone?

Takeaways

Stronger bonds are shorter bonds: triple bonds are the strongest and shortest, while single bonds are the longest and weakest.

Things to Watch Out For

pK_a (acid strength) is determined not only by the acid itself but also by the conjugate base that is formed upon the loss of a proton.

Key Concepts
Organic Chemistry Chapter 4
Acids and bases
Nucleophilicity
Polar solvents
Protic solvents

Nucleophilicity Trends

Rank the following compounds in order of increasing nucleophilicity toward the same electrophile in a polar protic solvent:

CH_3OH Et_3N Et_3P $CH_3O^\ominus$

1 Separate out nucleophiles with the same attacking atom and rank them first.

Let's look at the oxygen-containing nucleophiles first. Here, the methoxide anion is more basic than the acetate anion $\left(CH_3CO_2^-\right)$, which in turn is more basic than methanol. With the methoxide anion, the lone pair on oxygen is "stuck" on the oxygen atom, whereas with acetate, the negative charge can be delocalized through resonance; this makes methoxide more basic. Both molecules are more basic than methanol because methanol lacks a negative charge. When comparing nucleophiles with the same attacking atom, nucleophilicity parallels basicity. Therefore, the methoxide anion will be the most nucleophilic of the three oxygen-containing molecules.

2 Look next for nucleophiles where the attacking atom is in the same group.

Because phosphorus is directly below nitrogen in the Periodic Table, triethylphosphine is more nucleophilic than triethylamine. This is where the nature of the solvent makes a big difference. The more basic molecules are better hydrogen bond acceptors, which means that they will be surrounded by the polar protic solvent molecules and therefore less available to attack the electrophile. The differences in basicity are less pronounced when comparing attacking atoms that are the same or are in the same *period*; this effect is only notable when the attacking atoms are in the same *group*.

Comparing the basicity of triethylphosphine and triethylamine is a bit more complicated than the previous molecules. The key to determining their relative basicities is remembering that in triethylphosphine, the lone pair on phosphorus is contained in an sp^3-hybridized orbital that is made up of one $3s$ and three $3p$ orbitals. Contrast this with triethylamine, where the nitrogen lone pair is in an sp^3-hybridized orbital composed of one $2s$ and three $2p$ orbitals. The hybridized orbitals on phosphorus are composed of larger atomic orbitals, and as such are larger than the hybridized orbitals on nitrogen.

This, in turn, means that the electrons in the phosphorus lone pair are more stable because they have a larger volume of space in which to move around. If the phosphorus lone pair is more stable, then it is less basic (less likely to reach out and grab a proton). Therefore, triethylphosphine is a better nucleophile in a polar protic solvent than triethylamine. Again, this phenomenon is only relevant when the attacking atoms of two nucleophiles are in the same group.

If the solvent were polar aprotic, then the trend would be exactly the opposite. Here, the hydrogen bonding effect is removed, so the molecules with the most localized charge density—the most basic—will also be the most nucleophilic.

 ## Look for relationships between nucleophiles in the same period.

Now the question is between the two groups we have ordered separately. Which one is more nucleophilic? In most cases, this question is answered by realizing that for different nucleophiles where the attacking atoms are in the same period, nucleophilicity roughly parallels basicity. Nitrogen is less electronegative than oxygen. The less electronegative an atom, the less pull it will have on its attached electrons, making those electrons more available to act as a basic pair. Therefore, nitrogen is more basic than oxygen, and thus triethylamine is more nucleophilic than the oxygen-containing compounds. In summary, the compounds can be ranked by nucleophilicity toward the same electrophile in a polar protic solvent:

$$CH_3OH < CH_3CO_2^- < CH_3O^- < Et_3N < Et_3P$$

This trend is borne out experimentally. The relative reactivities of each nucleophile toward CH_3I in CH_3OH are as follows:

Nucleophile	Relative Rate
CH_3OH	1
$CH_3CO_2^-$	20,000
CH_3O^-	1,900,000
Et_3N	4,600,000
Et_3P	520,000,000

Takeaways

Sort out differences in nucleophilicity two or three molecules at a time. Don't try to order all the molecules at once or you risk confusing yourself.

Things to Watch Out For

Remember that basicity sometimes *parallels* nucleophilicity (comparing nucleophiles with the same attacking ion, in the same period, or in polar aprotic solvents) but sometimes opposes it (comparing nucleophiles in the same group in a polar protic solvent).

Related Questions

1. Place the following molecules in order of increasing nucleophilicity: pyridine (benzene with one of the carbons in the ring replaced by a nitrogen), triethylamine, acetonitrile (CH_3CN), and 4-dimethylaminopyridine (DMAP). (Note that the solvent doesn't impact nucleophilicity here because the same atom is nucleophilic in all four compounds.) Which of the two nitrogens in DMAP is more nucleophilic, and why?

2. How would the nucleophilicity of fluoride, chloride, bromide, and iodide rank in an S_N2 reaction with methyl iodide in methanol? In dimethyl sulfoxide (DMSO)?

3. How would you order the nucleophilicity of the following molecules in methanol: Et_3N, Ph_3P, Et_3P, Ph_3N, and Et_3As? Provide a rationale for your ordering.

High-Yield Problem-Solving Guide questions continue on the next page. ▶ ▶ ▶

Key Concepts

Organic Chemistry Chapter 5

Isomers

Important reactions of alcohols

Protecting groups

Tosylates

Reactions of Alcohols

Determine the identities of products 3 and 4. What is the relationship between the two products?

1 Identify the intermediate, 2.

Before **3** and **4** can be identified, the structure of **2** must be found. Interestingly, no reagents are given in this reaction aside from the solvent (DMF), so we will have to look more closely at the starting reactant. The molecule we are given has two reactive groups that immediately stand out: –OTs, a tosylate group, and –OH, a hydroxyl group. Tosylate is a very good leaving group; the hydroxyl substituent is a poor leaving group and a good (but not great) nucleophile.

Because we have a leaving group but no strong base or nucleophile, the reaction is likely to proceed through an S_N1 mechanism (or E1, although elimination reactions are not tested directly on the MCAT). The first step is the loss of the leaving group, leaving a carbocation intermediate, as shown below:

This carbocation intermediate has the formula $C_8H_{15}O$—that's just one hydrogen more than what we're given for intermediate **2**. What's the next step? Next, the nucleophilic hydroxyl group can attack the carbocation. This still leaves us with an intermediate containing an extra hydrogen, which the tosylate group can remove, giving us the structure of intermediate **2**.

2 Using the structure of 2, identify products 3 and 4.

Starting with the structure that we figured out for **2**, we can work through the next set of reagents and determine products **3** and **4**. Our intermediate, **2**, only has one particularly reactive group, the epoxide. While epoxides are not on the official MCAT content lists, it makes sense that the oxygens they contain make good leaving groups. In **2**, the three-membered oxygen-containing ring has a high degree of angle strain, which can be relieved by opening the ring.

Epoxides can open under acidic or basic conditions, but don't do much else. Looking at the reactants, we have sodium methoxide in methanol. Methoxide is both a good base and a good nucleophile. In this case, the less reactive methanol will act as the solvent.

Methoxide can attack at either of two positions, performing our predicted ring-opening reaction:

Protonating these molecules gives us our final products, **3** and **4**. The overall reaction is shown below:

Takeaways

Reactivity in the presence of a good leaving group depends on the quality of the nucleophile. Identifying the quality of a leaving group and the strength of the nucleophile will help determine what happens during the reaction.

Things to Watch Out For

Be sure to keep in mind the stereochemistry of a given reaction; backside attack and planar intermediates both indicate specific changes to stereochemistry. Know how to distinguish between different types of isomers.

3 Find the relationship between 3 and 4.

Because **3** and **4** share a molecular formula, they are isomers of one another. These molecules have the same connectivity, so they are stereoisomers—not configurational isomers:

While the connectivity is the same, the stereochemistry is different. These two molecules are nonsuperimposable mirror images, and are therefore enantiomers.

Related Questions

1. How would the reaction be affected by changing the hydroxyl group to a stronger nucleophile?

2. How would the reaction be affected by changing the tosylate to a hydroxyl group?

3. Is it possible to favor one product over the other in this reaction?

High-Yield Problem-Solving Guide questions continue on the next page. ▶ ▶ ▶

Identifying the Structure of an Unknown Oxy Compound

A student carried out the following series of transformations in the lab:

Upon **A**'s reaction with catalytic acid and benzylamine, the student obtained a mixture of two products, **B** and **C**. The mixture of **B** and **C** was subjected to lithium aluminum hydride. Following a dilute acid workup and chromatographic separation, two more products, **D** and **E**, were obtained in unequal yield.

Identify the structures of compounds **A** through **E**, given their molecular formulas.

Key Concepts
Organic Chemistry Chapter 6
Reaction mechanisms
Oxidation–reduction reactions
Aldehydes and ketones
Oxygen-containing functional groups
Carbonyl chemistry

1 React the alcohol with PCC.

The first step of this process is to take the secondary alcohol and subject it to pyridinium chlorochromate (PCC) oxidation, which results in a ketone:

Subject the ketone to an acid catalyst and benzylamine.

You should suspect that some sort of nucleophilic addition is going to take place. Recall that a ketone that reacts with a primary amine gives an imine:

 Determine the other product of this reaction.

Remember that any time there is an immovable bond (like a double bond), there exists the possibility of having *cis–trans* isomers. The immovable bond doesn't have to be a carbon–carbon double bond; it can also be between different constituent atoms, like the imine here. Thus, the other product must be the other geometric isomer:

4 **React the imines with LiAlH$_4$.**

Reacting each of the imines with lithium aluminum hydride (LiAlH$_4$ or LAH) will result in an amine. Note that you should be able to identify LiAlH$_4$ as a reducing agent because it contains a large number of hydrides (H$^-$) attached to a metal (aluminum):

Once reduced, the carbon atom from the imine can assume one of two different stereochemistries, resulting in two possible products:

The methyl stereocenter has the same orientation in both molecules because it has remained unchanged since the beginning of the reaction. Therefore, the difference in stereochemistry must be at the nitrogen-bearing carbon atom.

Related Questions

1. How many stereoisomers exist for product **E** (whether or not they were obtained in this particular reaction)?

2. The final amine products were mixed, in equal amounts, with an achiral solvent. The solution was placed in a polarimeter and found to rotate plane-polarized light. Why is this finding not surprising?

3. In addition to compounds that contain double bonds, what other class of compounds can have *cis–trans* isomers?

High-Yield Problem-Solving Guide questions continue on the next page. ▶ ▶ ▶

Key Concepts

Organic Chemistry Chapter 7

Enolate chemistry
Aldehydes and ketones
α-Hydrogen acidity
Keto–enol tautomerization

Enolate Chemistry

Enolate chemistry has blossomed in the last few decades, becoming one of the most powerful tools in organic synthesis. In reactions involving enolates, small structural differences in reactants can result in vastly different products. Take, for instance, the reaction of cyclohexanone, a common synthetic precursor, with methyl vinyl ketone; what are the products of this reaction?

1 Form the enolate.

Whether you recognize the reaction of cyclohexanone and methyl vinyl ketone as what is called a Robinson annulation, you should recognize that the use of ketones under basic conditions means we'll be doing enolate chemistry. Whenever you see a base and an aldehyde or ketone, look for the most acidic proton and deprotonate. In this case, the most acidic protons are on the cyclohexanone. Deprotonating one of the α-carbons results in the cyclohexyl enolate:

2 React the enolate with an electrophile.

Enolates are nucleophilic species. Therefore, the next step will require an electrophile. The only electrophile present in this reaction is the methyl vinyl ketone. It would be reasonable to assume that the enolate will attack the methyl vinyl ketone at the carbonyl carbon, its most electrophilic region, as shown below:

However, this requires a very crowded transition state to form. Instead, the enolate could attack C-4 on the methyl vinyl ketone because the primary carbon is signifi- cantly easier to reach. Indeed, this is what happens, resulting in the enolate shown below:

3 React the second enolate with an electrophile.

Again, we're left with an enolate and a carbonyl. In theory, we could have the enolate attack the carbonyl immediately. However, this results in the rather unfavorable formation of a four-membered ring. The cyclization is significantly slower than the isomerization of the enolate, shown below.

This isomerization is important because the newly formed primary enolate can attack the carbonyl carbon and form a six-membered ring—much more favored than the formation of a four-membered ring. It should be noted that the isomerization is a multistep acid–base reaction, involving protonation of one α-carbon, followed by deprotonation of the other.

Attack of the carbonyl carbon by the primary enolate is shown below. This results in alkoxide and ketone functionalities, as well as creating a second ring structure. Generally, alkoxides under basic conditions can be protonated; the result in this case is the alcohol shown below:

Is this our final product? It is important to check if any of the remaining functional groups will react under basic conditions. Alcohols can do one of two things under basic conditions: they can deprotonate to form alkoxides, or they can act as leaving groups in an elimination reaction to form double bonds. There are three possible isomers from an elimination reaction of our last product, shown below:

Takeaways

Enolates can allow the formation of cyclic products in molecules that contain both a carbonyl and the enolate functionality.

Things to Watch Out For

Keep track of nucleophiles and electrophiles to understand how the reaction will progress. Make sure you've reached the end of the mechanism and that nothing else will react!

At first, one might assume that the tetrasubstituted double bond (the middle structure) would be preferentially formed because more-substituted double bonds tend to be more stable than less-substituted ones. However, the rightmost compound, while having only three substituents on the double bond, also puts the double bond in conjugation with the carbonyl. This conjugation trumps the extra substitution, so elimination of the alcohol will result preferentially in the final product, shown below:

Related Questions

1. Cyclohexanone does not have a proton present on its oxygen atom. How does the first step of this reaction mechanism proceed?

2. What does it mean for a molecule to be conjugated? Why does conjugation increase the stability of a molecule?

3. When 2,2,6,6-tetramethylcyclohexanone reacts with 4,4-dimethylhexanal, which molecule serves as the nucleophile? Which molecule serves as the electrophile?

Nucleophilic Acyl Substitution Reactions

Carboxylic acid derivatives are found in a vast array of organic molecules. Luckily, these can often be prepared from a few common intermediates. Take, for instance, the following reactions with methyl pivalate. Each of these produces a unique product. What are the products of each of these reactions?

Key Concepts

Organic Chemistry Chapter 8
Nucleophilic acyl substitution reactions
Carbonyl chemistry
Carboxylic acids
Carboxylic acid derivatives

1 **Complete the reaction of an ester with an alkoxide (transesterification).**

In the first reaction, the ethoxide anion is a strong nucleophile and the carbonyl carbon in the pivalate is a good electrophile. The likely first step is an attack on the carbonyl carbon by ethoxide, as shown below:

The first intermediate after the nucleophilic attack is a tetrahedral alkoxide. The lone pair of electrons on the oxygen can push back down and reform the carbonyl if there is a good leaving group. In this case, both ethoxide and methoxide are reasonable leaving groups under basic conditions. Displacing ethoxide would simply return the original compound; to get a new product, the methoxide must leave, as shown in the following mechanism, to give us an ethyl ester as the final product:

Complete the reaction of an ester with an amine (amide formation).

Unsurprisingly, when one treats an ester with a nitrogen-containing anion as opposed to an alkoxide, the overall reactivity is similar; this process forms an amide. The nitrogen-containing anion is extremely nucleophilic, much like the alkoxide anion. In fact, the electron pushing is identical, as shown below:

In this case, the reaction is driven by the inherent stability of the final product. Amides, such as the final product shown, are relatively robust and nonreactive compounds.

 Complete the reaction of an ester with water (hydrolysis).

Whenever the conditions for a reaction call for a strong acid (or base) and water, your first thought should be hydrolysis. When esters are treated with a strongly acidic aqueous solution, they rapidly undergo hydrolysis to form the analogous carboxylic acid. As usual, the first step in acidic media is protonation of the most basic part of the molecule. In this case, it is the carbonyl oxygen:

Once the oxygen is protonated, the carbonyl carbon becomes significantly more electrophilic, allowing attack from the relatively non-nucleophilic water. Note that the initially produced cation is in equilibrium, via proton transfer, with the cation on the right:

The rightmost cation contains an excellent leaving group: methanol. If methanol leaves, one of the remaining oxygens can push one of its lone pairs to reform a protonated carbonyl. This cation can then be deprotonated to give the final product, a neutral carboxylic acid:

Related Questions

1. Which is a better leaving group, methanol or ethanol?

2. What is a lactone? What reactant(s) would be required to make a lactone through a nucleophilic acyl substitution mechanism?

3. What is a lactam? What reactant(s) would be required to make a lactam through a nucleophilic acyl substitution mechanism?

High-Yield Problem-Solving Guide questions continue on the next page. ▶ ▶ ▶

Key Concepts
Organic Chemistry Chapter 9
Anhydrides
Esters
Amides
Leaving group ability
Steric hindrance

Properties of Carboxylic Acid Derivatives

In an ideal reaction, there is exactly one nucleophile present that can react with exactly one electrophile. In practice, though, there are often multiple nucleophiles (and electrophiles) that compete with one another. Rank the carbonyl carbons in the following compounds in order of increasing electrophilicity toward a single nucleophile in a single polar protic solvent.

1 Order the reactivities of the molecules by the identity of the acyl derivative.

In the compounds listed above, there are three types of carbonyl functional groups: amides, esters, and anhydrides. These functional groups can be ranked by electrophilicity, which is based on the stability of their leaving groups. Anhydrides (**1** and **4**) are the most reactive (that is, most electrophilic) because their leaving groups are carboxylic acids, which can delocalize the lone pair left behind after heterolysis through resonance. Esters (**2** and **3**) are the next most reactive, while amides (**5**) are the least reactive. This is because the leaving group of an ester is an alkoxide ion or alcohol, which is less nucleophilic than the nitrogen-containing anion or amine leaving group of an amide. Leaving groups should be unreactive, so stronger nucleophiles generally make poorer leaving groups.

2 Account for steric hindrance.

Next, we can rank within these groups. The more steric hindrance an electrophile presents to a nucleophile, the less reactive that molecule will be. Of the two anhydrides, **1** has significantly more steric hindrance, caused by its bulky phenyl groups, and is therefore less reactive than **4**, which has hydrogen atoms instead. Of the esters, the additional phenyl group on **3** means it will not react as readily as the less sterically hindered **2**.

③ Order according to these rules.

With these rules in mind, we can order our compounds. The sterically hindered, least reactive amide **5** will be the least electrophilic; the unhindered and most reactive anhydride **4** will be the most electrophilic. **1**, **2**, and **3** fall in the middle. It is important to keep in mind that reactivity based on functional group may be counterbalanced by steric hindrance. In this case, although it is an anhydride, **1** will be significantly impeded by sterics, and will therefore be less reactive than the esters. On the MCAT, you would not be expected to know the relative contribution of each of these trends, but could be tested on any of them in isolation. This gives us our final order:

$$5 < 1 < 3 < 2 < 4$$

Related Questions

1. Why is it important that the peptide bonds in proteins, which are a special form of amide bonds, are relatively stable?

2. Which would you expect to be more reactive toward a given nucleophile, an aldehyde or a comparable ketone? Why?

3. Which carboxylic acid derivatives can participate in hydrogen bonding with themselves?

Takeaways

Ordering carboxylic acid derivatives by reactivity depends not only on the identity of the functional group (which is indicative of the resulting leaving group), but also on the characteristics of the substituents; sterics are important to keep in mind when analyzing reactivity.

Things to Watch Out For

Remember that on Test Day you can refer to the Periodic Table; periodic trends, like electronegativity, can help you figure out relative electrophilicity or nucleophilicity.

Key Concepts

Organic Chemistry Chapter 10

Phosphorus-containing compounds

pK_a

Polyprotic acids

Acid–base reactions

Zwitterions

Phosphorus-Containing Compounds

Physiologically, phosphoric acid may be found as a neutral compound or as a mono-, di-, or trivalent anion. Accordingly, it has three pK_a values: 2.15, 7.20, and 12.35. What are the relative concentrations of phosphoric acid and its ions at physiological pH (around 7.4)? If a pure sample of phosphoric acid were dissolved in *n*-butanol, would there be a reaction? If so, what would the products be?

1 Determine the most abundant forms of phosphoric acid from the pK_a values.

The question gives us three pK_a values: 2.15, 7.20, and 12.35. Remember, the concentration of an acid and its conjugate base are equal when pH = pK_a. For example, $[H_3PO_4] = [H_2PO_4^-]$ at pH = 2.15. As the pH increases above 2.15, the concentration of H_3PO_4 will decrease as the concentration of $H_2PO_4^-$ increases. A pH of 7.4 is sufficiently far from 2.15 that there is essentially no H_3PO_4 present at all. Similarly, PO_4^{3-} is also present in negligible quantities at pH 7.4 because pK_{a3} is so high (12.35).

The two intermediate forms, $H_2PO_4^-$ and HPO_4^{2-}, predominate at physiological pH because this pH is close to pK_{a2} for phosphoric acid (7.20). We could predict that because 7.4 is slightly more basic than 7.20, there will be a slightly higher concentration of HPO_4^{2-}, the conjugate base, than $H_2PO_4^-$ at this pH. Indeed, we can determine the relative concentrations from the Henderson–Hasselbalch equation:

$$pH = pK_a + \log\frac{\left[HPO_4^{2-}\right]}{\left[H_2PO_4^-\right]}$$

$$7.4 = 7.20 + \log\frac{\left[HPO_4^{2-}\right]}{\left[H_2PO_4^-\right]}$$

$$0.2 = \log\frac{\left[HPO_4^{2-}\right]}{\left[H_2PO_4^-\right]}$$

$$10^{0.2} = \frac{\left[HPO_4^{2-}\right]}{\left[H_2PO_4^-\right]} \approx 1.58$$

In summary, the relative concentrations of the various conjugates can be expressed as a ratio ($H_3PO_4{:}H_2PO_4^-{:}HPO_4^{2-}{:}PO_4^{3-}$):

$$\sim 0{:}1{:}1.58{:}\sim 0$$

2 Determine the possible reaction(s) of phosphoric acid with *n*-butanol.

This part of the question is asking whether phosphoric acid can react with alcohols. The answer to this question is undoubtedly *yes*, but what is the reaction? Any time an acid is present, we should look for a group to protonate—in this case, the hydroxyl group on *n*-butanol is the best candidate.

Alternatively, phosphoric acid can be viewed as the hydrolyzed form of an organic phosphate. It is reasonable to think that this reaction might be reversible, creating mono-, di-, or tri-*n*-butyl phosphates. Let's examine these two reactions to determine what products can result.

3 Consider the reaction that occurs when phosphoric acid protonates *n*-butanol.

As described in Step 2, phosphoric acid could protonate the hydroxyl group of the alcohol. When this happens, the hydroxyl group (which is now a water molecule) becomes a good leaving group, forming a carbocation. While elimination reactions are not tested directly on the MCAT, it is reasonable to predict that the molecule will seek to stabilize or reduce the positive charge; formation of a double bond through an elimination reaction would be one way to accomplish this goal:

4 Consider the reaction that occurs when *n*-butanol attacks phosphoric acid.

Another potential mechanism is the formation of a phosphate ester, which could occur if the butanol attacked the phosphate group. Elimination of a hydroxyl group as water could then follow.

Takeaways

The different forms of phosphoric acid have different pK_a values; phosphoric acid commonly reacts by protonating a leaving group to improve that group's ability to leave.

Things to Watch Out For

When comparing two plausible reactions, consider the relative nucleophilicity, electrophilicity, and leaving group abilities of the reacting compounds.

Note the similarity between this reaction and nucleophilic acyl substitution (specifically, esterification). Given the two additional hydroxyl groups on the phosphorus, one could imagine two more iterations of this mechanism to produce the di- and tributyl esters.

Related Questions

1. Which class of biomolecules *always* contain phosphorus? Which ones *sometimes* contain phosphorus?

2. One way to increase blood pH is to increase the excretion of *titratable acid* (protonated phosphates) from the kidney. Urine is usually slightly more acidic than physiological pH. What would happen to the relative concentrations of the different forms of phosphoric acid at this slightly lower pH?

3. $H_2PO_4^-$ is a Brønsted–Lowry acid because it can give up a proton. Would $H_2PO_4^-$ react in the same fashion with butanol as H_3PO_4 did?

High-Yield Problem-Solving Guide questions continue on the next page. ▶ ▶ ▶

Spectroscopy

An unknown compound was discovered in an old, unused laboratory. Its molecular formula was determined to be $C_6H_9NO_2$ by high-resolution mass spectrometry. The following IR stretches were recorded: 3300 (sharp), 2890 (medium), 2220, 1740 (sharp), 1220, 984, 700, and 650 cm^{-1}.

The ^{1}H–NMR spectrum of the compound is as follows:

Given this information, determine the structure of the unknown compound.

Key Concepts

Organic Chemistry Chapter 11

IR spectroscopy
^{1}H–NMR spectroscopy
Equivalent hydrogens
Splitting

 1 **Look at the IR stretches to determine what functional groups are present.**

Here, the most important signal is the sharp peak at 1740 cm^{-1}, which indicates the presence of a carbonyl. A carbonyl indicates that there must be one of the following functional groups in our molecule: aldehyde, ketone, carboxylic acid, anhydride, ester, or amide. It can't be an aldehyde because there are no aldehyde signals in the NMR (a single proton around 9–10), and it can't be a carboxylic acid because there is no hydroxyl group stretch in the IR (a broad absorption around 2800–3200). Nor can it be an anhydride because there are not enough oxygen atoms in the molecular formula—anhydrides require at least three. Because the stretch is close to 1750, it is most likely to be an ester. This is also supported by the ^{1}H–NMR data, as discussed below.

2 **Look at the ^{1}H–NMR data to determine the structure of the esterifying group.**

The signal for the esterifying group should be the furthest downfield (to the left) in the ^{1}H–NMR spectrum because it is attached to the most electronegative element in the molecule. The peak farthest to the left is composed of two hydrogens, which are split into four peaks. Keeping in mind the $n + 1$ rule, this implies that there are two hydrogens on the carbon closest to the ester oxygen, and three hydrogens on the next one. This is supported by the three hydrogens split into a triplet around 1.3 ppm. Thus, we know the molecule must contain the following structure:

 ## Use the molecular formula to discern the presence of unsaturation in the parent chain.

So far, we have determined that there is an ester with an ethyl esterifying group. This accounts for three carbon atoms (the carbonyl carbon and two in the esterifying group), two oxygen atoms, and five hydrogen atoms. Subtracting these from the molecular formula, $C_6H_9NO_2$, we are left with three carbon atoms, four hydrogen atoms, and a nitrogen atom. Immediately, we should recognize that there must be at least one multiple bond in the molecule because there are not enough hydrogens to create an alkyl chain. There are three possibilities for the parent chain to get the right numbers: a carbon–carbon triple bond, a carbon–nitrogen triple bond, or two carbon–carbon double bonds.

Use the ^{1}H–NMR data to determine which option for unsaturation is the correct one.

We can immediately eliminate the two carbon–carbon double bonds as an option because this would mean that at least one carbon is sp^2-hybridized; sp^2-hybridized carbons absorb in the range of 4.6–6, and there are no peaks in this range. Between the carbon–carbon triple bond and the carbon–nitrogen triple bond, then, we can determine that it must be the latter. If there was a carbon–carbon triple bond, the nitrogen would have two hydrogens on it to form an amine, and there are no peaks remaining that consist of only two hydrogens. Therefore, this compound must contain a nitrile.

Takeaways

With these combined structure problems, make sure to utilize all of the data at your disposal. The process is very much like taking the pieces of a jigsaw puzzle and putting them together.

Things to Watch Out For

Be sure to avoid overinterpreting the IR data. Many peaks can correspond to multiple functional groups or are inconclusive. ^{1}H–NMR data, on the other hand, is a wealth of information that, when interpreted carefully, can provide nearly all the information to figure out a molecule's structure.

5 ## Determine the backbone of the parent chain.

If we account for all of the atoms in the ester and nitrile functionalities, we are left with two carbons and four hydrogens. There can only be two possibilities, structurally:

Note that the protons in the structure on the left would have to give rise to two triplets because each is adjacent to a carbon with two protons. However, the only signals we haven't accounted for in the NMR are a doublet integrating for three protons and a quartet integrating for one. These signals exactly match the structure on the right, so that must be the unknown.

Related Questions

1. Why is it unlikely that the compound in the original question is cyclic?

2. If the molecule were a methyl ketone rather than an ester (that is, replacing the ethoxy group with a methyl group), where would you expect that the carbonyl IR stretch would appear? Why?

3. In the compound described in the previous question, where would the signal for the methyl ketone protons show up in the ^{1}H–NMR spectrum, relative to the signal for the protons adjacent to the oxygen in the ester?

High-Yield Problem-Solving Guide questions continue on the next page. ▶ ▶ ▶

Key Concepts

Organic Chemistry Chapter 12
Extraction (liquid–liquid separation)
Acid–base properties
Separation and purification schemes
Polarity

Extraction

A student wishes to separate methyl phenyl ketone, aniline ($C_6H_5NH_2$), and phenol from a solution. To perform the separation, the solution is dissolved in 500 mL H_2O and 500 mL dichloromethane. The solution is then washed with water three times, and the aqueous layer (**A**) is extracted. The remaining solution is then washed with 20% aqueous Na_2CO_3 three times, and the aqueous layer (**B**) is collected. The remaining organic layer is finally washed with 10% aqueous HCl three times and the aqueous layer (**C**) is once again collected, leaving behind the organic layer (**D**). What are the contents of samples **A**, **B**, **C**, and **D**?

1 Determine the differences between the molecules being separated.

Methyl phenyl ketone, aniline, and phenol are all organic compounds. However, aniline is a weak base (it contains an amine group) whereas phenol is a weak acid (it contains a hydroxyl group). Methyl phenyl ketone is the most hydrophobic of the three compounds because it doesn't possess any functional groups capable of making hydrogen bonds.

2 Determine into which phase each of the compounds will dissolve after the first set of washings.

All three compounds are uncharged organic compounds and will dissolve in the organic layer, dichloromethane. Thus, the first set of washings will not aid in separating any of the three compounds, and sample **A** will contain only water and water-soluble impurities.

3 Determine into which phase each of the compounds will dissolve after the second set of washings.

When the sample is washed with Na_2CO_3—a base—phenol will be deprotonated to yield phenoxide (the conjugate base of phenol). Because this molecule is charged, it will move into the aqueous layer. After the washing, the deprotonated phenol will move into the aqueous phase (**B**), while methyl phenyl ketone and aniline will remain in the organic layer. In general, washing a mixture with a base is an effective way to move acidic compounds from the organic layer into the aqueous layer.

4 **Determine into which phase each of the compounds will dissolve after the third set of washings.**

At this point, the only remaining compounds in the organic layer are methyl phenyl ketone and aniline. When the sample is washed with HCl—a strong acid—aniline will be protonated to yield anilinium (the conjugate acid of aniline). After the washing, the protonated compound will move into the aqueous phase (**C**), while methyl phenyl ketone will remain in the organic layer (**D**). In general, washing a mixture with an acid is an effective way to move basic compounds from the organic layer into the aqueous layer.

Related Questions

1. What would be an appropriate extraction procedure to separate a mixture of phenol and benzoic acid dissolved in ether?

2. In order to extract *p*-nitrophenol from phenol in an ether solution, a student washes the organic layer with 10 mL of a 5% aqueous solution of NaOH. After the washing, what will be left in the organic layer?

3. Why does the student perform three sets of washings in each step of the extraction?

Takeaways

In an extraction problem, each compound will either be dissolved in the aqueous layer or the organic layer. However, if a compound is acidic or basic, it is possible to transpose it to the aqueous layer by using basic or acidic washes, respectively.

Things to Watch Out For

Don't assume that the organic phase will be on top—this depends on the densities of the two phases. For example, dichloromethane $\left(1.3 \frac{\text{g}}{\text{mL}}\right)$ is denser than water $\left(1.0 \frac{\text{g}}{\text{mL}}\right)$; dichloromethane will sink to the bottom of the separatory funnel, with the water floating on top.

Solutions to Related Questions

1. Nomenclature

1. The alkyl group on the ester oxygen is called the esterifying group. It is named as a separate word before the rest of the compound name. This word should be viewed as an adjective describing the ester; the compound we named was the *ethyl* ester. Therefore, if the ethyl (alkyl) group of ethyl 2-methoxy-3-(2-oxocyclohexyl)propanoate contained substituents, the word *ethyl* would be replaced with whatever group was attached to the ester oxygen, using the suffix –*yl*.

2. Sodium borohydride (NaBH$_4$) is a reducing agent; as such, it will reduce the ketone in this molecule to a secondary alcohol. The two products of the reduction reaction would be (1R,2S)-2,5,5-trimethylcyclohexanol and (1S,2S)-2,5,5-trimethylcyclohexanol, which are shown below:

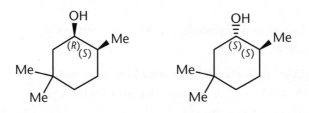

3. Lithium aluminum hydride (LiAlH$_4$) is an even stronger reducing agent than sodium borohydride and will reduce the imine in the molecule to a secondary amine. It is not strong enough to reduce the alkene to an alkane, however. The two products of the indicated reaction would be (S,Z)-6-chloro-6-cyclopentyl-N-methylhex-5-en-2-amine and (R,Z)-6-chloro-6-cyclopentyl-N-methylhex-5-en-2-amine, which are shown below:

2. Stereoisomers

1. The D- and L-isomers of a compound are enantiomers of each other, which means that they have opposite stereochemistry at all chiral carbons and no internal plane of symmetry. As such, they are nonsuperimposable mirror images. Enantiomers always have opposite specific rotation, so the specific rotation of the L-isomer must be −140°. Racemic mixtures contain equal concentrations of both enantiomers. The specific rotations from the two enantiomers cancel each other, resulting in an optically inactive solution (0° rotation).

2. Only the middle compound would give rise to an achiral polyol upon reduction. The other two would not contain a plane of symmetry.

3. For the purposes of the MCAT, it is not possible to have a chiral compound that does not contain chiral centers. Chiral compounds not only need to contain chiral centers, but must also have the right geometry, such that the chiral centers do not cancel each other out (as occurs in a *meso* compound). There are rare examples of complex polyaromatic compounds and certain allenes that do show chirality despite a lack of chiral centers, but such compounds are outside the scope of the MCAT.

3. Hybridized Orbitals

1. The lower the pK_a of a compound, the more acidic it is. Similarly, the lower the pK_b, the more basic it is. Compounds with low pK_b values are stronger bases. As such, they are not good proton donors (Brønsted–Lowry acids), preferring to accept protons (Brønsted–Lowry bases). Therefore, the higher the pK_b, the more acidic (less basic) the compound.

2. Carbon dioxide contains two double bonds. This requires two unhybridized *p*-orbitals—one to participate in each of the π bonds. Therefore, the hybridization of the carbon must be *sp*. Be careful not to fall into the trap of assuming that the presence of double bonds automatically means sp^2 hybridization. Indeed, because there are only two areas of electron density in carbon dioxide, the carbon must be *sp*-hybridized.

3. Careful reading of this compound's name indicates that there is only one double bond in the molecule, implied by the suffix *–one*. If we draw out the structure of 5-hydroxy-2,6-dimethyl-3-heptanone, it confirms that the highest bond order is 2 (double bond):

4. Nucleophilicity Trends

1. Because all of the nucleophiles contain the same attacking atom (nitrogen), nucleophilicity will parallel basicity, irrespective of the solvent used. Here, resonance delocalization and hybridization each play a role.

First, we will compare pyridine, triethylamine, and acetonitrile, as they each have only one nitrogen atom with one isolated lone pair. It may appear that the lone pair on the pyridine nitrogen may be resonance-stabilized, but in fact that lone pair does not engage in the aromatic ring delocalization. The nitrogen in acetonitrile is sp-hybridized, the nitrogen in pyridine is sp^2-hybridized, and the nitrogen in triethylamine is sp^3-hybridized. In a similar manner to the carbon atoms discussed in the *Hybridized Orbitals* question, the sp-hybridized lone pair will be the most stable (least basic), while the least stable (most basic) is the pair on triethylamine. The basicity order for these three compounds is acetonitrile < pyridine < triethylamine.

Now we must consider DMAP. The heterocyclic nitrogen (the nitrogen in the ring) is similar to pyridine, while the other nitrogen looks similar to that of triethylamine. However, while the lone pair of the ring-bound nitrogen is not delocalized (similar to pyridine), the lone pair of the tertiary nitrogen does form resonance structures with the ring. This resonance delocalization makes those electrons much less basic, and so the heterocyclic nitrogen is the one that acts as the base. Now we must decide whether DMAP is more or less basic than pyridine. When DMAP gains a proton, the positive charge is stabilized via resonance with the amino substituent, making DMAP more likely to gain a proton than pyridine, thereby making it more basic (and nucleophilic).

The final order is acetonitrile < pyridine < DMAP < triethylamine.

2. Methanol is a polar protic solvent, so we should be careful when considering how nucleophilicity and basicity relate. The halogens are all in the same group, so the stronger the base, the *weaker* the nucleophile in a polar protic solvent. To assess the basicity of the halogens, consider the strength of their conjugate acids, HF, HCl, HBr, and HI. The strongest acid (HI) has the weakest conjugate base, and the weakest acid (HF) has the strongest conjugate base. Therefore, the nucleophilicity for the halogens in a polar protic solvent like methanol is $I^- > Br^- > Cl^- > F^-$.

   DMSO is a polar aprotic solvent. Nucleophilicity always parallels basicity in polar aprotic solvents, so the nucleophilicity trend in DMSO is $F^- > Cl^- > Br^- > I^-$.

3. The order of increasing nucleophilicity in methanol is $Ph_3N < Et_3N < Ph_3P < Et_3P < Et_3As$. Triphenylamine and triphenylphosphine are less nucleophilic than triethylamine and triethylphosphine, respectively, because in the phenyl analogs, the lone pair can be delocalized into the three phenyl rings, making it less reactive and less nucleophilic. As for comparing the nitrogen, phosphorus, and arsenic compounds, the amine is more basic than the phosphine, which is more basic than the arsine. Because these are all in the same group and the solvent (methanol) is protic, the nucleophilicity is backwards from basicity, making arsenic the most nucleophilic of the group.

5. Reactions of Alcohols

1. Changing the hydroxyl group to a stronger nucleophile would change the mechanism by which it proceeds to S_N2 (or E2). S_N2 reactions proceed via a one-step (concerted) mechanism. While S_N1 and S_N2 reactions often have pronounced differences in stereochemistry, in this case the stereochemistry would be the same. This is because the nucleophile in the first step will have to attack from above the ring, resulting in an epoxide (or other three-membered ring intermediate) sticking out of the plane of the page, regardless of the nucleophilic substitution mechanism used. Thus, while the mechanism would be different with a stronger nucleophile, the products would be the same.

2. Changing the tosylate group to a hydroxyl would leave us without a good leaving group. While this reaction could still occur under acidic conditions (because acid would protonate they hydroxyl groups, making them better leaving groups), it would no longer occur under the conditions given.

3. In this case, it is not possible to favor one product over the other without changing the reactant molecule. The two compounds are almost identical in stability, meaning that both will form in approximately equal amounts. If the reactant molecule could be altered by changing one of the methyl substituents, or by adding another substituent to the ring, this could sterically impede the ring-opening nucleophile and favor one product over the other.

6. Identifying the Structure of an Unknown Oxy Compound

1. Product **E** is one of four possible stereoisomers. While **D** and **E** are diastereomers of each other, each also has an enantiomer that has opposite absolute configurations at both the nitrogen-bearing carbon and the methyl group on C-3. Looking just at the stereocenters, we could describe these compounds as: (1*R*,3*R*), (1*R*,3*S*), (1*S*,3*R*), and (1*S*,3*S*).

2. The products in this reaction are diastereomers of each other. While a racemic mixture (equimolar concentrations of two enantiomers) should have no optical activity, this is because enantiomers always have specific rotations with equal magnitude but opposite sign—canceling each other in solution. Diastereomers do not have the same predictable relationship; knowing the specific rotation of one diastereomer gives no indication of the specific rotation of another. Therefore, we would not expect the specific rotations of the two diastereomers to cancel, and a solution containing equimolar concentrations of two diastereomers *should* have optical activity.

3. *Cis–trans* isomers differ by the positions of groups around an immovable bond. This can refer to a double bond (C=C, C=N, C=O), but can also refer to the bonds in a cyclic molecule. Cycloalkanes can also have *cis–trans* isomers.

7. Enolate Chemistry

1. The most acidic atoms in cyclohexanone are the α-carbons, which readily give up a proton in the presence of a base. This results in the formation of a secondary carbanion, which can push its lone pair to form a double bond with the carbonyl carbon. This converts the carbonyl to the enolate intermediate.

2. Conjugation refers to alternating single and multiple bonds, which necessarily means that there are unhybridized *p*-orbitals aligned with each other. This allows delocalization of π electrons throughout those *p*-orbitals, resulting in a cloud of electron density above and below the plane of the molecule. Delocalization of these electrons stabilizes a molecule because electrons are able to spread out over a larger volume of space, decreasing their energy. Conjugated molecules can stabilize charges, as well, by delocalizing them throughout the π-electron clouds.

3. 2,2,6,6-Tetramethylcyclohexanone does not have any α-hydrogens because both α-carbons are quaternary carbons, as shown below:

4,4-Dimethylhexanal, on the other hand, has α-hydrogens on its α-carbon because the α-carbon is secondary, as shown below:

Because 2,2,6,6-tetramethylcyclohexanone does not contain any α-hydrogens, it cannot be deprotonated at the α-carbon to form forming the nucleophilic enolate. Thus, it must act as the electrophile. 4,4-Dimethylhexanal will form the enolate and will serve as the nucleophile in this reaction.

8. Nucleophilic Acyl Substitution Reactions

1. Methanol is generally a better leaving group than ethanol. Alkyl chains are electron-donating and therefore destabilize the negative charge that remains on the alkoxide oxygen after heterolysis. (They also destabilize the lone pairs that remain on the hydroxyl oxygen, under acidic conditions). This effect is less pronounced for the shorter alkyl chain of methanol than for the longer alkyl chain of ethanol.

2. Lactones are cyclic esters. They can be synthesized by intramolecular attack in a molecule that contains both a hydroxyl group and a carboxylic acid. The nucleophilic hydroxyl group attacks the carbonyl carbon, as shown below:

3. Lactams are cyclic amides. They can be synthesized by intramolecular attack in a molecule that contains both an amine and a carboxylic acid, in a similar mechanism to lactone formation. An example of a lactam is shown below:

9. Properties of Carboxylic Acid Derivatives

1. Peptide bonds join amino acids together in proteins. Many proteins in the body serve a structural role or must withstand tension, both of which require that the integrity of the amino acid sequence be maintained. The body is also an aqueous environment. Under normal conditions, water does not react with an amide to form a carboxylic acid and an amine (hydrolysis). Amide bonds are stable and relatively nonreactive; were they more reactive than carboxylic acids, life as we know it would not exist.

2. Aldehydes are always terminal groups and, as such, have less steric hindrance than comparable ketones, which are always internal in a compound. By extension, an aldehyde will be more reactive toward a nucleophile.

3. Hydrogen bonding occurs in molecules containing a hydrogen bound to a very electronegative atom (N, O, or F). Amides may have hydrogens on the amide nitrogen, and can therefore hydrogen bond. Carboxylic acids can also hydrogen bond because they have a hydrogen on the acyl oxygen. Under normal circumstances, neither anhydrides nor esters can hydrogen bond.

10. Phosphorus-Containing Compounds

1. Out of the four major classes of biomolecules (carbohydrates, lipids, proteins, and nucleic acids), only nucleic acids *require* phosphorus. It is a component of adenosine triphosphate (ATP), which is used for energy storage, and also of organic phosphates, like the nucleotides that make up RNA and DNA. On the other hand, phosphate groups can be found attached to at least *some* lipids, proteins, and carbohydrates (for example, the phospholipids in the cell membrane).

2. As the pH drops slightly from physiological pH, the concentration of $H_2PO_4^-$ will increase and the concentration of HPO_4^{2-} will decrease; lower pH means more protons are available in solution, so the protonated form will become more favorable. At a pH of 7.20 (pK_{a2} of phosphoric acid), the concentrations of these two species will be equal. At a pH of 7, the ratio between the two species will be reversed from the ratio at 7.4. That is, $H_2PO_4^-$: HPO_4^{2-} = 1.58:1. Note that the concentrations of phosphoric acid and phosphate anion will remain essentially zero; the pH is still far away from the pK_a.

3. $H_2PO_4^-$ is not nearly as strong of an acid as H_3PO_4—pK_{a2} is over five pH scale values higher than pK_{a1}! As a much weaker acid, $H_2PO_4^-$ cannot protonate the alcohol to any significant extent, so the dehydration reaction will not occur.

11. Spectroscopy

1. There are only six carbon atoms in the molecular formula, which means that any rings present would have to be small. Small rings have a high degree of angle strain (especially if there are double or triple bonds in the ring), which would make having one or multiple rings in the unknown very unlikely.

2. If the molecule were a methyl ketone rather than an ester, the carbonyl IR stretch would be closer to 1700 cm^{-1}. The resonance donation of the ester alkoxide makes the C=O bond more unstable and therefore higher in energy.

3. The methyl ketone protons would be further upfield in the ^{1}H–NMR spectrum (closer to 2 ppm than 4 ppm). This is because the alkyl group in the ketone is less electron-withdrawing than the highly electronegative oxygen in the ester.

12. Extraction

1. To separate a mixture of benzoic acid and phenol dissolved in ether, it would be best to take advantage of their relative acidities. Benzoic acid is a stronger acid than phenol, so a weak base (NaHCO$_3$, for example) can be used to deprotonate benzoic acid and move it into the aqueous phase, while leaving phenol in the organic phase.

2. After washing the mixture with 5% NaOH, *p*-nitrophenol and phenol will both be deprotonated by the strong base and will move into the aqueous phase. Nothing will be left in the organic layer except for the ether solvent and water-insoluble impurities.

3. Each compound has a given solubility in water, which may be exceeded if it has a high concentration in the organic solvent. Further, not all of the desired product necessarily comes into contact with the water during the first extraction and may remain dissolved in the organic solvent. In general, it is more effective to perform multiple small washes, as done by this student, than to try to extract all of a desired product in one step with a larger amount of solvent.

Physics
and Math

Inclined Plane

A block with a mass of 2 kg is sliding down a plane that is inclined at 30° to the horizontal. The coefficient of kinetic friction between the block and the plane is 0.3. Starting from rest, how far does the block travel in 2 seconds?

Key Concepts

Physics and Math Chapter 1

Newton's laws

Friction

Kinematics

Newtonian mechanics

1 **Draw a free body diagram of the forces present.**

There are three forces acting on the block: the force of gravity ($\mathbf{F}_g$, the magnitude of which is mg), which always acts straight down; kinetic friction (labeled $\mathbf{f}_k$), which always acts opposite the direction of motion; and the normal force (labeled $\mathbf{N}$), which is always perpendicular to the plane:

2 **Break the weight into parallel and perpendicular components.**

Orient the axes in this question to be parallel and perpendicular to the plane; this will make calculations much easier because we can solve for the acceleration in the parallel direction. $\mathbf{N}$ points in the positive perpendicular direction, and $\mathbf{f}_k$ points in the negative parallel direction. The weight, $\mathbf{F}_g$, must be broken into components along these axes:

The parallel component of the gravitational force, $\mathbf{F}_{g,\parallel}$, is equal to $mg\sin\theta$. The perpendicular component of the gravitational force, $\mathbf{F}_{g,\perp}$, is equal to $mg\cos\theta$.

 ## Write the sum of the forces in each direction.

The sum of the forces in a given direction is always equal to $m\mathbf{a}$ according to Newton's second law:

$$\mathbf{F}_{net,\parallel} = m\mathbf{a}_{\parallel} = mg\sin 30° - \mathbf{f}_k$$

$$\mathbf{F}_{net,\perp} = m\mathbf{a}_{\perp} = \mathbf{N} - mg\cos 30°$$

 ## Solve for the normal force.

We know that the block is not accelerating in the perpendicular direction because it is not sinking into the plane or coming off of the plane; thus, we can set $\mathbf{a}_{\perp} = 0$ and solve for $\mathbf{N}$:

$$\mathbf{a}_{\perp} = 0$$

$$\mathbf{N} - mg\cos 30° = 0 \rightarrow \mathbf{N} = mg\cos 30°$$

Solve for the acceleration of the block.

The force of friction depends on the magnitude of the normal force, N, and the coefficient of kinetic friction, μ_k. Plug in the expression for normal force from Step 4 to determine the frictional force:

$$f_k = \mu_k N = \mu_k mg\cos 30°$$

Then, plug this expression for frictional force into the forces in the parallel direction expression from Step 3 to determine the acceleration:

$$m\mathbf{a}_{\parallel} = mg\sin 30° - \mathbf{f}_k$$

$$m\mathbf{a}_{\parallel} = mg\sin 30° - \mu_k mg\cos 30°$$

$$\mathbf{a}_{\parallel} = g(\sin 30° - \mu_k\cos 30°)$$

$$\approx \left(10\,\frac{m}{s^2}\right)\left(\frac{1}{2} - 0.3 \times 0.866\right)$$

$$\approx \left(10\,\frac{m}{s^2}\right)\left(\frac{1}{2} - 0.27\right) = 10 \times 0.23 = 2.3\,\frac{m}{s^2}\left(\text{actual} = 2.40\,\frac{m}{s^2}\right)$$

Note that the mass cancels out completely.

6 **Use a kinematics formula to calculate the displacement.**

We are given an acceleration, an initial velocity (starting from rest), and a time. Thus, we can determine the displacement:

$$\Delta \mathbf{x} = \mathbf{v}_0 t + \frac{\mathbf{a}t^2}{2}$$

$$= 0 + \frac{\left(2.4 \, \frac{\mathrm{m}}{\mathrm{s}^2}\right)\left(2\,\mathrm{s}\right)^2}{2} = 4.8\,\mathrm{m}$$

Related Questions

1. A block of mass 5 kg is placed on an inclined plane at 45° to the horizontal. What is the minimum coefficient of static friction so that the block remains at rest?

2. A block is given an initial velocity of $2 \, \frac{\mathrm{m}}{\mathrm{s}}$ up a frictionless plane inclined at 60° to the horizontal. What is the highest point above the original height reached by the block?

3. What is the velocity of a 10 kg block sliding down a frictionless inclined plane at 30° to the horizontal 5 seconds after it is released from rest?

High-Yield Problem-Solving Guide questions continue on the next page. ▶ ▶ ▶

Projectile Motion and Air Resistance

> An arrow with a mass of 80 g is fired at an angle of 30° to the horizontal. It strikes a target located 5 m above the firing point and impacts the target traveling at a speed of $20\,\frac{\text{m}}{\text{s}}$. If 10 percent of the initial energy of the arrow is lost to air resistance, what was the initial speed of the arrow?

Key Concepts

Physics and Math Chapter 2
Conservation of energy
Kinetic energy
Potential energy
Nonconservative forces
Kinematics

 Write an expression for the final energy of the arrow.

The total energy of the arrow is its potential energy plus its kinetic energy. The potential energy of the arrow is mgh. For simplicity, make the height at the firing point the datum ($h = 0$) so that the final height is 5 m. Remember that finding a numerical value at this point is not necessary. Writing a variable expression will save you time because some term (usually the mass) may cancel out in a later step. Thus, the final energy is:

$$E_{\text{f}} = K_{\text{f}} + U_{\text{f}} = \frac{1}{2}mv_{\text{f}}^2 + mgh_{\text{f}}$$

 Write an expression for the initial energy of the arrow.

As stated in Step 1, the initial height is assigned the value of zero, so the potential energy at this point is also zero:

$$E_{\text{i}} = K_{\text{i}} + U_{\text{i}} = \frac{1}{2}mv_{\text{i}}^2 + mgh_{\text{i}} = \frac{1}{2}mv_{\text{i}}^2$$

3 **Relate the change in energy to the energy lost to air resistance.**

The conservation of energy equation tells us that all of the energy of a system must be accounted for. Whatever energy is lost between the beginning and the end must have been due to air resistance:

$$\begin{aligned}
W_{\text{nonconservative}} &= E_{\text{i}} - E_{\text{f}} \\
&= \frac{1}{2}mv_{\text{i}}^2 - \left(\frac{1}{2}mv_{\text{f}}^2 + mgh_{\text{f}}\right)
\end{aligned}$$

Relate the energy lost to the initial energy.

The question states that 10 percent of the initial energy is lost. Thus, the energy lost is the initial energy times 0.1:

$$W_{\text{nonconservative}} = 0.1 \times E_i = 0.1\left(\frac{1}{2} \times mv_i^2\right)$$

5 **Solve for the initial speed.**

$$W_{\text{nonconservative}} = \frac{1}{2}mv_i^2 - \left(\frac{1}{2}mv_f^2 + mgh_f\right)$$

$$0.1 \times v_i^2 = v_i^2 - \left(v_f^2 + 2gh_f\right)$$

$$0.9 \times v_i^2 = v_f^2 + 2gh_f$$

$$v_i = \sqrt{\frac{v_f^2 + 2gh_f}{0.9}} \approx \sqrt{\frac{\left(20\,\frac{m}{s}\right)^2 + 2 \times 10\,\frac{m}{s^2} \times 5\,m}{0.9}}$$

$$= \sqrt{\frac{400 + 100}{0.9}} \approx \sqrt{529} = 23\,\frac{m}{s}\left(\text{actual} = 23.5\,\frac{m}{s}\right)$$

Related Questions

1. A rock is dropped from the top of a 100 m tall building and lands while traveling at a speed of $30\,\frac{m}{s}$. How much energy was lost due to air resistance?

2. Two different objects are dropped from rest off of a 50 m tall cliff. One lands going 30 percent faster than the other. The two objects have the same mass. How much more kinetic energy does one object have at the landing than the other?

3. A projectile is fired vertically at a speed of $30.0\,\frac{m}{s}$. It reaches a maximum height of 44.1 m. What fraction of its initial energy has been lost to air resistance at this point?

Takeaways

Note that the angle and the mass were never used in the calculation. This will often be the case when using the conservation of energy equation to solve problems. These problems can be worded in many different ways, but the problem-solving process is the same for all of them:

1. Write an expression for the initial energy and an expression for the final energy.
2. If there is friction, air resistance, or viscous drag, the difference between final and initial energy is the energy lost due to these forces.
3. If there is no friction, air resistance, or viscous drag, the energy lost is zero, so set the two expressions equal to each other.
4. Solve for the quantity of interest.

Keep a realistic view of these problems to check your answers for math errors. Note that the initial speed is faster than the final speed, which we expect because the target is higher than the firing point and some energy is lost due to air resistance.

Things to Watch Out For

The mention of lost energy in the question stem should tip you off that you need to use the conservation of energy equation. In general, unless you are asked for an acceleration or time value, the energy approach is easier and faster than the kinematics and Newton's laws approach for these questions.

Key Concepts

Physics and Math Chapter 3
State functions
Thermodynamic processes
Heat
Work
Internal energy

Thermodynamics

A theoretical ideal engine, known as a Carnot engine, uses the thermodynamic properties of a closed gas piston system. The cycle involves two isothermal steps—one of expansion and one of compression—as well as an expansive and a compressive adiabatic step. This four-step system is shown in a pressure–volume diagram below:

What is the total heat, work, and internal energy change over the course of a single cycle beginning at point **A** and moving through points **B**, **C**, and **D**?

 Identify the types of processes involved and their properties.

First, we must identify the individual steps as well as the entire process as known thermodynamic functions. Both isothermal and adiabatic processes appear hyperbolic on a pressure–volume graph, but adiabatic processes are steeper than isothermal ones. The path from **A** to **B** is not very steep and thus is an isothermal process; because the volume increases, it is an expansion. The path from **B** to **C** is steeper and is an adiabatic expansion. The cycle then proceeds through an isothermal compression and an adiabatic compression to return to **A**.

In addition to the four steps of this process, we must note that it is a closed system as stated in the question stem; thus, only energy may be exchanged between the system and the environment. It is also a closed cycle, which means that the internal energy at the start and finish must be the same.

2 Set up any known mathematical relationships.

For thermodynamic relationships, we have certain known quantities. The first law of thermodynamics can be stated as $\Delta U = Q - W$, where ΔU is the change in internal energy, Q is the heat entering the system, and W is the work done by the system.

For the closed cycle from **A** to **B** to **C** to **D** and back to **A**, $\Delta U = 0 = Q - W$; thus, $Q = W$. We need only determine one quantity to determine the second as well. For the isothermal processes between **A** and **B** and between **C** and **D**, the same relationship is true. Because temperature remains constant, internal energy also remains constant and $\Delta U = 0 = Q - W$; thus, $Q = W$.

For the adiabatic processes between **B** and **C** and between **D** and **A**, there is no heat exchange with the environment. The first law can simplify to $\Delta U = 0 - W$; thus, $\Delta U = -W$.

Finally, we know that work can be calculated from the area under the curve in a pressure–volume graph; thus, we can obtain work from the graph by approximating the area using trapezoids.

3 Determine the work from each process and the total work.

Work is determined graphically as the area under a pressure–volume curve. For Test Day, it is useful to approximate the area under the curve using trapezoids. The area of a trapezoid is given by:

$$A_{\text{trapezoid}} = \left(\frac{b_1 + b_2}{2}\right)h$$

Keep in mind that the bases b_1 and b_2 are vertical in this graph and the height h is the distance along the x-axis. For the isothermal expansion from **A** to **B**, the calculation of the area under the curve is modeled here:

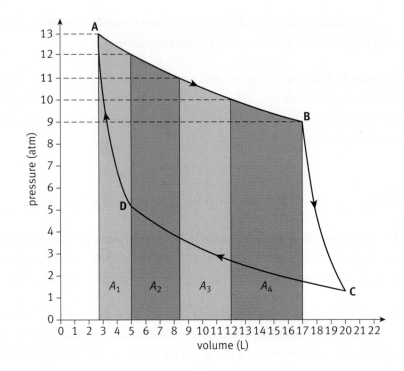

Work is done by the gas as it expands. This is considered positive work. Heat is also added to the gas. To calculate the area, take the average of the bases and multiply by the height:

$$A_1 = \frac{13\,\text{atm} + 12\,\text{atm}}{2}\left(5 - 2.5\,\text{L}\right) = 31.25\,\text{L} \cdot \text{atm}$$

$$A_2 = \frac{12\,\text{atm} + 11\,\text{atm}}{2}\left(8.5 - 5\,\text{L}\right) = 40.25\,\text{L} \cdot \text{atm}$$

$$A_3 = \frac{11\,\text{atm} + 10\,\text{atm}}{2}\left(12 - 8.5\,\text{L}\right) = 36.75\,\text{L} \cdot \text{atm}$$

$$A_4 = \frac{10\,\text{atm} + 9\,\text{atm}}{2}\left(17 - 12\,\text{L}\right) = 47.5\,\text{L} \cdot \text{atm}$$

The total area is $A_1 + A_2 + A_3 + A_4 = 31.25 + 40.25 + 36.75 + 47.5 = 155.75$ L • atm.

This is an unusual unit for work, and even more unusual for heat. It makes sense to convert this answer to joules. Using the conversion factor 1 atm = 101,325 Pa, we can obtain the work in joules:

$$1 \text{ atm} \approx 10^5 \text{ Pa}$$
$$1 \text{ L} \cdot \text{atm} = 10^5 \text{ L} \cdot \text{Pa}$$
$$= 10^5 \text{ L} \cdot \text{Pa} \times \left[\frac{1000 \text{ mL}}{1 \text{ L}} \right] \times \left[\frac{1 \text{ cm}^3}{1 \text{ mL}} \right] \times \left[\frac{1 \text{ m}}{100 \text{ cm}} \right]^3 \times \left[\frac{1 \frac{\text{N}}{\text{m}^2}}{1 \text{ Pa}} \right]$$
$$= \frac{10^5 \times 10^3}{10^6} = 100 \text{ J}$$

Thus, 155.75 L • atm ≈ 15.5 kJ (actual = 15.8 kJ).

This process must be repeated for the path from **B** to **C**. The same method is used for the path from **C** to **D** and from **D** to **A**, but the values calculated are negative because the gas is undergoing compression. The total work is the sum of the work for these four paths:

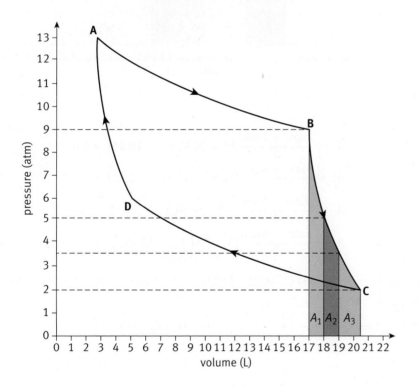

$$A_1 = \frac{9 \text{ atm} + 5 \text{ atm}}{2}\left(18 - 17 \text{ L}\right) = 7 \text{ L} \cdot \text{atm}$$

$$A_2 = \frac{5 \text{ atm} + 3.5 \text{ atm}}{2}\left(19 - 18 \text{ L}\right) = 4.25 \text{ L} \cdot \text{atm}$$

$$A_3 = \frac{3.5 \text{ atm} + 2 \text{ atm}}{2}\left(20.5 - 19 \text{ L}\right) = 4.125 \text{ L} \cdot \text{atm}$$

The total area for **B** to **C** is 7 + 4.25 + 4.125 = 15.375 L • atm ≈ 1.5 kJ (actual = 1.56 kJ).

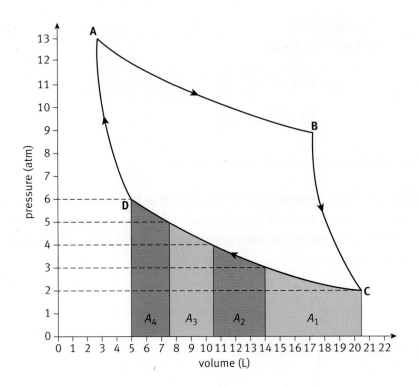

$$A_1 = \frac{2\,\text{atm} + 3\,\text{atm}}{2}\left(14 - 20.5\,\text{L}\right) = -16.25\,\text{L} \bullet \text{atm}$$

$$A_2 = \frac{3\,\text{atm} + 4\,\text{atm}}{2}\left(10.5 - 14\,\text{L}\right) = -12.25\,\text{L} \bullet \text{atm}$$

$$A_3 = \frac{4\,\text{atm} + 5\,\text{atm}}{2}\left(7.5 - 10.5\,\text{L}\right) = -13.5\,\text{L} \bullet \text{atm}$$

$$A_4 = \frac{5\,\text{atm} + 6\,\text{atm}}{2}\left(5 - 7.5\,\text{L}\right) = -13.75\,\text{L} \bullet \text{atm}$$

The total area for **C** to **D** is $-16.25 - 12.25 - 13.5 - 13.75 = -55.75\,\text{L} \bullet \text{atm} \approx -5.6\,\text{kJ}$ (actual = $-5.65\,\text{kJ}$).

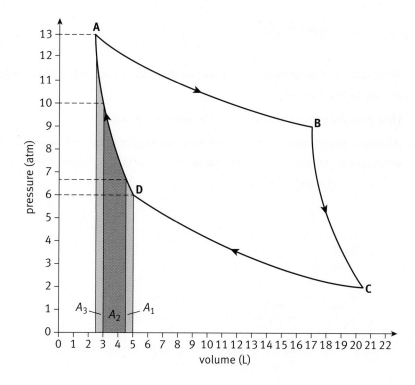

$$A_1 = \frac{6\,\text{atm} + 6.5\,\text{atm}}{2}\left(4.5 - 5\,\text{L}\right) = -3.125\,\text{L} \cdot \text{atm}$$

$$A_2 = \frac{6.5\,\text{atm} + 10\,\text{atm}}{2}\left(3 - 4.5\,\text{L}\right) = -12.375\,\text{L} \cdot \text{atm}$$

$$A_3 = \frac{10\,\text{atm} + 13\,\text{atm}}{2}\left(2.5 - 3\,\text{L}\right) = -5.75\,\text{L} \cdot \text{atm}$$

The total area for **D** to **A** is $-3.125 - 12.375 - 5.75 = -21.25$ L • atm ≈ -2.1 kJ (actual $= -2.15$ kJ).

The total work throughout the cycle is the sum of the work for each portion of the cycle:

$$15.8 + 1.56 - 5.65 - 2.15 = 9.54\,\text{kJ}$$

4 Insert work into the earlier relationships to determine heat.

As established earlier, for a closed-loop process, $\Delta U = 0 = Q - W$; thus, $Q = W$. If the system has performed 9.54 kJ of work, then it has also absorbed 9.54 kJ of heat during the process.

Related Questions

1. What is the minimum number of processes that must be accomplished in order to have a closed cycle?

2. How does the entropy change during an adiabatic process?

3. A thermometer immersed in very hot water undergoes expansion as it changes temperature. Describe the thermodynamic processes that are taking place within the thermometer and the water.

High-Yield Problem-Solving Guide questions continue on the next page. ▶ ▶ ▶

Key Concepts

Physics and Math Chapter 4
Pressure
Density
Bernoulli's equation
Continuity equation

Fluid Dynamics

A water storage tank is located 300 m away from a water outlet, as shown in the diagram below:

The empty space in the water tank is held at a pressure of 3 atm. The storage tank has a diameter of 5 m, and the outlet has a diameter of 1 cm. What is the speed of the water exiting the outlet? (Note: 1 atm = 101.325 kPa; $\rho_{water} = 1000 \frac{kg}{m^3}$)

1 Write an expression using Bernoulli's equation.

Bernoulli's equation is a statement of the conservation of energy for fluids. It has three terms—one for pressure (a form of stored energy), one analogous to kinetic energy, and one analogous to gravitational potential energy:

$$P_1 + \frac{1}{2}\rho v_1^2 + \rho g h_1 = P_2 + \frac{1}{2}\rho v_2^2 + \rho g h_2$$

Write the expression for Bernoulli's principle at the two points of interest, just as you would write the total energy of a mechanical system at two points. For this problem, the two points are the top of the water level in the storage tank and the outlet.

2 Use the continuity equation.

In almost all applications of Bernoulli's equation, you will need to eliminate some of the terms in order to solve the problem. A common one here is speed. The continuity equation relates linear flow speed to area:

$$A_1 v_1 = A_2 v_2$$

This shows that the product of the cross-sectional area and linear flow speed is a constant. Given that the diameter of the water tank is 5 m and of the spout is 1 cm, the linear flow speed at the surface is near zero. Think about it like this: as this vessel drains, the surface will drop at a nearly negligible speed compared to the speed of the fluid leaving the spout. This simplifies the equation:

$$P_1 + \rho g h_1 = P_2 + \frac{1}{2}\rho v_2^2 + \rho g h_2$$

 ### Plug in the given information, and solve.

The pressure inside the tank is 3 atm. Convert this to pascals, the SI unit for pressure:

$$P_1 = 3\,\text{atm}\left[\frac{101\,\text{kPa}}{1\,\text{atm}}\right] = 3.03 \times 10^5\,\text{Pa}$$

$$P_2 = 1.01 \times 10^5\,\text{Pa}$$

The pressure at the outlet is 1 atm (101,325 Pa) because the outlet is exposed to outside air.

Now we have all the necessary variables:

$$h_1 = 20 - 0.2 = 19.8\,\text{m}$$

$$h_2 = 50\,\text{cm} = 0.5\,\text{m}$$

$$\rho = 1000\,\frac{\text{kg}}{\text{m}^3}$$

Plug into Bernoulli's equation:

$$P_1 + \rho g h_1 = P_2 + \frac{1}{2}\rho v_2^2 + \rho g h_2$$

$$3.03 \times 10^5\,\text{Pa} + \left(1000\,\frac{\text{kg}}{\text{m}^3}\right)\left(10\,\frac{\text{m}}{\text{s}^2}\right)(19.8\,\text{m}) = 1.01 \times 10^5\,\text{Pa} + \frac{1}{2}\left(1000\,\frac{\text{kg}}{\text{m}^3}\right)v_2^2$$

$$+ \left(1000\,\frac{\text{kg}}{\text{m}^3}\right)\left(10\,\frac{\text{m}}{\text{s}^2}\right)(0.5\,\text{m})$$

$$3.03 \times 10^5 + 1.98 \times 10^5 = 1.01 \times 10^5 + 0.05 \times 10^5 + 500v_2^2$$

$$3.95 \times 10^5 = 500v_2^2$$

$$790 = v_2^2$$

$$v_2 \approx 28$$

Takeaways

Bernoulli's equation looks complicated, but it is really just a statement of the conservation of energy. The process is the same for every problem:
1. Write Bernoulli's equation at the two points of interest.
2. Eliminate any variables if possible (often via the continuity equation).
3. Solve for the unknown quantity.

Things to Watch Out For

A common use of Bernoulli's equation is with no change in height, so that $P + \frac{1}{2}\rho v^2 = $ constant. In this situation, a decrease in pressure is associated with an increase in velocity. This is known as the Bernoulli effect and is responsible for balls curving in flight, windows exploding during hurricanes, and (partially) for airplane wings experiencing lift.

Related Questions

1. The pressure at one point in a horizontal pipe is triple the pressure at another point. How do the linear flow speeds compare at these two points?

2. A tapered pipe has two points labeled. At point A, the radius is twice that at point B. The pipe is horizontal and is subjected to a fluid pressure of 1.6 atm. What is the ratio of linear flow speeds these two points in the pipe?

3. A water storage tank is open to air on the top and has a height of 1 m. If the tank is completely full and a hole is made at the center of the wall of the tank, how fast will the water exit the tank?

High-Yield Problem-Solving Guide questions continue on the next page. ▶ ▶ ▶

Key Concepts

Physics and Math Chapter 5
Work
Electrostatics
Electrical potential energy
Charge distributions

Electrostatics

Three charges are lined up along the x-axis at 1 mm intervals. Charge 1 has a charge of $+1\,\mu C$. Charge 2 has a charge of $-2\,\mu C$. Charge 3 has a charge of $+4\,\mu C$. How much work was required to assemble this distribution of charges, assuming that the charges were initially very far apart? $\left(\text{Note: } k = 9 \times 10^9\ \dfrac{\text{N} \cdot \text{m}^2}{\text{C}^2}\right)$

1 Find the work required to place Charge 1.

The work done to move a charge equals the magnitude of the charge times the change in electrical potential. The work done to place Charge 1 is zero because there is no change in electrical potential:

$$W = \Delta U = q\Delta V = 0$$

As a matter of convention, the work to place the first charge is always zero.

2 Find the work required to place Charge 2.

The same formula is used in this step as in Step 1. Here, Charge 2 has an initial electrical potential of zero because it is very far away from Charge 1. The final electrical potential is given by the formula $V = \dfrac{kQ}{r}$ where Q is the stationary charge and r is the distance between the charges.

$$W = \Delta U = q\Delta V = \frac{kQq}{r}$$

$$W = \frac{\left(9 \times 10^9\ \dfrac{\text{N} \cdot \text{m}^2}{\text{C}^2}\right)\left(1 \times 10^{-6}\ \text{C}\right)\left(-2 \times 10^{-6}\ \text{C}\right)}{1 \times 10^{-3}\ \text{m}}$$

$$= -18\ \text{J}$$

3 Find the work required to place Charge 3.

Just like in Step 2, the work to place Charge 3 equals the magnitude of Charge 3 times the change in the electrical potential. Once again, the initial electrical potential is 0. The final potential is the potential due to Charge 1 plus the potential due to Charge 2. Be careful, because the distances must be from Charge 1 to Charge 3 (call this r_1) and from Charge 2 to Charge 3 (call this r_2), respectively:

$$W = \Delta U = q\Delta V_1 + q\dot{\Delta}V_2 = \frac{kQ_1 q}{r_1} + \frac{kQ_2 q}{r_2} = kq\left(\frac{Q_1}{r_1} + \frac{Q_2}{r_2}\right)$$

$$W = \left(9 \times 10^9 \; \frac{N \cdot m^2}{C^2}\right)\left(4 \times 10^{-6}\; C\right)\left(\frac{1 \times 10^{-6}\; C}{2 \times 10^{-3}\; m} + \frac{-2 \times 10^{-6}\; C}{1 \times 10^{-3}\; m}\right)$$

$$= 36 \times 10^3 \left(-1.5 \times 10^{-3}\right) = -54 \; J$$

Takeaways

To find the work required to assemble a distribution of charges, find the work required to place each charge individually, and then add them together. The work to place the first charge is always zero.

 4 Add the work from Steps 1, 2, and 3.

Add the work from Steps 1, 2, and 3 to find the net work. The net work is negative, meaning that the potential energy of the system has been lowered:

$$W_{net} = 0 - 18 - 54 = -72 \; J$$

Related Questions

Things to Watch Out For

It is common to make errors with the sign convention on these types of problems. Keep this in mind when checking your work: like charges increase in potential energy as they are brought closer to each other; unlike charges decrease in potential energy as they are brought closer to each other.

1. A +1 μC charge sits 1 cm from a −2 μC charge. How much work is done in tripling the distance between these charges?

2. How much work is done in assembling a square-shaped charge distribution with a side length of 1 μm if all of the charges have a charge of 5 nC?

3. Charges 1, 2, and 3 are lined up, in that order, at 1 mm intervals along the y-axis. Charge 1 has a charge of +4 μC. Charge 2 has a charge of −2 μC. Charge 3 has a charge of −3 μC. What is the change in potential energy of the system if Charge 1 is removed?

Key Concepts

Physics and Math Chapter 6

Ohm's law
Resistors in series
Resistors in parallel
Voltage sources

Resistor Circuits

What is the current through R_1 in the circuit shown below?

(Note: $R_1 = 30\ \Omega$; $R_2 = 6\ \Omega$; $R_3 = 20\ \Omega$; $R_4 = 10\ \Omega$; $R_5 = 30\ \Omega$; V = 30 V)

1 Find the equivalent resistance of the network.

The first part of this problem is to find the equivalent resistance of the entire circuit. This will take several steps. Begin by combining R_1 and R_2 using the equation for the equivalent resistance of two parallel resistors:

$$\frac{1}{R_{eq1}} = \frac{1}{R_1} + \frac{1}{R_2} = \frac{1}{30\ \Omega} + \frac{1}{6\ \Omega} = \frac{1}{30} + \frac{5}{30} = \frac{6}{30} = \frac{1}{5}$$

$$R_{eq1} = 5\ \Omega$$

Now, combine R_3 and R_4, which are in series:

$$R_{eq2} = R_3 + R_4 = 20\,\Omega + 10\,\Omega$$

$$R_{eq2} = 30\,\Omega$$

Now, combine the equivalent resistance R_{eq2} with R_5. These resistors are in parallel:

$$\frac{1}{R_{eq3}} = \frac{1}{R_{eq2}} + \frac{1}{R_5} = \frac{1}{30\,\Omega} + \frac{1}{30\,\Omega} = \frac{2}{30}$$

$$R_{eq3} = 15\,\Omega$$

Finally combine R_{eq1} and R_{eq3}. These resistors are in series:

$$R_{eq4} = R_{eq1} + R_{eq3} = 5\,\Omega + 15\,\Omega$$

$$R_{eq4} = 20\,\Omega$$

2 Find the current through the circuit.

The point of finding the equivalent resistance is so that we can find the current through the circuit. This is also often referred to as the current through or leaving the battery. Use Ohm's law to find the current from the source voltage and equivalent resistance:

$$V = IR \rightarrow I = \frac{V}{R} = \frac{30 \text{ V}}{20 \text{ }\Omega} = 1.5 \text{ A}$$

3 Expand the circuit.

Now expand the circuit back out and apply what we know about resistors in series and parallel to find the current and voltage through individual resistors. All resistors in series must have the same current, so we know that the current from Step 2 must equal the current through R_{eq1} and R_{eq3}:

Use Ohm's law to find the voltage across R_{eq1}:

$$V_{eq1} = I_{eq1}R_{eq1}$$
$$= (1.5\text{ A})(5\,\Omega)$$
$$= 7.5\text{ V}$$

Because R_{eq1} is a parallel combination of R_1 and R_2, we know that R_1 and R_2 must have the same voltage as R_{eq1}. Any two (or more) circuit components in parallel must have the same voltage as the others:

Takeaways

There is a standard process for solving these types of resistor problems:
1. Find the equivalent resistance by combining series and parallel resistors.
2. Find the current through the circuit.
3. Expand the circuit back out, step by step.
4. Apply knowledge of series and parallel resistors to find the quantity of interest.

Things to Watch Out For

The arithmetic for calculating the equivalent resistance in parallel can be confusing. Another version of the formula is $R_p = \dfrac{R_1R_2}{R_1 + R_2}$. Note, however, that this only works for two resistors and cannot be easily expanded to account for three resistors.

Use the voltage and resistance of R_1 to find the current through R_1:

$$V_1 = I_1R_1 \rightarrow I_1 = \frac{V_1}{R_1}$$
$$= \frac{7.5\text{ V}}{30\,\Omega} = 0.25\text{ A}$$

Related Questions

1. In the circuit shown in the original question, what is the voltage across R_4?

2. Four resistors are attached in parallel to a voltage supply of 9 V. If the resistances of the resistors are $10\,\Omega$, $20\,\Omega$, $30\,\Omega$, and $40\,\Omega$, what is the current through the battery?

3. There are six resistors in a circuit. R_1, R_2, R_3, R_4, and R_5 are all in parallel with each other, and they are all in series with R_6. If the current leaving the battery is 10 A and each of the resistors has a resistance of $1\,\Omega$ except for R_6, which is unknown, what is the resistance of R_6 if $V = 20$ V?

Key Concepts

Physics and Math Chapter 7
Doppler effect
Wavelength
Frequency
Speed

Doppler Effect

Two cars, Car A and Car B, are moving toward each other, with each car traveling at $50 \frac{m}{s}$ when Car B starts to beep its 475 Hz horn. Assuming that the speed of sound is $343 \frac{m}{s}$, what is the wavelength of the horn as perceived by the driver of Car A?

1 Identify this as a Doppler effect problem and determine the source and detector of the wave.

This problem has the classic setup of a Doppler effect question. Whenever you see a setup in which one object emits a wave and another object detects it, think about the Doppler effect—especially if those two objects are moving relative to each other. First, let's define our terms. The source is the object that emits the sound wave; this is Car B. The detector or observer is the object that detects the wave; this is the person in Car A.

2 Determine the effect of the velocity of the detector on the perceived frequency.

Every Doppler effect problem can be solved using the Doppler effect equation:

$$f' = f \frac{(v \pm v_{\mathrm{D}})}{(v \mp v_{\mathrm{s}})}$$

where f' is the observed frequency, f is the emitted frequency, v is the speed of sound in the medium, v_{D} is the speed of the detector, and v_{s} is the speed of the source. The most complicated aspects of using the Doppler effect equation are remembering where to place the variables and the sign convention. While we present the logic for the sign convention throughout this explanation, a mnemonic can be used: if memorized in this form, the **t**op sign should be used when the detector or source is moving *toward* the other object, whereas the bottom sign should be used when the detector or source is moving *away* from the other object.

Let's start with the detector (the person in Car A). The detector is moving toward the source; therefore, the observed frequency, f', will be greater than if the detector were stationary. The numerator of the Doppler effect equation represents the motion of the detector; the fact that the detector is moving toward the source implies that a plus sign should be used in the numerator. Remember: the top sign in the numerator (plus) should be used when the detector is moving toward the source:

$$f' = f \frac{(v + v_{\mathrm{D}})}{(v \mp v_{\mathrm{s}})}$$

Determine the effect of the velocity of the source on the perceived frequency.

Now, let's consider the source (the horn on Car B). The source is moving toward the detector; therefore, the observed frequency, f', will be greater than if the source were stationary. The denominator of the Doppler effect equation represents to motion of the source; the fact that the source is moving toward the detector implies that a minus sign should be used in the denominator. Remember: the top sign in the denominator (minus) should be used when the source is moving toward the detector:

$$f' = f\frac{(v + v_D)}{(v - v_s)}$$

4 **Plug the values into the Doppler effect equation.**

We are given the following values:

$$f = 475 \text{ Hz}$$

$$v = \text{speed of sound} = 343\,\frac{\text{m}}{\text{s}}$$

$$v_D = v_s = 50\,\frac{\text{m}}{\text{s}}$$

Plugging these into the equation, we get:

$$f' = f\frac{(v + v_D)}{(v - v_s)}$$

$$= (475 \text{ Hz})\frac{\left(343\,\frac{\text{m}}{\text{s}} + 50\,\frac{\text{m}}{\text{s}}\right)}{\left(343\,\frac{\text{m}}{\text{s}} - 50\,\frac{\text{m}}{\text{s}}\right)}$$

$$= 475 \times \frac{393}{293} \approx 480 \times \frac{4}{3} = 640 \text{ Hz (actual} = 637.1 \text{ Hz)}$$

5 **Convert frequency to wavelength.**

This question asks for the wavelength of the observed wave, not its frequency. We can use the relationship between wave speed, frequency, and wavelength to determine the answer:

$$v = f\lambda \rightarrow \lambda = \frac{v}{f}$$

$$\lambda = \frac{343\,\frac{\text{m}}{\text{s}}}{637\,\text{Hz}} \approx 0.5\,\text{m}\,(\text{actual} = 0.54\,\text{m})$$

Takeaways

As the detector approaches the source, the observed frequency will be higher than the emitted frequency, and when the detector moves away from the source, the observed frequency will be lower than the emitted frequency. The same rule applies to the motion of the source. Therefore, when determining the right sign convention of the Doppler equation, use the sign in the equation that will yield the appropriate observed frequency.

Things to Watch Out For

Always separate Doppler effect questions into two parts: the effect of the source and the effect of the observer. Be careful in problems where the object and the source are moving in the same direction. If the source is ahead of the detector, the source will be moving away from the detector while the detector is moving toward the source, regardless of their relative speeds. If the detector is ahead of the source, the detector will be moving away from the source while the source is moving toward the detector.

Related Questions

1. Suppose a policeman running at $5\frac{m}{s}$ is firing his gun at a rate of 20 bullets per minute while chasing a bank robber who is driving away at $50\frac{m}{s}$. At what rate do the bullets reach the bank robber? (Note: Use $500\frac{m}{s}$ for the speed of a bullet.)

2. A bungee jumper yells at 350 Hz as he falls off a bridge toward a river at a rate of $20\frac{m}{s}$. What are the frequencies heard by the observers on the bridge and a boat on the river? (Note: The speed of sound is $343\frac{m}{s}$.)

3. Some animals use echolocation to navigate three-dimensional space and find prey. During echolocation, what is the detector and what is the source? What signs would be used in the Doppler effect equation in this case?

High-Yield Problem-Solving Guide questions continue on the next page. ▶ ▶ ▶

Key Concepts

Physics and Math Chapter 8

Refraction

Snell's law

Index of refraction

Trigonometry

Snell's Law

A gold doubloon rests on a rock 1 m below the surface of the ocean. A glass-bottom boat passes over the area, and a passenger spots the coin at a 60° angle from the normal. If the glass layer is 3 cm thick, find the apparent depth of the coin. (Note: The indices of refraction are as follows: air, $n = 1$; glass, $n = 1.5$; ocean water, $n = 1.34$.)

1 **Sketch the situation.**

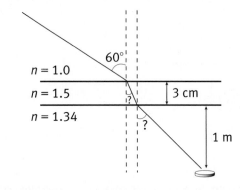

Light bends toward the normal when going from a medium with a lower index of refraction to one with a higher index of refraction. Your sketch need not be to scale; we use it to approximate what is going on and to keep track of the important data.

2 **Apply Snell's law.**

Snell's law shows mathematically that light bends toward the normal (decreasing θ) when it enters a medium with a higher refractive index. Here, we work through the formula to find the angles of light entry and exit for the glass and salt water.

$$n_{air} \sin \theta_{air} = n_{glass} \sin \theta_{glass}$$

$$\theta_{glass} = \sin^{-1} \frac{n_{air} \sin \theta_{air}}{n_{glass}}$$

$$= \sin^{-1} \frac{1 \times \sin 60°}{1.5} \approx \sin^{-1} \frac{0.866}{1.5} \approx \sin^{-1} 0.577$$

$$\theta_{glass} \approx 35°$$

While exact calculation of an inverse trigonometric function is outside the scope of MCAT math, we would be able to predict this value with reasonable accuracy on Test Day. If the sine of 30° is 0.5, then the inverse sine of 0.577 should be just a bit larger than 30°.

Now, plug into Snell's law for the second refraction step (from glass to salt water):

$$n_{glass} \sin \theta_{glass} = n_{water} \sin \theta_{water}$$

$$\theta_{water} = \sin^{-1} \frac{n_{glass} \sin \theta_{glass}}{n_{water}}$$

$$= \sin^{-1} \frac{1.5 \times \sin 35^\circ}{1.34} \approx \sin^{-1} \frac{0.866}{1.34} \approx \sin^{-1} 0.646$$

$$\theta_{water} \approx 40^\circ$$

Alternatively, realize that when light passes through multiple layers, the final angle can be determined merely by comparing the first and final media. The glass in this example alters the distance that the light travels in the *x*-direction but has no bearing on the final angle because the light enters and exits the glass at the same angle:

$$n_{air} \sin \theta_{air} = n_{water} \sin \theta_{water}$$

$$\theta_{water} = \sin^{-1} \frac{n_{air} \sin \theta_{air}}{n_{water}}$$

$$= \sin^{-1} \frac{1 \times \sin 60^\circ}{1.34} \approx \sin^{-1} \frac{0.866}{1.34} \approx \sin^{-1} 0.646$$

$$\theta_{water} \approx 40^\circ$$

 3 ## Use trigonometry to determine how far the light goes in the *x*-direction.

We know the thickness and depth of the glass and water, respectively, so we can use that information to determine how far the coin is from the ray of light the passenger sees. Light travels through a total of three media, but the distance of the observer from the glass doesn't actually matter. As long as he is looking 60° from the normal, he will see the coin. The trigonometry here is direct, using the relationship:

$$\tan \theta = \frac{\text{opposite}}{\text{adjacent}} = \frac{x}{y}$$

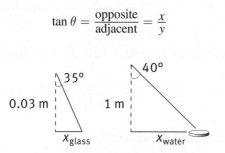

The value of *x* in the triangle within the glass can be determined as follows:

$$x_{glass} = y \tan \theta = 0.03 \,\text{m} \times \tan 35^\circ \approx 0.02 \,\text{m}$$

The triangle in the water is solved the same way:

$$x_{\text{water}} = y \tan \theta = 1\,\text{m} \times \tan 40° \approx 0.84\,\text{m}$$

The ray of light escapes the water and glass $0.02 + 0.84 = 0.86$ meters from the coin.

4 Find the object's image.

When the passenger sees the coin, his brain interprets light as a straight line. In other words, his brain doesn't consider the bending of light due to the indices of refraction, and he perceives the coin to be closer than it actually is. We previously determined the x-component of the light ray from the air–glass interface to the coin to be $0.86\,\text{m}$. The observer sees the coin at a $60°$ angle from the normal, so set up a new triangle with this angle:

We are trying to find the apparent depth of the coin—the y-component of this triangle:

$$\tan 60° = \frac{0.86}{y} \rightarrow y = \frac{0.86}{\tan 60°} \approx \frac{0.86}{1.732} = 0.50\,\text{m}$$

Thus, the apparent depth of the coin is $0.50\,\text{m}$.

Related Questions

1. A firefighter shines her flashlight through a smoky room at a 45° angle to a window. What angle does the beam of light make with the pane of glass on the outside? (Note: The indices of refraction are as follows: air, $n = 1$; glass, $n = 1.5$; smoke, $n = 1.1$.)

2. A jeweler is appraising the stone on a ring. He aims a beam of light 35° from the normal at a flat edge of the gem. What angle would he observe in the gem if the stone were diamond ($n = 2.4$)? What angle would he observe if the stone were zircon ($n = 1.9$)?

3. If light were traveling from salt water into air, what would be the associated critical angle?

Key Concepts

Physics and Math Chapter 9

Atomic number

Mass number

Isotopes

Radioactive decay

Nuclear Reactions

A neutral U-238 atom absorbs a neutron and then immediately undergoes two alpha decays, three beta decays, one positron decay, and two gamma decays (not necessarily in that order). Describe the resulting nucleus using isotopic notation. The resulting atom is an isotope of what element?

1 Find the mass number and atomic number of the parent nucleus.

The notation U-238 indicates a uranium atom with a mass number (A) of 238. The letter is always the element's symbol, as listed on the Periodic Table. From the Periodic Table, the atomic number of uranium (Z) is 92: all uranium atoms, by definition, have 92 protons.

The mass number, A, is the sum of the number of protons and neutrons. The mass number is given in the question because a given element may have many different isotopes, which all have the same number of protons but vary in the number of neutrons they contain.

Isotopes may be written in shorthand notation as $_Z^A X$, where X is the element's symbol, A is the mass number, and Z is the atomic number. Here, this uranium isotope could be written as $_{92}^{238}U$.

2 Find the result of the neutron absorption.

A neutron has a mass number of 1 and an atomic number of 0 because it has no protons. In these problems, make sure to balance both the atomic numbers and the mass numbers in the decay equation:

$$_Z^A X + {}_0^1 n \rightarrow {}_Z^{A+1} X$$
$$_{92}^{238}U + {}_0^1 n \rightarrow {}_{92}^{239}U$$

The result of the absorption is the formation of a different isotope of uranium.

3 Find the result of the alpha decays.

An alpha particle is a helium nucleus: two protons and two neutrons. Thus, for a single alpha decay, A decreases by 4 and Z decreases by 2. Because there are two alpha decays, multiply these numbers by two to find the change in the values of Z and A:

$$\ _Z^A X \rightarrow\ _{Z-2}^{A-4} X +\ _2^4 \alpha$$
$$\ _{92}^{239} U \rightarrow\ _{88}^{231} Ra + 2\ _2^4 \alpha$$

4 Find the result of the beta decays.

Beta decay comes in two forms: beta-minus and beta-plus (also called positron emission). In β^- decay, a neutron decays into a proton, a β-particle, and an antineutrino. The β-particle, which is nothing more than an electron, is ejected from the nucleus. Thus, the mass number stays the same, while the atomic number of the daughter nucleus increases by 1. There are three beta decays in this question:

$$\ _Z^A X \rightarrow\ _{Z+1}^A X +\ _{-1}^0 \beta$$
$$\ _{88}^{231} Ra \rightarrow\ _{91}^{231} Pa + 3\ _{-1}^0 \beta$$

5 Find the result of the positron decay.

Positron decay is the exact opposite of beta decay and is often called β^+ decay. In positron decay, a proton decays into a neutron, a positron, and a neutrino. The positron (an anti-electron—a particle with a positive charge and negligible mass) is ejected from the nucleus. Thus, the mass number stays the same, and the atomic number decreases by 1:

$$\ _Z^A X \rightarrow\ _{Z-1}^A X +\ _{+1}^0 \beta$$
$$\ _{91}^{231} Pa \rightarrow\ _{90}^{231} Th +\ _{+1}^0 \beta$$

6 Find the result of the gamma decays.

In gamma decay, a gamma ray (an electromagnetic wave) is ejected from the nucleus. There is no change in atomic number or mass number:

$$\ _Z^A X^* \rightarrow\ _Z^A X + \gamma$$
$$\ _{90}^{231} Th^* \rightarrow\ _{90}^{231} Th + 2\gamma$$

The daughter nucleus of these eight decay processes is a thorium-231 atom, with 90 protons and $231 - 90 = 141$ neutrons.

Takeaways

It is important to know the decay types and the identities of the decay particles themselves. Once you have these down, these problems are relatively simple.

Things to Watch Out For

Fission occurs when a large nucleus splits into smaller nuclei. Fusion is the combination of smaller nuclei to form a larger particle. Transmutation, or radioactive decay resulting in a change of atomic number, is a specific type of fission reaction. β-particles (electrons) and positrons are very easy to confuse; make sure that you understand the differences between them.

Related Questions

1. Is it possible for neptunium to decay into an isotope of lead through a series of alpha decays?

2. How many β-particles are ejected when polonium-214 decays into radon-214?

3. Uranium-226 decays radioactively into radon-218 through two positron decays and an unknown number of alpha decays. How many alpha particles must be emitted in this reaction?

High-Yield Problem-Solving Guide questions continue on the next page. ▶ ▶ ▶

Dimensional Analysis

Key Concepts

Physics and Math Chapter 10
Dimensional analysis
Frequency
Density
Force
Surface tension

Water is dripping from a leaky faucet. As the drops fall, they oscillate as shown in the diagram above. Given that the frequency depends only on the surface tension T of the water (measured in $\frac{N}{m}$), the radius of the drops r, and the density of the water, use dimensional analysis to find a proportionality expression for the frequency f of the drops.

 Identify all of the relevant physical quantities and their SI units.

As given in the problem, surface tension has units of newtons per meter. We can convert this to SI units by remembering that $1 \text{ N} = 1\frac{\text{kg} \cdot \text{m}}{\text{s}^2}$. Density can be given in the units of $\frac{\text{kg}}{\text{m}^3}$. Radius is a distance with the units of meters. Frequency has the units of Hz, or $\frac{1}{\text{s}}$. In summary:

$$T : \frac{\text{N}}{\text{m}} = \frac{\text{kg}}{\text{s}^2}$$

$$\rho : \frac{\text{kg}}{\text{m}^3}$$

$$r : \text{m}$$

$$f : \text{Hz} = \frac{1}{\text{s}}$$

Write a hypothetical formula for the frequency.

The frequency is related to the surface tension, T, the radius, r, and the density, ρ. Write an equation for these using variables (like x, y, and z) as exponents:

$$f = kT^x r^y \rho^z$$

where k is a unitless constant

 ## Plug the units into the hypothetical formula.

Plug the units into the hypothetical formula from Step 2:

$$f = kT^x r^y \rho^z$$

$$\frac{1}{s} = \left[\frac{kg}{s^2}\right]^x [m]^y \left[\frac{kg}{m^3}\right]^z$$

4 Solve for the values of x, y, and z.

We know that the units on the left must equal the units on the right. Only the first term on the right side contains seconds, so we know x must be $\frac{1}{2}$; thus, we end up with $\frac{1}{s}$ on both sides.

Only the first and third terms contain kilograms; there are no units of kilograms on the left side of the equation. Therefore, the last term (density) must have an exponent of $z = -\frac{1}{2}$ so that the units of kilograms divide on the right side of the equation.

Finally, only the second and third terms contain meters; there are no units of meters on the left side of the equation. If the value of $z = -\frac{1}{2}$, then the middle term (radius) must have an exponent of $y = -\frac{3}{2}$ so that the units of meters divide on the right side of the equation.

Takeaways

It is often possible to determine an equation by concentrating on the units of the variables involved. This is a good approach on Test Day if you find yourself unable to remember a particular equation.

Things to Watch Out For

If you are short on time, you can at least determine general trends using a common-sense approach. The larger the radius, the slower the drop will oscillate. The denser the fluid, the slower the drop will oscillate. The surface tension is supplying the force to keep the drop oscillating, so if it is stronger, the drop will oscillate more quickly.

5 Convert these exponents to a simple equation.

All of our exponents are fractions, which means that a radical will be involved in the equation. Remember that a quantity raised to a negative exponent is the same as dividing by the same quantity raised to a positive exponent of the same magnitude. Putting this together, we can determine the equation:

$$f = kT^{\frac{1}{2}}r^{-\frac{3}{2}}\rho^{-\frac{1}{2}}$$

$$= k\frac{T^{\frac{1}{2}}}{r^{\frac{3}{2}}\rho^{\frac{1}{2}}}$$

$$= k\sqrt{\frac{T}{r^3\rho}}$$

Related Questions

1. What are the SI units of G in the universal law of gravitation?

2. An electric dipole is initially at rest in a uniform electric field. The torque provided by the electric field causes the dipole to oscillate back and forth. For the period of motion, the physicist derives the formula $T = kE^{\frac{1}{2}}$, where T is the period, E is the electric field, and k is a quantity with the appropriate units. Is this equation physically reasonable?

3. What are the units for the permeability of free space, μ_0?

High-Yield Problem-Solving Guide questions continue on the next page. ▶ ▶ ▶

Study Design

A student wishes to document the effects of two different drugs in hypertensive patients. He obtains permission to contact all of the patients on propranolol and all of the patients on diltiazem from a certain pharmacy, and sends out written surveys asking for the patient's most recent blood pressure reading, age, and gender. Forty percent of respondents return their surveys. The student then compiles the diastolic blood pressure readings from each group. The mean systolic blood pressure in the propranolol group is 129 mmHg, and the mean in the diltiazem group is 127. The student concludes that diltiazem should be used as a first line treatment, rather than propranolol. Identify the errors that this student has made or the additional information that is needed to support his conclusion.

Key Concepts

Physics and Math Chapter 11
Causality
Statistical analysis
Support for interventions
Study design

1 Identify the steps in research design where error may be introduced.

Break the components of any study down into phases; the list of question design, experimental method, data collection, data analysis, conclusions, and execution is generally a good place to start. Next, determine where error is likely to be introduced. Question design is not likely to lead to errors, but should be kept in mind during a discussion of the experimental method. Data collection is also relatively unlikely to lead to erroneous conclusions (although it can with systematic bias and inaccurate instruments) and execution is almost always free from errors that impact the study. Therefore, we should focus our evaluations of most studies on the experimental method, data analysis, and conclusions.

2 Compare the known execution of each step to ideal study design protocols.

To determine what errors have been made, we should compare the study to an ideal study of the same topic. Keep in mind that not all deviations from the ideal study are necessarily errors; some deviations may be deemed necessary because of practicality or financial concerns that may not substantially affect the data.

When considering the experimental method, one should always compare the study to the gold standard in biomedical research: the double-blind randomized controlled trial. The study that was conducted is not randomized, and does not have pre- and post-intervention data. The study was conducted from a single location and used self-report as the measurement instrument.

For data analysis, consider potential sources of bias. Studies with high response rates and sample sizes are ideal because they minimize selection bias. In this study, there was a very low response rate, which may have contributed to selection bias—only those who responded to the medication (or did not respond to the medication) may have replied to the survey, for example. Only one of the four collected variables was analyzed, and statistical findings were not provided. Whenever multiple variables may impact the measured outcomes, they should be considered as part of the analysis, and determinations of significance as well as *p*-values should be reported. This student did not account for other potential variables, such as severity of hypertension; demographic differences such as race, socioeconomic status, or access to healthcare; allergies to other study medications; and comorbid medical conditions.

To act upon a study, it should meet the requirements of the FINER approach and Hill's criteria. It should also demonstrate both clinical and statistical significance. In this study, we do not have sufficient information to draw the conclusions that the author makes for the reasons given above.

3 **Determine whether the flaw is one of omission or design and consider appropriate ways to correct it.**

The study is designed poorly, and requires a complete revision. However, there are several data points that could improve its relevance. An analysis that includes relevant *p*-values and adjusts for the collected variables could improve this study. Additionally, information about the clinical value of the different blood pressures would be worthwhile for study analysis in supporting the author's conclusion.

Takeaways

Research errors are pervasive and compound one another. It is not enough to look for sample size or an overt bias because there may be issues that arise before any data is even collected.

Things to Watch Out For

Statistical significance and clinical significance are often used interchangeably in common parlance, but they are two different topics. In study analysis we must look for errors in interpretation of data and experimental design, not just data analysis.

Related Questions

1. It is found that the number of shark attacks appears to correlate with the national gross sales of ice cream on a monthly basis. Why would it be a flawed conclusion to state that there is a causal relationship between purchasing ice cream and a shark attack?

2. How is respect for persons maintained in a study about the effects of electroconvulsive therapy?

3. How is causality established in an experimental study *vs.* an observational study?

Key Concepts

Physics and Math Chapter 12
Measures of central tendency
Measures of distribution
Charts, tables, and graphs
Comparative statistics

Graphical Analysis

Given the following data sets for age of mortality in these imaginary countries, construct a series of box-and-whisker plots. Use these plots to determine which countries have the best and worst life expectancies:

Physia	Orgostan	United Biology	GCS
69	65	91	56
74	87	56	89
52	55	82	65
63	69	44	47
70	66	62	85
71	59	53	39
65	72	68	98
81	72	85	71
64	58	65	52
70	71	59	65

 Order the data sets and calculate meaningful statistics.

Median, mode, range, quartiles, and interquartile range (IQR) are easiest to calculate if the data are ordered, so this is the first step in generating comparisons. The reordered data are shown below:

Physia	Orgostan	United Biology	GCS
52	55	44	39
63	58	53	47
64	59	56	52
65	65	59	56
69	66	62	65
70	69	65	65
70	71	68	71
71	72	82	85
74	72	85	89
81	87	91	98

Now, it is possible to calculate the median, mean, and quartiles for this data. The median will be the average of the fifth and sixth data points for each set. Thus the medians are 69.5, 67.5, 63.5, and 65 for Physia, Orgostan, United Biology, and GCS, respectively.

We will calculate the mean by summing each column and dividing by ten. The means are 67.9, 67.4, 66.5, and 66.7 for Physia, Orgostan, United Biology, and GCS, respectively.

To find the quartile positions, we multiply the number of data points by $\frac{1}{4}$ and by $\frac{3}{4}$. If these are whole numbers, the quartiles are the averages of these data values and the ones above them. If they are not, then round up to find the positions of the quartiles. Here, $10 \times \frac{1}{4} = 2.5$ (round up to 3), and $10 \times \frac{3}{4} = 7.5$ (round up to 8). These data points are highlighted in green the following chart, with the median, mean, and IQR listed below the data.

Physia	Orgostan	United Biology	GCS
52	55	44	39
63	58	53	47
64	59	56	52
65	65	59	56
69	66	62	65
70	69	65	65
70	71	68	71
71	72	82	85
74	72	85	89
81	87	91	98

	Physia	Orgostan	United Biology	GCS
Median	69.5	67.5	63.5	65
Mean	67.9	67.4	66.5	66.7
IQR	7	13	26	33

Already, this data is more accessible than the initial presentation, but using a graphical form is even easier to interpret.

 Construct the appropriate box-and-whisker plots on the same axis.

Using an axis that contains the minimum and maximum data points (39 and 98, respectively), construct a box-and-whisker plot that is divided according to the quartiles and median for each data set. The box plots can be constructed with or without outliers. Including outliers is useful information, but does require additional mathematics:

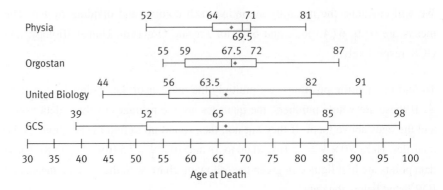

An outlier is any data point that is more than 1.5 × IQR away from the closest quartile. The one outlier in this data set is highlighted in red in the data table.

Takeaways

Graphical representations of data are generally more informative than text or tables. As long as the axes are the same between graphs, they provide comparative as well as absolute information.

Things to Watch Out For

Be careful not to rely on a single statistic or data point as a decision-making tool when evaluating graphs. In this case, outliers or erroneous data collection could cause a flawed result.

3 **Compare the data using the constructed box-and-whisker plots.**

Using the box-and-whisker plots, determine how countries compare to one another. For example, three quarters of the people in Physia live longer than half of the people in United Biology, so they have a longer life expectancy despite having similar mean and median values. In this data set, Physia has the best longevity outcomes when compared to the other groups; both United Biology and GCS are very similar and have the poorest outcomes.

Related Questions

1. Provide at least three criticisms of the following chart:

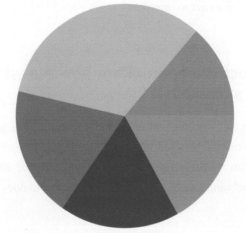

2. What are the appropriate first steps when analyzing any graph or table?

3. Determine the equations for the two lines below. At what point do they intersect?

Solutions to Related Questions

1. Inclined Plane

1. The only two forces acting on this block in the parallel dimension are the force of static friction pointing up the plane and the parallel component of gravity pointing down the plane. If the block is at rest, then it is in translational equilibrium and the magnitudes of these two forces must be equal:

$$f_s = F_{g,\parallel}$$
$$\mu_s N = mg \sin \theta$$
$$\mu_s mg \cos \theta = mg \sin \theta$$
$$\mu_s = \frac{\sin \theta}{\cos \theta} = \tan \theta = \tan 45° = 1$$

2. This question can be solved with kinematics equations, but it is actually easier to use conservation of energy to arrive at the answer. If the ramp is frictionless, then there are no nonconservative forces and all of the kinetic energy will be converted to gravitational potential energy. The initial gravitational potential energy can be assigned the value of zero because the question asks for the height above the initial point. The final kinetic energy is also zero because the block has zero speed when it reaches its highest point. Therefore, the initial kinetic energy and final gravitational potential energy are equal:

$$K_1 = U_2$$
$$\frac{1}{2}mv_1^2 = mgh_2$$
$$h_2 = \frac{v_1^2}{2g} \approx \frac{\left(2\,\frac{m}{s}\right)^2}{2 \times 10\,\frac{m}{s^2}} = 0.2\,m$$

3. Start by determining the acceleration. Because the only force in the parallel direction is the parallel component of gravity, the acceleration will be $g \sin \theta = 10\,\frac{m}{s^2} \times 0.5 = 5\,\frac{m}{s^2}$. Now, use a kinematics equation:

$$v = v_0 + at$$
$$= 0 + \left(5\,\frac{m}{s^2}\right)(5s) = 25\,\frac{m}{s}\left(\text{actual} = 24.5\,\frac{m}{s}\right)$$

2. Projectile Motion and Air Resistance

1. The rock starts with zero kinetic energy and a gravitational potential energy of mgh_i. It ends with a kinetic energy of $\frac{1}{2}mv_f^2$ and zero gravitational potential energy. We are asked how much energy is lost, which would be the difference between these two terms:

$$W_{\text{nonconservative}} = E_i - E_f$$

$$= mgh_i - \frac{1}{2}mv_f^2$$

$$= m \times 10\,\frac{m}{s^2} \times 100\,m - \frac{1}{2} \times m \times \left(30\,\frac{m}{s}\right)^2$$

$$= 1000\,m - 450\,m = 550\,m$$

We cannot say an exact value for the amount of energy lost without knowing the mass of the rock, but $550m$ joules of energy have been lost, where m is the mass of the rock. We could also say that $\frac{550\,m}{1000\,m} = 55\%$ of the energy has been lost.

2. Let's call the speed of the slower rock v. This means that the speed of the faster rock is $1.3\,v$. The difference in kinetic energy between the rocks is:

$$\frac{1}{2}m(1.3v)^2 - \frac{1}{2}mv^2 = 0.69 \times \frac{1}{2}mv^2$$

The question asks how much more kinetic energy the faster rock has. We cannot give an exact value, but can compare it to the kinetic energy of the slower rock—the faster rock has 69% more kinetic energy than the slower rock.

3. First, find the difference in energy between the initial and final point:

$$W_{\text{nonconservative}} = E_i - E_f$$

$$= \frac{1}{2}mv_i^2 - mgh_f$$

Now, divide that by the initial energy:

$$\frac{\frac{1}{2}mv_i^2 - mgh_f}{\frac{1}{2}mv_i^2} = \frac{v_i^2 - 2gh_f}{v_i^2}$$

$$\approx \frac{\left(30\,\frac{m}{s}\right)^2 - 2 \times 10\,\frac{m}{s^2} \times 44.1\,m}{\left(30\,\frac{m}{s}\right)^2} = \frac{900 - 882}{900} = \frac{18}{900} = 0.02 = 2\% \ (\text{actual} = 4\%)$$

3. Thermodynamics

1. A minimum of three processes is required to have a closed cycle. This requires either an adiabatic or an isothermal process as well as an isobaric process (one with a constant pressure) and an isovolumetric process (one with a constant volume; also called an isochoric process). This creates a shape like a right triangle on a pressure–volume graph. While three-process cycles are seen, it is most common for closed-cycle processes to have four steps as seen in the Carnot cycle.

2. Entropy change can be given by the equation $\Delta S = \frac{Q_{\text{rev}}}{T}$. During an adiabatic process, $Q = 0$, thus $\Delta S = 0$. During an adiabatic process, there is no entropy change.

3. The liquid (usually mercury in older thermometers) is undergoing expansion. Because there is a change in temperature, this process is not isothermal. Because the change in temperature is accompanied by heat exchange, it is not adiabatic

either. This process is likely to be isobaric, taking place under constant pressure. The water is cooling very slightly as a result of the distribution of heat to the thermometer, and consequently will experience some compression.

4. Fluid Dynamics

1. If the pipe is horizontal, then $h_1 = h_2$ in Bernoulli's equation. This simplifies the equation:

$$P_1 + \frac{1}{2}\rho v_1^2 = P_2 + \frac{1}{2}\rho v_2^2$$

We are told that $P_1 = 3P_2$. We can now solve for the linear flow speed at Point 1 in terms of the linear flow speed at Point 2:

$$3P_2 + \frac{1}{2}\rho v_1^2 = P_2 + \frac{1}{2}\rho v_2^2$$

$$\frac{1}{2}\rho v_1^2 = \frac{1}{2}\rho v_2^2 - 2P_2$$

$$v_1^2 = v_2^2 - \frac{4P_2}{\rho}$$

$$v_1 = \sqrt{v_2^2 - \frac{4P_2}{\rho}}$$

2. This question can be solved using the continuity equation. The radius at Point A is twice the radius at Point B, meaning that cross-sectional area at Point A is four times that at Point B:

$$A_A v_A = A_B v_B$$

$$\left(\pi r_A^2\right) v_A = \left(\pi r_B^2\right) v_B$$

$$\frac{v_A}{v_B} = \left(\frac{r_B}{r_A}\right)^2 = \left(\frac{1}{2}\right)^2 = \frac{1}{4}$$

Thus, $v_A : v_B = 1 : 4$.

3. We can solve this question with Bernoulli's equation again. In this case, the pressure is the same (atmospheric pressure) because the tank is open to the air. We can again assume the linear flow speed at the surface is essentially zero. Thus, Bernoulli's equation simplifies to:

$$\rho g h_1 = \frac{1}{2}\rho v_2^2 + \rho g h_2$$

$$\frac{1}{2}v_2^2 = g h_1 - g h_2$$

$$v_2 = \sqrt{2g(h_1 - h_2)} = \sqrt{2 \times 10\, \frac{m}{s^2} \times (1\,m - 0.5\,m)} = \sqrt{10} \approx 3.16\, \frac{m}{s}$$

5. Electrostatics

1. The amount of work done is equal to the change in electrical potential energy:

$$\Delta U = \frac{kQq}{r_2} - \frac{kQq}{r_1} = kQq\left(\frac{1}{r_2} - \frac{1}{r_1}\right)$$

$$= \left(9 \times 10^9 \, \frac{\text{N} \cdot \text{m}^2}{\text{C}^2}\right)\left(1 \times 10^{-6}\text{C}\right)\left(-2 \times 10^{-6}\text{C}\right)\left(\frac{1}{3 \times 10^{-2}\text{m}} - \frac{1}{1 \times 10^{-2}\text{m}}\right)$$

$$= -18 \times 10^{-3}\left(\frac{1}{3 \times 10^{-2}} - \frac{3}{3 \times 10^{-2}}\right)$$

$$= -18 \times 10^{-3}\left(-\frac{2}{3 \times 10^{-2}}\right) = 1.2 \text{ J}$$

2. The amount of work can be determined by summing the work to move each charge into the configuration:

$$W_1 = 0 \text{ V}$$

$$W_2 = \frac{kQq}{r_1} = \frac{kQq}{1 \times 10^{-6}\text{m}}$$

$$W_3 = \frac{kQq}{r_1} + \frac{kQq}{r_2} = \frac{kQq}{1 \times 10^{-6}\text{m}} + \frac{kQq}{1.4 \times 10^{-6}\text{m}}$$

$$W_4 = \frac{kQq}{r_1} + \frac{kQq}{r_2} + \frac{kQq}{r_3} = \frac{2kQq}{1 \times 10^{-6}\text{m}} + \frac{kQq}{1.4 \times 10^{-6}\text{m}}$$

$$W_{\text{total}} = \frac{4kQq}{1 \times 10^{-6}} + \frac{2kQq}{1.4 \times 10^{-6}} = \frac{kQq}{10^{-6}}\left(4 + \frac{2}{1.4}\right)$$

$$\approx \frac{\left(9 \times 10^9 \, \frac{\text{N} \cdot \text{m}^2}{\text{C}^2}\right)\left(5 \times 10^{-9}\text{C}\right)\left(5 \times 10^{-9}\text{C}\right)}{10^{-6}\text{m}}(5.4)$$

$$\approx 225 \times 10^{-3} \times 5.4 \approx 1.22 \text{ J}$$

3. The initial potential energy of the system is:

$$U_i = \frac{kq_1q_2}{r_{1,2}} + \frac{kq_1q_3}{r_{1,3}} + \frac{kq_2q_3}{r_{2,3}}$$

$$= \left(9 \times 10^9 \, \frac{\text{N} \cdot \text{m}^2}{\text{C}^2}\right)\left[\frac{\left(4 \times 10^{-6}\text{C}\right)\left(-2 \times 10^{-6}\text{C}\right)}{1 \times 10^{-3}\text{m}} + \frac{\left(4 \times 10^{-6}\text{C}\right)\left(-3 \times 10^{-6}\text{C}\right)}{2 \times 10^{-3}\text{m}} + \frac{\left(-2 \times 10^{-6}\text{C}\right)\left(-3 \times 10^{-6}\text{C}\right)}{1 \times 10^{-3}\text{m}}\right]$$

$$= \left(9 \times 10^9\right)\left[-8 \times 10^{-9} - 6 \times 10^{-9} + 6 \times 10^{-9}\right]$$

$$= -72 \text{ J}$$

The final potential energy of the system is:

$$U_f = \frac{kq_2q_3}{r_{2,3}}$$

$$= \left(9 \times 10^9 \; \frac{\text{N} \cdot \text{m}^2}{\text{C}^2}\right)\left[\frac{(-2 \times 10^{-6}\text{C})(-3 \times 10^{-6}\text{C})}{1 \times 10^{-3}\text{m}}\right]$$

$$= (9 \times 10^9)(6 \times 10^{-9})$$

$$= 54 \text{ J}$$

The change in electrical potential energy is therefore $54 - (-72) = +126$ J.

6. Resistor Circuits

1. We know that the current through the circuit is 1.5 A and the equivalent resistance of the portion of the circuit including R_3, R_4, and R_5 is 15 Ω. Thus, the voltage across this part of the circuit is $V = IR = (1.5 \text{ A})(15 \text{ Ω}) = 22.5$ V. The same voltage drop will be seen across the branch including R_3 and R_4. The total voltage drop will be the sum of the voltage drop across R_3 plus the voltage drop across R_4. The current is the same through each resistor, so the ratio of their resistances will be the same as the ratio of their voltage drops. There is a 2:1 ratio of resistance, so the voltage drop must be 15 V across R_3 and 7.5 V across R_4.

2. Use the equation for equivalent resistance of resistors in parallel:

$$\frac{1}{R_p} = \frac{1}{10 \text{ Ω}} + \frac{1}{20 \text{ Ω}} + \frac{1}{30 \text{ Ω}} + \frac{1}{40 \text{ Ω}}$$

$$= \frac{12 + 6 + 4 + 3}{120} = \frac{25}{120} = \frac{5}{24}$$

$$R_p = \frac{24}{5} = 4.8 \text{ Ω}$$

Now, use Ohm's law:

$$V = IR \rightarrow I = \frac{V}{R}$$

$$I = \frac{9 \text{ V}}{4.8 \text{ Ω}} \approx 2 \text{ A (actual} = 1.88 \text{ A)}$$

3. We know the current and voltage of the circuit, which allows us to find the equivalent resistance:

$$V = IR \rightarrow R = \frac{V}{I} = \frac{20 \text{ V}}{10 \text{ A}} = 2 \text{ Ω}$$

Now determine the equivalent resistance of R_1 through R_5:

$$\frac{1}{R_p} = \frac{1}{R_1} + \frac{1}{R_2} + \frac{1}{R_3} + \frac{1}{R_4} + \frac{1}{R_5} = \frac{5}{1 \text{ Ω}}$$

$$R_p = 0.2 \text{ Ω}$$

Because R_1 through R_5 are in series with R_6, the resistance of R_6 must be $2 - 0.2 = 1.8$ Ω.

7. Doppler Effect

1. We are given all of the necessary variables to plug into the Doppler effect equation. Here, $f = 20$ bullets per minute, $v = 500\frac{m}{s}$, $v_D = 50\frac{m}{s}$, $v_S = 5\frac{m}{s}$. The detector (the bank robber) is moving away from the source, so a minus sign is used in the numerator. The source (the policeman's gun) is moving toward the detector, so a minus sign is used in the denominator, as well:

$$f' = f\frac{(v - v_D)}{(v - v_S)}$$

$$= \left(20\,\frac{bullets}{min}\right)\frac{\left(500\,\frac{m}{s} - 50\,\frac{m}{s}\right)}{\left(500\,\frac{m}{s} - 5\,\frac{m}{s}\right)} = 20 \times \frac{450}{495} \approx 20 \times \frac{9}{10} = 18\,\frac{bullets}{min}$$

2. In this question, $f = 350$ Hz, $v = 343\,\frac{m}{s}$, $v_D = 0\,\frac{m}{s}$, and $v_S = 20\,\frac{m}{s}$. There are two scenarios. In one case, the source is moving away from observers on the bridge, so a plus sign would be used in the denominator for this Doppler effect equation. In the other case, the source is moving toward observers on the river, so a minus sign would be used in the denominator for this Doppler effect equation:

$$f'_{bridge} = f\frac{v}{(v + v_S)} = (350\text{ Hz})\frac{343\,\frac{m}{s}}{\left(343\,\frac{m}{s} + 20\,\frac{m}{s}\right)} = 350 \times \frac{343}{363} = 331\text{ Hz}$$

$$f'_{river} = f\frac{v}{(v - v_S)} = (350\text{ Hz})\frac{343\,\frac{m}{s}}{\left(343\,\frac{m}{s} - 20\,\frac{m}{s}\right)} = 350 \times \frac{343}{323} = 372\text{ Hz}$$

3. During echolocation, the same animal serves as both the source and the detector. The sound wave bounces off of some surface and returns to the same animal that emitted the original frequency. In this case, as the animal flies toward some object, it could be said that the source is moving toward the detector and the detector is also moving toward the source. Thus, the top sign would be used in both the numerator (plus) and denominator (minus), and the general form of the Doppler effect equation would be:

$$f' = f\frac{(v + v_D)}{(v - v_S)}$$

8. Snell's Law

1. This is another application of Snell's law. Consider only the initial and final media because light enters and exits the pane of glass at the same angle:

$$n_{smoke}\sin\theta_{smoke} = n_{air}\sin\theta_{air}$$

$$\theta_{air} = \sin^{-1}\frac{n_{smoke}\sin\theta_{smoke}}{n_{air}}$$

$$= \sin^{-1}\frac{1.1 \times \sin 45°}{1} \approx \sin^{-1}0.778$$

$$\theta_{air} \approx 51°$$

2. This question requires another two applications of Snell's law:

$$n_{air} \sin \theta_{air} = n_{diamond} \sin \theta_{diamond}$$

$$\theta_{diamond} = \sin^{-1} \frac{n_{air} \sin \theta_{air}}{n_{diamond}}$$

$$= \sin^{-1} \frac{1 \times \sin 35°}{2.4} \approx \sin^{-1} 0.239$$

$$\theta_{diamond} \approx 13.8°$$

and

$$n_{air} \sin \theta_{air} = n_{zircon} \sin \theta_{zircon}$$

$$\theta_{zircon} = \sin^{-1} \frac{n_{air} \sin \theta_{air}}{n_{zircon}}$$

$$= \sin^{-1} \frac{1 \times \sin 35°}{1.9} \approx \sin^{-1} 0.301$$

$$\theta_{zircon} \approx 17.6°$$

3. The critical angle is the angle at which light can no longer exit a medium, and instead is totally internally reflected. This implies that the refracted angle must be greater than or equal to 90°. The critical angle can be found as follows:

$$n_1 \sin \theta_c = n_2 \sin 90° \rightarrow \theta_c = \sin^{-1} \frac{n_2}{n_1}$$

We are given the relevant indices of refraction in the original question:

$$\theta_c = \sin^{-1} \frac{1}{1.34} \approx 48°$$

9. Nuclear Reactions

1. It is not possible for neptunium to decay into lead through a series of alpha decays. Each alpha decay reduces the atom's atomic number by two, but the difference between neptunium and lead's atomic numbers ($93 - 82 = 11$) is not divisible by two.

2. Balance the decay equation to determine how many β-particles are ejected:

$$^{214}_{84}Po \rightarrow \,^{214}_{86}Rn + 2\,^{0}_{-1}\beta$$

Two β-particles are ejected during this decay reaction.

3. Balance the decay equation to determine how many α-particles are ejected:

$$^{226}_{92}U \rightarrow \,^{218}_{86}Rn + 2\,^{0}_{+1}\beta + 2\,^{4}_{2}\alpha$$

Two α-particles are ejected during this decay reaction.

10. Dimensional Analysis

1. First, rearrange the universal law of gravitation to solve for G:

$$F_g = \frac{Gm_1m_2}{r^2} \rightarrow G = \frac{F_g r^2}{m_1 m_2}$$

Now, plug in the relevant units:

$$[G] = \frac{N \cdot m^2}{kg \cdot kg} = \frac{\left(\frac{kg \cdot m}{s^2}\right)m^2}{kg^2} = \frac{m^3}{s^2 \cdot kg}$$

2. The stronger the electric field, the stronger the electrostatic force. Because the electrostatic force is the restoring force in this question, we would expect that the larger its magnitude, the faster the dipole oscillates. Hence, the period should *decrease* as a function of the electric field—not *increase*. This makes the given equation unreasonable.

3. First, rearrange an equation that uses the permeability of free space:

$$B = \frac{\mu_0 I}{2r} \rightarrow \mu_0 = \frac{2rB}{I}$$

The units for r, a distance, are meters. The units for magnetic field are teslas, where $1 \, T = 1\frac{N}{m \cdot A}$. (If you did not remember this conversion factor, it can be determined from the equation $F = ILB \sin \theta$, where F is force in newtons, I is current in ampères, and L is length in meters.) Finally, the units for current are ampères. Now, plug in the relevant units:

$$[\mu_0] = \frac{[m]\left[\frac{N}{m \cdot A}\right]}{[A]} = \frac{N}{A^2} = \frac{\frac{kg \cdot m}{s^2}}{\left(\frac{C}{s}\right)^2} = \frac{kg \cdot m}{C^2}$$

11. Study Design

1. Correlation does not necessarily indicate causation. In this case, confounding likely explains the relationship between shark attacks and ice cream sales—namely, both of these variables are likely increased in summer months, when more individuals visit the beach, and when salt water climes may be more habitable for sharks. Ice cream sales also likely increase during summer months.

2. Respect for persons is maintained in any research context by providing the opportunity for informed consent, by allowing subjects to withdraw at any time, and by providing a debriefing at the end of the study period. Electroconvulsive therapy is still used in many psychiatric illnesses, including severe depression and suicidality, as well as psychotic disorders.

3. Causality in an experimental study is established through the use of at least one positive or negative control. Causality in an observational study cannot be proven, but can be supported through the use of Hill's criteria (temporality, strength, dose–response relationships, consistency, plausibility, consideration of alternative explanations, experiments, specificity, and coherence).

12. Graphical Analysis

1. Pie charts are generally poor at information dissemination with more than four categories, and for information that is not meant to add up to a whole. In addition, the colors have poor contrast and there is no written explanation or key. The chart is unlabeled, which leaves it uninterpretable.

2. For graphs, always start by checking the axes, including the relevant quantities, the units, and if there are any interruptions in the axes (indicated by wavy lines). Then, look for points of intersection, maxima, minima, differences in slope, or anything else noteworthy in the graph. For tables, always check for unusual values (zero, infinity, and so on) and make sure that the referenced categories are comparable.

3. These lines can be written in slope–intercept form. The slope of the red line is:

$$m_{red} = \frac{\Delta y}{\Delta x} = \frac{10 - 9}{-1 - 0} = \frac{1}{-1} = -1$$

This line's y-intercept is $(0,9)$, so the equation of the line is $y = -x + 9$.

The slope of the blue line is:

$$m_{blue} = \frac{\Delta y}{\Delta x} = \frac{0 - 1}{-0.33 - 0} = \frac{-1}{-0.33} = 3$$

This line's y-intercept is $(0,1)$, so the equation of the line is $y = 3x + 1$.

To determine their point of intersection, set the two equations equal to each other:

$$y = -x + 9$$
$$y = 3x + 1$$
$$-x + 9 = 3x + 1$$
$$4x = 8$$
$$x = 2$$
$$y = -x + 9 = -2 + 9 = 7$$

Thus, these lines intersect at the point $(2,7)$.